Challenges to European Legal Scholarship:
Anglo-German Legal Essays

Law in its Social Setting

Challenges to European Legal Scholarship: Anglo-German Legal Essays

Edited by
Geoffrey Wilson
Professor of Law, University of Warwick

and

Rolf Rogowski
Senior Lecturer in Law, University of Warwick

BLACKSTONE
PRESS LIMITED

First published in Great Britain 1996 by Blackstone Press Limited,
9–15 Aldine Street, London W12 8AW.   Telephone 0181-740 2277

© Legal Research Institute 1996

ISBN: 1 85431 603 6

British Library Cataloguing in Publication Data
A CIP catalogue record for this book is available from the British Library.

Printed by Bell & Bain Ltd, Glasgow

Contents

General Editor's Preface

Law in its Social Setting aims to foster the established commitment of Warwick to the contextual study of law. The series brings together authors from other research centres in Britain and abroad to enrich debates on issues of contemporary importance in the area of socio-legal studies.

The immediate inspiration for this volume of essays is a conference held at Warwick in 1995 involving scholars drawn from the Law Faculty of Giessen and the School of Law at Warwick. But the true source is to be found in the prescient links forged between scholars from the two countries more than twenty years ago and which found formal expression in the partnership between Warwick and Giessen. The enterprise shows the value of bringing together scholars from the two most influential countries in Europe representing very different legal traditions. The essays make important contributions to debates at a variety of levels and raise interesting questions about legal theory and comparative methods across a broad range of subject areas.

Mike McConville
University of Warwick
February 1996

Introduction – Anglo-German Essays

When Warwick Law School was set up in 1967 it was unusual in including in its undergraduate curriculum a course in German Law. In spite of the arrival from the mid-30s onward of a number of distinguished German legal scholars in the United Kingdom they did not manage or even it seems desire to shift the Francocentric and even Francophile focus that was dominant at the time among those few who saw advantages in looking at other European systems. In this British scholars reflected the position at comparative law conferences at international level. French was the dominant language and French private lawyers dominated the agenda.

Thankfully those times are past. The days of the hegemony of the Code Civile and the Conseil d'Etat are past, though language remains a major barrier. German still lags behind French as the second language of the English legal scholar. But the introduction of the study of German law into the Warwick curriculum was prophetic. Germany has become an increasingly important subject for discussion and analysis and an increasingly important player on the European stage, not only within the European Community, of which the United Kingdom was not even a member when Warwick opened its doors, but in Europe at large. And this importance has, of course, increased with unification. Germany has not only become, once again, a Central European state. It is the Central European state, and there is a desperate and urgent need to know more about it, even more about it perhaps than German legal scholars themselves know.

Two important events have given a particular boost to the study of German law at Warwick. One has been the steady, generous support for a visiting German lecturer by the German Academic Exchange Service (DAAD). Times have changed since offering German law as a subject of study was a major pioneering effort. Even in the remotest parts of the United Kingdom law schools have become aware that, even where they do not feel the need to become more European-minded, there is a need to become more Community-minded and hence show an interest in things German. This is quite apart from the growing pressures on academic institutions to obtain financial support wherever it seems to be available for ventures which might otherwise have not come to mind. And yet the DAAD has continued to keep faith with Warwick and support its German programme. And the venture has turned out well not only for Warwick but for the visiting lecturers themselves. Former German lecturers are now to be found working at the Community's Commission, as public prosecutors, in banks, insurance companies, and in one of the country's leading law publishers. It has been a considerable relief to discover that the risk they took in making what was often regarded as a step off the escalator towards further promotion in the German career system has paid off for them as well as Warwick.

The second major event was the signing of an agreement between the Law Schools of the University of Warwick and the University of Giessen in 1986 and the inauguration of student exchanges under the umbrella of the Community's Erasmus programme. Anyone who has had experience of student exchange programmes knows that two factors are of utmost importance in making such exchanges a success. One is the preparation of the students before they leave. It is here that the DAAD supported German lawyer has played a vital role from the arrival in 1972 of Dr Rainer Maschmeier, now one of Düsseldorf's leading private lawyers, to our current visiting lecturer, Frau Heike Simon. The second major factor making for successful student exchanges is the care and attention given to the exchange students by the host law school. Here Warwick could not have been more fortunate than it has been in having the Giessen Law Faculty as its German partner. From Professor Dr Steiger to Professor Dr Weick at least one of their Faculty has taken the responsibility for making the exchange work, not only in the selection of German students to come to Warwick, but in also seeing that Warwick students at Giessen have had the opportunity to make the most of their year abroad.

The good fortune of Warwick in its choice of partner however has not stopped at the exchange of students. Important steps have been made towards bringing together members of the staff as well, on what is almost a regular biennial basis, each Law school taking it in turn to act as host. One volume of papers has already been published under the title 'National and European law on the threshold to the Single Member'(ed. Professor G. Weick. Peter Lang. 1993). The essays in this book are the product of their latest meeting at Warwick in the Spring of 1995. In fact the prospect of the extension of contact between staff on the basis of the exchange of students was enhanced on this occasion by the presence at the conference of two representatives from one of our partner institutions in France, the University of Bordeaux, Professor Jean du Bois du Gaudusson and Doctor Sonia Dubourg-Lavroff.

The general theme was 'Challenges to European legal scholarship'. As will be seen one major response was in the field of Community law, already an area which is both seen as a challenge and which attracts scholars who are ready to show an interest in European systems other than their own. But even where on the face of it a second group of topics deal with what look like domestic issues, it is easy to see their relevance across frontiers. A third group raise more directly some of the problems and choices associated with a readiness to look at other legal systems. The paper on Japan is an important marker in this respect. There is a sense in which the readiness to look into the law and culture of Japan in the 80s and 90s is equivalent to the boldness needed to look at Germany in the 60s. It both marks the extent to which we have moved on, at the same time as providing a reminder of about how much has still to be done by way of reorientation of legal studies.

Exchanges of the Giessen and Warwick kind have, of course, a special character and a distinctive contribution to make to the variety of cross-border contacts that are now common throughout the world. The fact that they speak as representatives of the two major European legal traditions of the world, the civil and common law systems means that they are confronting on a small scale what is still one of the major divisions of legal understanding and practice in the world at large. Their bilateral character also gives them a special quality. They are conferences of colleagues who have come to know one another on a personal basis and as a result have come slowly to understand more about the cultural and legal differences between them which goes behind the bare exchange of papers. It is a slow business but it differs in kind from the kind of contact that results from more diffuse international conferences. They also differ from a conference of specialists in a particular subject area. The fact that specialists in a bilateral conference have to explain the subject matter of their contributions, not only to colleagues with a different scholarly background and motivation, but across subject areas as well, gives them a very special quality. It is hoped it also makes them of interest to a wider audience.

There is an important footnote to all this. As was mentioned earlier, German is not the natural second language of the British legal scholars. The success of this symposium as of the others held in the past rested on the ability and willingness of the contributors from Giessen to write, make their presentations and conduct discussions in English. It is a measure of the progress we still have to make that the publication of the proceedings at this conference in German for an audience in the United Kingdom able to read it is still unthinkable.

Geoffrey Wilson
University of Warwick

1. Challenges to the Law of Contract

Professor Günter Weick – University of Giessen

I DEATH OF CONTRACT?

About 20 years ago Grant Gilmore, a professor of Law at Yale University, published a monograph with the dramatic title 'The Death of Contract'.[1] The book became a famous example of American legal literature. Is Contract dead and, consequently, the present occupation with Contract Law nothing but *'Nachlaßabwicklung'* – a kind of probate proceedings? At a closer look you find that under the sensational title Gilmore described and analyzed the decline of 19th century – so-called classical – theory of contract in the U.S.A., represented by scholars like Langdell or Williston. It is the Law of Contract which had grown out of political and economic Liberalism and was based on the pillars of strict individualism, freedom of decision and the fiction of 'homo oeconomicus'.[2] One has to realize that in the United States Liberalism reached a late and radical peak when its credo had already faded in Western Europe. And one has to realize too, that the 'American Dream', an ideology that is still fascinating generations of Americans – and not a few Europeans – is realised through contracts, be it sale, purchase, investment, securities, joint ventures etc. On the other hand Gilmore's diagnosis fits well into the environment of the last phase of the Vietnam War, which marked a deep crisis of American society: the very medium of success and making a fortune, contract itself, was in a state of agony or even decay, a gloomy perspective welcomed by the critical student generation of 1974. At that time there was indeed a whole 'Contract is Dead Movement' in the United States.[3] Since the 1970s, however, the patient believed to be dead has shown a remarkable vitality. If contract had

---

[1] G. Gilmore, The Death of Contract, Columbus, Ohio 1974. The book is based on lectures held in 1970 in Ohio State University, so Gilmore's ideas are now at least 25 years old.

[2] Cf. e.g., the characteristic given by L. Friedman, Contract Law in America, Madison and Milwaukee 1965, pp. 20-24.

[3] Cf. Gilmore, op. cit., n. 1, p. 3.

died, it had - like Phoenix - a marvellous resurrection.[4] To give just a few examples: there is a bulk of new theoretical literature on contract with programmatic titles like 'The Many Futures of Contract'[5] or 'Toward a General Theory of Contractual Obligations'[6], high-ranking conferences[7] and brain-storming workshops on contracts and a plethora of new ideas and concepts, for example 'relational contract'[8], 'symbiotic contract'[9] , 'administered contract',[10] 'Netzverträge' (network contracts)[11] etc. The resurrected bird is iridiscent and perhaps still uncoordinated in its movements, but obviously very much alive.

Let us have a short look at some of the phenomena Gilmore took as symptoms of decline and death: the growing importance of 'essentially factual questions as good faith, reasonableness, observance of commercial standards, change of circumstance'[12], the transcending of privity of contract and the extension of contractual effects to third persons,[13] the erosion of the doctrine of consideration and even the shifting from case Law of Contract to statute Law.[14]   To start with the last two symptoms: a jurist from Germany or France can imagine a sound Law of Contract without a doctrine of consideration and without the predominance of case Law. Looking at other alleged symptoms of decline and death there is no doubt that all of them were – in their time – serious challenges to traditional Contract Law. But I would say that they are also examples of successful responses by legal scholarship and the courts. It is also interesting to observe that – at least in German Law – the solutions have been found in

---

[4]   Gilmore himself (p. 103), however sceptical, gave at the end of his book a vague hint at a possible renaissance: 'Contract is dead – but who knows what unlikely resurrection the Easter-tide may bring?'

[5]   I.R. Macneil, The Many Futures of Contract, 47 South.Cal.L.Rev. 691 (1974).

[6]   Goetz / Scott, The Mitigation Principle: Toward a General Theory of Contractual Obligations, 69 Va.L.Rev. 967 (1983); cf. also Levin, McDowell, The Balance-Theory of Contracts: Seeking Justice in Contractual Obligations, 29 McGill L.J. 24 (1983).

[7]   Cf. e.g., the following published conference papers: Nicklisch (ed.), Der komplexe Langzeitvertrag, Heidelberg 1987; C. Joerges (ed.), Franchising and the Law – Theoretical and Comparative Approaches in Europe and the United States, Baden-Baden 1991; Weyers (ed.) Die Verflechtung von Verträgen – Planung und Risikoverteilung bei Großprojekten, Baden-Baden 1991.

[8]   Macneil, op. cit., n. 5, pp. 694, 720 et seq. and 1985 Wisc.L.Rev. 483.

[9]   Schanze, in: Joerges (ed.), op. cit., n. 7, pp. 67.

[10] V.P. Goldberg, Regulation and administered contract, 7 Bell J. of Econ. 426 (1976).

[11] W. Möschel, Netzverträge im bargeldlosen Zahlungsverkehr, AcP 186 (1986), 187; see also G. Teubner, in: Joerges (ed.), op. cit., n. 7, pp. 105, 115 et seq.

[12] Gilmore, op. cit., n. 1, p. 100.

[13] Ibid., pp. 90 et seq.

[14] Ibid., pp. 68/69.

the context of the Law of Contract.[15] In Germany the doctrines of *Treu und Glauben, Wegfall der Geschäftsgrundlage, Vertrag zugunsten Dritter, Vertrag mit Schutzwirkung für Dritte, Drittschadensliquidation*, which have been responses to the challenges mentioned above, have become well-established parts of the contemporary Law of Contract. The relevant battles are part of legal history. True, they have changed the character of this field of law, but they are far from having caused its demise. Gilmore's thesis is a nice example of the often experienced identification of the decline and fall of a certain conception of a legal or social institution as the total death of the institution itself.[16]

II RECENT CHALLENGES

When I said that contract is far from being dead, I did not want to pretend that Contract Law is in perfect order and harmony. There is no doubt that during the last fifty years Contract Theory and Contract Law have been faced with disturbing economic and social problems which they were not well prepared for and, which, having regard to their traditional approaches and instruments, put quite a strain on them. The facts are probably well known, so I can confine myself to a brief enumeration of some features:
– the usurpation of the freedom to determine the contract terms by one party, particularly by means of one-sided standard terms of contract;
– the development of new types of long-term contracts which require a continuous cooperation of the parties;
– hence the impossibility of anticipating all future difficulties and problems and of regulating the future relationship in clear-cut provisions;
– the tasks of filling the gaps in such contract documents and to settle the inevitable conflicts of interest in the course of a long-term relationship without upsetting it;
– the necessity of a smooth and fair 'contract administration';
– the adaptation of long-term contracts to changing political, economic and technical conditions;
– the 'complex contract' including many different, although interrelated, obligations (e.g. turnkey contracts concerning complete industrial plants including training of staff and start of production);

---

[15] The pre-contractual liability for culpa in contrahendo is based on contractual principles. In this area Contract Law sometimes attracts cases which belong to the field of torts.

[16] Another example is the confusion of the demise of the patriarchal family structure with the 'death of the family'.

– open-ended contracts without a clearly defined result, e.g. in relation to co-operation in research and development;
– the relationship between contracts between different parties in 'networks' (e.g. employer – main contractor – sub-contractors) and the protection of weaker parties in such a system (e.g. franchising or dealership contract networks).

Although most of these problems are still far from having perfect solutions, courts and arbitration tribunals, legal scholarship, occasional legislation and, last but not least, practitioners and institutions such as the ICC, have made significant progress in dealing with them, doing so in the context of, and by means of, the Law of Contract. It goes without saying that the problems are either similar in all Western industrialized countries or have specific international dimensions.

In this paper I would like to deal with two examples of fairly recent challenges and responses. The first is a very short outline of problems with networks including a main contract and sub-contracts. The second example is a closer look at specific aspects of unreasonableness or unconscionability of contracts.

III RELATIONS BETWEEN EMPLOYER – MAIN CONTRACTOR AND SUB-CONTRACTORS

As mentioned in section II, the relationship of several contracts in a 'network' can pose legal problems which are not easily solved by traditional Contract Law. Such a network can, for example, be necessary for a major project, such as the design and turn-key construction of a whole industrial plant or an airport. The typical contractual structure is a main contract between the employer and a main contractor for the whole project and a number of sub-contracts with more or less specialized sub-contractors who are often obliged to undertake part of the design work. Frequently the employer has a further contract with a consulting engineer who is responsible for planning and design overall and for the administration of the contract. Particularly in contracts influenced by English Law and British standard conditions of contract the consulting engineer has a number of different roles in the system. He is not only the agent of the employer but also certifier and even 'quasi-arbitrator' in relation to the contract between the employer and the main contractor and sometimes even to the sub-contracts. In the last-mentioned roles he has a neutral position between the parties. Sub-contractors are normally chosen by the main contractor, but it frequently happens that the choice is influenced by the employer who may go so far as to nominate a particular sub-contractor ('the nominated sub-contractor') and to determine the contents of the sub-contract. Sometimes the sub-contractors even employ sub-sub-contractors. So we are faced with a sophisticated system or network – I prefer the German term *'Vertragsgefüge'*. The various contracts are interrelated, at least in an economic sense, but, as we shall see, also in a legal sense. They all aim at one project. Frequently the performance of one contract is a precondition of the performance of other contracts. Mistakes and defective work are not only a matter of the relevant bilateral contract but will normally affect and impair other contracts and their performance.

For obvious reasons the main contract and the sub-contract terms should be harmonized. But if the parties fail to do so or the harmonization is incomplete, can courts make adaptations and corrections? Are there limits to harmonization, for example can a sub-contract term extend the defects liability period until the end of the respective period under the main contract, i.e. for the whole project? Is a main contractor fully liable for bad performance of a nominated sub-contractor, even if he had objected to his nomination? Is the employer entitled to make direct payments to sub-contractors if the cash flow is disturbed by the main contractor, thus endangering the progress of the whole project? Has a sub-contractor a direct claim against the employer in cases of insolvency or other failure of the main contractor? [17] This enumeration of problems could easily be extended. Courts and arbitrators have had a lot of troubling experience with questions like those mentioned above.[18] Meanwhile there is also scholarly literature on the problems and possible solutions.[19] Various approaches have been suggested and followed by the courts. In France there is even a

---

[17] See for these and further problems the 11 questions by J. Sweet, The American Construction Network and Its Linked Set of Contracts: Some Legal Questions and Solutions, in: Weyers (ed.), op. cit., n. 7, pp. 9, 12 et seq.

[18] See e.g., BGHZ 83, 197; Cass. Ass.Pl. 7.2.1986, D.S. 1986, 293; Cass.civ.I 21.6.1988, D.S. 1989, 5 note Larroumet; Thomas J Dyer Co. v. Bishop Intern. Eng. Co., 303 F.2d 655 (1962). Westminster Corp. v. J. Jarvis & Sons Ltd. (1970) 1 W.L.R. 637; Bickerton & Son Ltd. v. NW Metrop. Region. Hospital Board (1970) 1 All ER 1039.

[19] See e.g., the articles by Hager, Légeais, Sweet and Vékás in: Weyers (ed.), op. cit., n. 7; Dubisson, dpci 1983, 429 ; Nicklisch, NJW 1985, 2361 et seq.; Vetter, RIW 1986, 81; Parris, Default by Sub-Contractors and Suppliers, London 1985; Keating, Sub-Contracts under English Law, in Gauch, Sweet (eds.), Selected Problems of Construction Law, Fribourg/London 1983, pp. 213; Lloyd, Thornton, Clay, in: Halsbury's Laws of England, 4th ed., vol. 4 (2), Reissue 1992, par. 339-352; Weick, Vereinbarte Standardbedingungen im deutschen und englischen Bauvertragsrecht, München 1977, pp. 197 et seq.

special statute which deals with some of the problems, particularly the protection of the sub-contractor.[20]

It is evident that adequate solutions cannot be achieved on the basis of strict privity of contract. By now, however, approaches taken by legislators, courts and most of the literature are half-hearted and typically piecemeal.[21] They lack a sound theoretical basis and framework. A little analogy here, extensive interpretation of specific provisions there, or the odd statutory claim – but most frequently the advice that most problems could be tackled by suitable provisions in the relevant contracts. The latter approach, that the contracting parties should take care to make provision, is obviously insufficient, because then solutions are found at the expense of the weakest participants, in most cases the sub-contractors. Apart from that, one cannot reasonably expect the parties to anticipate all the manifold situations and intricate legal questions that may arise in such a network.

The reality of contractual networks cannot be assessed by following the bilateral relations, and not even by reluctant extensions to third parties, for example the application of *'Drittschadensliquidation'* or *'Vertrag mit Schutzwirkung für Dritte'* in German Law. The individual contracts must be seen in their social and economic context. A helpful general basis is the theory of complex systems with its premise that the system as a whole is more than the sum of its single components (i.e. here the bilateral contracts). As in an ant-heap – a natural example of a complex system and a sophisticated cooperational 'project' – there must be something that makes the system work, something which is beyond the interests and possibly the comprehension of its single participants. In the case of complex contractual systems there is a little more certainty about the 'something' than with natural complex systems. We know that the various contracts in a project network are connected by a man-made common plan, an organizational framework and, hopefully, a cooperational spirit. But the law is still lagging behind this comprehension. The approach from the law of bilateral contracts is inadequate to assess the reality of a complex contractual system. I do not expect substantial solutions from Tort Law or Company Law. The Law of Contract is the suitable framework, but it

---

[20] Loi de 31.12.1975, J.O. 3.1.1976 pf. 80 with amendments of 1981 and 1984.

[21] Of course, there are some exceptions: Nicklisch NJW 1985, 2361, 2370 suggested a general approach which refers to the specific structure of sub-contracts combined in a common project. See also Austrian OGH, JBl 1990, 587 which considers a general view but does not apply it in order to decide the case. Significant transgression of the privity of contract doctrine also in Cass.civ.I, 21.6.1988, D.S. 1989, 5 and Cass.civ.I, 8.3.1988, J.C.P.1988 II 21070, cf. Légeais, in: Weyers (ed.), op. cit., n. 7, pp. 29, 41 et seq.

needs further development to comprehend and integrate the legal problems of contractual networks.

IV PROBLEMS WITH UNREASONABLE SURETY CONTRACTS AND OTHER CONSUMER OBLIGATIONS.

In this section I want to focus on problems which for the last six years have troubled several courts in Germany, among them two senates of the BGH (Federal Court of last instance in civil matters) and the Federal Constitutional Court, but which in my opinion represent a general problem of Contract Law. Obviously, it is a topic which causes strong feelings and unusually emotional arguments by lawyers, who are normally expected to keep cool. One court, the OLG Stuttgart (Court of Appeal in Stuttgart), based its decision on 'the inalienable right of hope and the pursuit of happiness'[22] and quoted the relevant sentence of the U.S. Declaration of Independence. The Federal Court (9th senate), however, was not impressed by this high authority and reversed the decision. It was in turn criticized by a professor of law as representing the 'ice-cold wind of private autonomy of the late 19th century'.[23] Lower courts refused to follow the Federal Court, something which is allowed because our legal system does not know a doctrine of stare decisis, and one of them condemned the Federal Court's decision as '*herzlos*' (heartless).[24] Two senates of the Federal Court (BGH) went different ways, and the Federal Constitutional Court (BVerfG) rendered two judgments reprimanding the BGH for having neglected a fundamental human right, Art.2(1) GG.[25]

1. The Facts and Background of the Surety Cases

What had happened? The typical facts of the cases are rather simple. A member of a family, normally the husband – or father as the case may be – wanted a bank loan. In most cases he was a businessman, and the desired loan was rather high. The bank required a surety (*'Bürgschaft'*) or a collateral obligation (*'Schuldbeitritt'*) from his wife or, in some cases, from

---

[22] OLG Stuttgart NJW 1988, 833 (835): '...Erhaltung des unveräußerlichen Menschenrechtes auf Hoffnung, auf das Streben nach dem Glück'.

[23] Honsell JZ 1989, 492 (495).

[24] LG Münster 1990, 1668; cf., also LG Osnabrück NJW-RR 1990, 306, which refused to follow the BGH as well.

[25] BVerfG NJW 1994, 36 = BVerfGE 89, 214; BVerfG NJW 1994, 2749.

his grown-up son or daughter. In all disputed cases the wife, son or daughter had no significant financial means and only a modest income, if any. Sometimes – but not in all cases – the wife, son or daughter hesitated and were only induced to sign the contract by the husband's or father's influence, emphasizing family solidarity. In a few cases the banker played down the dangers of the contract, for example with remarks such as that it was 'not a big obligation' or 'only for our files'[26]. When the main debtor later became insolvent, the wife, son or daughter were confronted with a liability which went far beyond their capability; if the obligation was valid, the poor person would have to work for the rest of her life to pay the debts living at subsistence level. At first glance it is hard to understand why the banks insisted on obtaining the surety or collateral obligation, as in most cases they were well aware of the miserable financial situation of the family member. The true reason was that the banks wanted to prevent the transfer of assets from the main debtor to the wife, son or daughter. This technique of shifting assets (so-called *'Vermögensverschiebung'*) is frequently used by businesspeople. In German Insolvency Law and the Law of Tort there are only limited possibilities of making a wife or child liable for her husband's or father's debts. The banks at least consider these statutory remedies as insufficient and have tried to reduce their risks by the above-mentioned practice.[27]

2. The Conflicting Responses by Civil Courts and the Federal Constitutional Court

Since the late 1980s the civil courts have been busy with such cases. Meanwhile there are at least ten decisions of the BGH,[28] and many more decisions of lower courts. The courts are split into two camps. One, including the 11th senate of the Federal Court, tends to help the poor family members. We can not go into the details of the various decisions. The main line of reasoning, however, is as follows: The contract of surety etc was void because of a violation of 'gute Sitten' *(bonae mores)* in the sense of § 138 (1) BGB (German Civil Code). The wife – or other family

---

[26] Cf. BGH NJW 1989,1605; LG Münster NJW 1989,1668.

[27] This practice to require sureties or collateral obligations from family members, even if they have no sufficient means, seems widespread. In the case LG Münster NJW 1990, 1668 (1670) the plaintiff argued that it was a common practice of banks ('banküblich').

[28] BGH NJW 1988, 2599; BGH NJW 1989, 830 = BGHZ 106, 269; BGH NJW 1989, 1276 = BGHZ 107, 92; BGH NJW 1989, 1605; BGH NJW 1991, 923 and 2015; BGH NJW 1992, 896; BGH NJW 1993, 322 = BGHZ 120, 272; BGH NJW 1994, 1278; BGH NJW 1995, 592; see also BGH NJW 1989, 1665 and NJW 1990, 1034 concerning unmarried partners.

member – took a financial burden which she was never capable of bearing unless she experienced a most unlikely change in her personal and economic situation. This, together with other special circumstances, can amount to a serious disturbance of the contractual balance (*'Vertragsparität'*). Relevant special circumstances were easily found by those courts: that the loan was only for the husband's business, or that the bank, by insisting on getting the surety, caused the husband to appeal to family solidarity, marital love etc.[29] The OLG Stuttgart, as mentioned above, based its decision on the wife's inalienable right to hope and the pursuit of happiness.[30]

The second group, lead by the 9th senate of the Federal Court, represents the hardliners. This senate delivered most of the relevant last instance decisions. Their starting points are the principle of freedom of contract and the principle of full capacity (*'volle Geschäftsfähigkeit'*), which in Germany as in most European countries begins at the age of eighteen. According to the Court freedom of contract (one aspect of private autonomy) includes the ability of every person of full capacity to enter into contractual obligations even if they are risky and even if the promisor can fulfil them only under especially favourable circumstances.[31] A person over eighteen is able to recognise that a surety is a risky contract, even if she does not have any special experience.[32] It is up to the promisor to evaluate her financial resources. The motive of family solidarity is not a reason for saying that of the surety contract is unconscionable.[33] This point of view can be summarized by the sentence 'a contract is a contract'. It was on this basis that the 9th senate of the BGH confirmed, for example, a surety signed by a pharmacy assistant for obligations of her former husband amounting to one million DM,[34] or a surety limited to 350 000 DM by two students, 20 and 21 years old, for debts of their father.[35] Another decision in favour of the bank concerned a surety signed by a 21 year old unskilled worker in a fish factory with a net income of 1150 DM per month for her father's debts.[36] The total sum of the debts at the time of his bankruptcy were 2.4 million DM, but 'fortunately' the surety was limited to 100 000 DM. This rigid position was maintained until October 1993 when the

---

[29] Cf. e.g., BGH (11th senate) NJW 1991, 923 (925).
[30] See op. cit., n. 22. The doctrinal approach was an analogy to § 310 BGB.
[31] BGH NJW 1989, 830 (831) and 1276 (1277).
[32] BGH NJW 1989, 830 (831).
[33] BGH NJW 1989, 830 (831); BGH NJW 1991, 2015 (2016).
[34] BGH NJW 1992, 869.
[35] BGH NJW 1989, 830.
[36] BGH NJW 1989, 1605.

Federal Constitutional Court entered the stage and rendered two decisions[37] forcing the hardliners to reconsider their decisions. One of the cases brought before the Constitutional Court was the case mentioned above of the 21 year old unskilled worker. According to the Federal Constitutional Court the core of these cases is a conflict of equal fundamental rights of the contracting parties, the rights to self-determination of the individual (*'freie Entfaltung der Persönlichkeit'*) in the sense of art. 2(1) GG. They are interrelated and have to be weighed against each other. This excludes a solution in the favour of the right of the stronger party. Contracts must not be used as instruments of heteronomy (*'Fremdbestimmung'*). It has to be avoided that one party, due to his or her totally dominant position, can de facto determine the contents of the contract. If civil courts have to decide cases where one party to the contract is in a position of 'structural inferiority' (*strukturelle Unterlegenheit*) and the consequences of the contract mean an unusual burden to the weaker party, the courts must not rely on the principle 'a contract is a contract' but have the duty to make corrections.[38] Without going into details of the law of obligations the Constitutional Court gives a hint that the solution could best be found on the basis of the general provisions of the Civil Code concerning bonae mores (§ 138 BGB) and good faith (§ 242 BGB). The Court recommends a control of the contents of the relevant contracts (*'Inhaltskontrolle'*).[39] In the case of the unskilled worker it came to the conclusion that the ninth senate of the BGH had violated the fundamental right to self-determination of the defendant by appraising the surety contract as if it were a normal contract without having regard to the unequal bargaining power of the parties and the special circumstances of the contract.[40]

The reaction of the BGH, in the shape of its hardliner ninth senate, has been a turn, but not a U-turn. The two judgments of the Constitutional Court concerned grown-up children of the main debtor, and a lot of criticism focussed on the heavy burden put on young people which could destroy their hope and future.[41] The first reaction of the BGH, worthy of a Solomon, is a nice distinction made between sons and daughters on one

---

[37] BVerfG NJW 1994, 36 and NJW 1994, 2749.

[38] BVerfG NJW 1994, 36 (38 et seq.).

[39] Ibid. at p. 38 (C.II.2.c).

[40] A similar decision of the Fed. Const. Court concerned contracts signed by a daughter and her fiancé, in order to secure her parents' debts. It was delivered in August 1994, BVerfG NJW 1994, 2749.

[41] E.g. Honsell JZ 1989, 495 et seq.; Wochner BB 1989, 1354 (1355).

side and a spouse on the other side. In a decision of February 1994,[42] four months after the spectacular first judgment of the Federal Constitutional Court, the same ninth senate of the BGH which had led the hardliners nullified a surety signed by a 24 year old soldier with a net income of 1500 DM per month. It was certainly a strong case, the total and final amount of his parents' debts amounting to more than 2 million DM. The Court did not make much fuss about its change of opinion.[43] True, it repeated the credo of former decisions that freedom of contract also included risky contracts and that normally a person of full capacity could evaluate the risks of becoming a surety and act accordingly. But now the ninth senate recognises 'special circumstances' which were neglected in earlier cases: firstly, the gross discrepancy between the extent of the obligation and the capability of the promisor, and secondly, the undue influence by the parents upon the son, which according to the Court could be attributed to the bank. In this case the influence was not exceptional, apparently only the normal allusion to family solidarity. So it is obvious that the hardliners of the BGH made an almost complete U-turn as far as grown-up children of the main debtor are concerned. The latest judgment of the BGH of January 5th 1995 [44]makes it clear that the same senate is determined to treat spouses differently. As to grown-up children the judges now go so far as to say that their sureties signed by reason of family solidarity and resulting in a long-term financial strain, are as a rule immoral (*'in aller Regel rechtlich und sittlich zu mißbilligen'*).[45] Marriage, however, as the Court sees it, is also a partnership with regard to economic risks; normally the wife should not complain about her participation in the liability for investments which are to benefit the family income, even if she has no other assets.[46]

Nevertheless, the Court has found a way to discharge the spouse as well under certain circumstances. This is not the Court's own idea; the judgment refers to suggestions in legal literature.[47] It is the most interesting and most questionable part of the new decision. The judges stick to the

---

[42] BGH NJW 1994, 1278. The aim of the bank, to avoid the disadvantages of a transfer of assets, which had been taken seriously in former decisions of the same senate, was now played down, cf., ibid., at p. 1279 (B.III.1.c).

[43] In its reasons there is only one sentence that the senate does not stick to its former decisions insofar as they neglected the freedom of decision of grown-up but inexperienced 'children' (Ibid., at p. 1280).

[44] BGH NJW 1995, 592.

[45] Ibid. at p. 593 (II.2.b).

[46] BGH, op. cit., n. 40.

[47] BGH, op. cit., n. 44, p. 594; cf. Reifner, ZIP 1990, 427, 434 et seq.; H.P. Westermann, FS H. Lange (1992), 995(1013 et seq.). See also Medicus, AcP 188 (1988), 489, 504 et seq. on the application of the doctrine to consumer cases in general.

opinion that the banks have a legitimate interest to prevent the transfer of assets from the main debtor to a spouse or unmarried partner, the true reason behind the bank's demand to get a surety or collateral obligation from a person of insufficient means. The Court has held that in such cases the surety etc. has a peculiar purpose: not to extend the capital subject to liability (*'Haftungsmasse'*), but to avoid damage to the bank by transfer of assets. Consequently, the essential question is: was there a transfer of assets between the spouses or is it still possible?[48] If so, the surety is valid. If not, the BGH has taken refuge in the established doctrine of cessation of the basis of the contract (*'Wegfall der Geschäftsgrundlage'*), a doctrine that has a certain similarity to the English 'frustration of contract'. In this case a 34 year old wife with three children, who had neither a training for a job nor other financial means, signed a surety for the debts of her husband with a limit of 280 000 DM. After their divorce the husband became insolvent. The bank claimed 280 000 DM plus interest from the wife and obtained an enforcement order for part of the amount, namely 50 000 DM. The Federal Court held – on the basis of the asserted new type of surety – that as a result of the divorce there was a clear case of cessation of the basis of the contract, as there was no further danger that the divorced husband would transfer assets, if he had any, to his former wife. One would expect that under these circumstances the Court would have discharged the lady from the surety burden. Surprisingly, it made another turn. The judges did not say 'valid' or 'not valid', but 'only 17,85 %'. How is that possible? The doctrine of *Wegfall der Geschäftsgrundlage* is based on the principle of good faith (§ 242 BGB) and is applied with caution and restraint. It is meant to avoid intolerable and absolutely unreasonable results. The normal remedy under this doctrine is a modification of the contract and only in exceptional cases the total termination of the contract. This is the formal justification for the Court's interference with the contents of the contract. The liability of the defendant is reduced from 280 000 DM to 50 000 DM, presumably because the bank itself had limited its first resort to litigation, i.e. the partial enforcement order, to this amount.

3. Comments on the Latest Decisions of the BGH

This is the present situation. In my opinion the decision of January 1995 is not the end of the story but only the beginning of a new act in the drama.[49]

---

48 BGH NJW 1995, 592, at p. 594 (II.3.b).

49 Cf. only the new article by Huff 'Die lebenslange Mithaftung' in the German newspaper Frankfurter Allgemeine Zeitung of 19 April 1995, p. 15, with a critical

Let me start my comment with some remarks as to the present position of our highest civil court. Its latest turns show that the original rigid approach is now considered to be untenable; on the other hand, the Court is not prepared to admit that its position was totally erroneous. Several aspects of the latest decision are doubtful. I want to make it clear: the Court does not protect a spouse charged with an exorbitant surety obligation for debts of her husband as long as the couple is not separated. There is only an obiter dictum that in cases of this special type of surety one might construe the contract in a way that it includes a tacit *pactum de non petendo* as long as the spouse has no significant means of her own. This is only a vague allusion, and banks will be quick to exclude such an interpretation by changing their standard contract terms. This construction is any way difficult to reconcile with the solution in the relevant case that the wife after her divorce, being as poor as before, was liable to pay 50 000 DM.[50] By taking refuge in the doctrine of *Wegfall der Geschäftsgrundlage* in cases of separation or divorce, the BGH has tried to evade the objections of the Federal Constitutional Court. However, as far as spouses are concerned, it is not prepared to go in the heart of the Constitutional Court's criticism. In my opinion the distinction between grown-up children and spouses is not convincing. There are good reasons for the opposite point of view. *Firstly,* with regard to the special purpose of the surety, namely the prevention of damage by a transfer of assets, there is little difference between the members of a family. Business people can achieve this with spouses as well as with children, and even with unmarried partners. *Secondly,* not is it only the spouse but also the children, as presumable heirs and as persons entitled to maintenance, who are beneficiaries of a flourishing enterprise of their father. *Thirdly,* the ninth senate of the BGH has always stressed that from the bank's perspective the value of the surety lay in the future, and one did not know how the economic situation of the family member would develop.[51] If this is so the chances of a 21 year old student of getting a good income are certainly better than those of a forty year old housewife.[52]

---

appraisal of the latest decision and the statement, that at the moment even bank lawyers cannot tell which surety contracts are valid.

[50] BGH NJW 1995, 592, at p. 593.

[51] Cf. e.g., BGH NJW 1991, 2015 (2017).

[52] The Federal Court's position regarding unmarried partners is also obscure. In 1989 the 3rd senate refused to apply § 138 (1) BGB to collateral obligations of unmarried partners in two cases of gross discrepancy between the amount of debts and the means of the partner (BGH NJW 1989, 1665; BGH NJW 1990, 1034). The new decision of the 9th senate appears to privilege the unmarried partner by emphasizing the economic solidarity of spouses and the character of marriage as a 'risk community' (Risikogemeinschaft), see BGH NJW 1995, 592 (593). This raises constitutional

The asserted specific type of surety is certainly a novelty. According to the BGH it is defined by its special purpose: to prevent the damaging effects of a transfer of assets from the main debtor to the person who is to sign the surety. But the Court does not follow this through, because it does not recognize the total cessation of the basis of the contract after a separation or divorce of the spouses, only being prepared to reduce the obligation. This implies a complicated mixed purpose: in the relevant case it treated 17,85 % genuine surety and 82,15 % is intended to prevent a tranfer of assets, a rather artificial creation! Nor is it plausible that in future the fate of commercial transactions, for example the surety of a bank credit granted to a businessman or the collateral obligation with the same purpose, should depend on the marital harmony of the two debtors. This, however, is the consequence if the basis of the contract is linked with the prognosis as to whether or not the main debtor will be inclined to transfer assets to his spouse. And to make it worse, the loyal and devoted wife who stands by the side of her husband even in times of financial desaster will be strangled (cf. the proverb *'Bürgen soll man würgen'*), while the opportunist who leaves the other partner in bad times will be protected. This is the result of the new approach.

4. Wider Context and Foreign Cases

These and other doubts raised by the latest decision of our Federal Court gives the impression that it is far from being a happy solution. I would, with respect, go even further to say that it does not get to the bottom of the problem. The crucial questions are not about the expectations of poor young people, undue influence by parents or the probability of a transfer of assets to a spouse. All these facts are peripheral. Nor is the core of the relevant cases a problem of specific German banking practice. The surety cases in German courts are only part of a more general problem. They put the spotlight on some actors in a play with a much larger cast. To show the wider and international dimensions I will refer two cases from England and the U.S.A.

In a sensational English case (which I know only from a newspaper report), a salesman had made a hire purchase contract with a customer who was obviously totally incapable of paying the instalments. When the purchaser failed to pay several instalments, the vendor made a claim for the

---

doubts, because Art. 6 (1) GG provides for special protection of marriage. Or are unmarried partners examples of the old legal proverb 'Bürgen soll man würgen' (he who signs a surety shall be strangled), because they have neither the special position of children nor the protection of *Wegfall der Geschäftsgrundlage* granted to the spouse?

total amount. The judge held that the defendant had to pay the total amount but allowed him to pay by instalments of one penny per month in order to show the nonsense of giving credit to people who do not have a minimum of credit-worthiness, who are'not good for a penny'.

In the case of *Williams v. Walker-Thomas Furniture Co.*[53] a U.S. Court of Appeals had to consider an instalment purchase of a stereo set by a woman who together with her seven children had to live on $ 218 monthly welfare payment. Although the vendor was aware of her financial situation he sold her the stereo set for $ 514, thus raising her debts together with a balance due from former sales to $ 678. A clause in the small print said that all payments made by the purchaser should be credited pro rata on all outstanding bills and accounts due.[54] The Court held that there were strong indications of the unconscionability of the contract and therefore its unenforceability, but remanded the case to the trial court for further proceedings.

The Williams case has a certain similarity to a German case decided by the Federal Court in 1982.[55] The plaintiff, a so-called 'Dowry Service', sold to a woman a 'dowry' of luxurious bed linen at a total price of 12,000 DM payable in monthly rates of 200 DM. The goods were to be delivered after the last payment, i.e. normally after five years. The snag was that the woman had six minor children and lived on social security payments of about 1100 DM per month. So she was not really in a position where one needs a luxurious dowry. She did not make any payments. The Federal Court (eighth senate) held that the contract was void because of a violation of bonae mores *('gute Sitten'),* § 138 (1) BGB, because of its imbalance, its one-sided terms, and the circumstances of its conclusion.

5. The Crucial Problem of the Cases

The common core of all the cases mentioned above is the old problem of contractual justice *('Vertragsgerechtigkeit').* However, it is suggested that the crucial point of the cases is more specific and, although not a new phenomenon, has been neglected for a long time. In order to show this you

---

[53] 350 F.2d 445 (1965) = 18 ALR 3d 1297.

[54] 350 F.2d 445, at p. 447. The result of the provision was to keep a balance due on every item purchased until the balance due on all items, whenever bought, was paid. So the vendor had a security giving him the right to repossess all the items. This is a possible explanation why the company sold the stereo set in spite of being aware of the incapability of the purchaser.

[55] BGH NJW 1982, 1455; cf. also BGH NJW 1982, 1457, a case concerning the 'dowry' of a 18 year old student.

need not go back to the sentence of the French scholar Fouillé,: 'Qui dit contractuel dit juste'.[56] Those times when scholars believed that the very instrument of contract was sufficient to guarantee justice are far away. Modern Contract Law is aware of the possibility of inherent injustice in contracts. For centuries the Law has tried to prevent a gross imbalance between the two sides of a reciprocal contract, particularly through the doctrine of *laesio enormis* and the prohibition of usury, but also on the basis of general principles such as *bonae mores*, good faith or reasonableness. With the spreading of standardized contracts, lawyers became sensitive to the possible injustice produced by unilaterally drafted contract terms. After a period of concealed control of contract terms by pretending that the relevant clauses had not become part of the agreement, the courts and legislators took the step towards direct control of the contents of contract terms. I refer to the well known statutes of the 1970s, for example the Unfair Contract Terms Act 1977 or the German AGB-Gesetz of 1976.[57] The latest initiative in this context is the EC Directive on unfair contract terms in consumer contracts of 5 April 1993 which has to be implemented by the Member States.[58] The normal method followed by the statutes and the EC Directive is to combine a ban of certain types of unfair clauses with general control standards based on principles such as 'reasonableness', *'Treu und Glauben'* or 'unconscionability'. Apart from that the legislators take different approaches to the problems of unfair contract terms. The German *AGB-Gesetz* is limited to the control of *'Allgemeine Geschäftsbedingungen'* (standard terms of contract). In addition § 242 BGB is used as a basis of control of unfair individual terms or standard terms outside the scope of the *AGB-Gesetz*. The EC Directive focusses on unfair terms in consumer contracts, i.e. contracts between businesspeople and consumers, and includes both standard terms and individual terms. German statute law has to be amended to include this European approach.

However, in a closer look we find that the crucial point of the cases dealt with in this paper (surety, dowry etc.) does not fit into these established patterns of unfairness and their treatment by enlightened contract lawyers. The cases are not about imbalance in reciprocal agreements. A surety contract is not a reciprocal contract at all; the obligation of the promisor

---

[56] Fouillé, La Science sociale contemporaine (1880), p. 410, quoted in Kahn-Freund, Levy, Rudden, Source-book in French Law, 2nd ed., Oxford 1979, p. 319.

[57] See also § 879 Austrian ABGB and §§ 1 et seq. of the Austrian Konsumenten-schutzgesetz; sec. 2-302 of the American UCC.

[58] Directive 93/13/EWG, ABl EG Nr. L 95/29 (German edition).

lacks a counter-obligation of the creditor.[59] Therefore the law of usury is not applicable.[60] Nor is the lack of proportion between the two main obligations a decisive factor in the above-mentioned instalment sales cases. For example, in the *Williams* case the contract may be unconscionable but not because of a gross discrepancy between the price and the value of the stereo set.

But what about unfairness of contract terms? True, some of the decisions lay some stress on unfair clauses in the contracts, for example the U.S. Court of Appeals in the *Williams* case or the eighth senate of the BGH in the dowry cases.[61] Courts in civil matters are inclined to do justice in the individual case; so if in the relevant case they find specific facts that fit into well-established patterns of reasoning they tend to use this track even if it is a side-track. In my opinion it was a side-track. If in the *Williams* contract the Court had nullified the clause concerning the pro rata crediting on all outstanding payments, the contract of sale of the stereo set would not be fair and reasonable. And if in the German dowry case the welfare mother had got the luxurious bed linen for 12,000 DM right at the beginning, serious doubts would remain regarding the validity of the contract. The accidental nature of the contents of contract terms becomes obvious in the surety cases. The standard terms of the surety contracts were the usual terms used by the German banks. There were no elements of unfairness of specific contract terms. One might argue that in all cases the limit of liability was too high. This, however, does not go to the root of the problem. If the banks were obliged to adapt the limit to the capability of the relevant partners they would have to reduce the sureties in most cases to ridiculously small amounts, and the sureties would loose their point. Hence the crucial point in the surety cases is not the unfairness of single terms but clearly the fact that the banks induced the poor person to sign the contract at all. I also suggest that even a clause in the surety discharging the wife in case of separation or divorce is not sufficient to remove the objections. Therefore I am not convinced by the recent approach of the BGH mentioned above.[62] The Constitutional Court's remarks concerning contractual disparity (*'gestörte Vertragsparität'*) and the instruction to apply in these cases the method of *'Inhaltskontrolle'* (control of the contents of the contract) fall short of the problem as well.[63]

---

[59] BGH NJW 1989, 830 (831); BGH NJW 1988, 2599.

[60] Wochner BB 1989, 1354 et seq., however, wants to apply at least the underlying principle ('Rechtsgedanke') of the usury provision § 138 (2) BGB.

[61] Cf. op. cit., n. 55.

[62] Cf. op. cit., n. 44 and pp. 15-16.

[63] BVerfG NJW 1994, 36 (38 et seq.).

Inhaltskontrolle makes sense with single contract terms or groups of contract terms, but not when the contract as such is opressive because it puts too much strain on a person and under normal circumstances can not be performed by him or her. Then the question is: valid or void? We should stop blurring the problem by evasive arguments concerning unfair terms, the bank's duty to warn or clarify, or frustration of purpose etc.

6. Steps Towards a Solution

The answer to the crucial question is not easy. Certainly the BGH is right in emphasizing that the freedom of contract includes also the freedom to enter into risky obligations.[64] To take risks is an essential element of a market economy. However, I am not equally sure of the Court's second premise that freedom of contract includes also the freedom to incur an obligation that could be fulfilled only under exceptionally favourable circumstances.[65] Here is the starting point for limitations. If an employee undertook to work 20 hours per day for even only one week this would, even in an extremely laissez-faire society, be considered to be an unenforceable obligation. And it is only in fairy tales that valid commitments are made to build a castle in one day; the deplorable building contractor can only rely on 'exceptionally favourable circumstances' such as the help of a fairy queen – or the devil as the case may be. So why should it be different with financial obligations? It is because of a deeply rooted dogma that no debtor is excused by a lack of financial means. German law students learn in their first year: *'Geld hat man zu haben'* (one has to have money).[66] I suggest that this dogma has blocked the understanding of our problem. Again, the sentence makes good sense when a person incurs a reasonable obligation and later runs out of money. But it is an exaggeration to consider the dogma 'one has to have money' as a cornerstone of freedom of contract.[67] In my opinion, it has nothing to do with the problem whether a contract is unfair from its very beginning because it charges a person with a burden that he or she is totally unable to bear.

Finally I would like to outline my approach to the problem. If the future situation of a person is only uncertain, for example the monthly income of a future solicitor after the completion of his legal education, there is no

---

[64] Cf. op. cit., n. 32 and n. 43.
[65] Cf. op. cit., n. 31 and BGH NJW 1994, 1278, 1279 (B.II.2.); BGH NJW 1995, 592 (II.1.).
[66] See for the origin and the meaning of the doctrine Medicus, AcP 188 (1988), 489.
[67] In English Law this is obviously not an insurmountable dogma; see the cases mentioned below in n. 71.

reason why he should not incur a financial obligation which he could fulfil under normal or even favourable circumstances. In many countries students take loans to finance their studies. But if an unskilled worker who is in her forties and has no other assets signs a surety contract amounting to half a million DM it would be naive to say: you never know how her financial situation will be in some years. She may hit the jackpot or inherit the fortune of a forgotten uncle in America. I hold that these are not serious arguments in a legal discussion. Turning to the underlying principles and basic values, I confess that I am not a friend of deciding questions of private law by weighing constitutional fundamental rights. But in this context it makes good sense to refer to the principles of human dignity and self-determination of the individual, which are embodied in our Constitution[68] and considered to be general value decisions (*'Wertentscheidungen'*) that are to be respected also in civil disputes. It is the advantage of the dramatic surety cases – promisor facing further fifty years of his life at subsistence level without any chance to get rid of the burden etc. – that may make this dimension perfectly clear, and it is to the credit of our Federal Constitutional Court that may have focussed attention on it.

If this is accepted as the basis of the suggested unconscionability test,[69] it has to be limited to obligations of natural persons. Legal persons (*personnes morales, juristische Personen*) or other corporations on the debtor's side have to be excluded.

How should the relevant standard of unconscionablity be defined? There is a nice, although vague, description of an unconscionable bargain in an English case of the 18th century:

...such as no man[70] in his senses and not under delusion would make on the one hand, and as no honest and fair man would accept on the other.[71]

These simple and plain words are a useful starting point. They make it clear that there must be irrational behaviour on both sides. The debtor must act hazardously, desperately or just foolishly in taking a burden which goes far beyond his or her capability. The creditor must behave irresponsibly and unfairly by inducing the promisor to bind himself or at least by

---

[68] See Articles 1 (1) and 2 (1) GG.

[69] I would prefer the notion 'unconscionability' to 'fairness', because it expresses the fact that the conclusion of the contract is contrary to good conscience.

[70] Today we would add 'and woman'.

[71] Earl of Chesterfield v. Janssen (1750) 2 Ves.Sen. 125, 28 E.R. 82 at p. 100. See also King v. Michael Faraday & Partners Ltd. (1939) 2 K.B. 753 at pp. 761-763, where Atkinson J. held that an obligation depriving the debtor of his sole means of support and being 'wholly impossible of performance from the common-sense point of view', was against public policy.

accepting his promise. This also means that the creditor must not close his eyes to the financial situation of the promisor. As a bank or salesman he will be normally well informed of the customer's financial means. A careful businessperson will seek information before he or she gives a major credit or accepts a surety. Apart from cases of clear fraud on the part of the customer, the creditor's knowledge can be assumed.

What about the additional requirement of 'structural inferiority' (*'strukturelle Unterlegenheit'*) of one party which is suggested by the Federal Constitutional Court.[72]   This is a relatively new and unusual concept. As far as I can see the Constitutional Court used it for the first time in the context of Contract Law, and it has given no explanation of it. Adomeit, in a harsh criticism of this new 'general clause'[73], traced it back to a book by the German professor Norbert Reich.[74]   His concept of structural inferiority is very wide and influenced by a general criticism of the capitalist market economy. Reich made the statement that the whole structure of communication (*'Kommunikationsstruktur'*) of modern markets was oriented to the interests of corporations, and the consumer had the role of a passive-receptive market participant. As a result of this structure of markets the consumer is almost always in an inferior position. The market power of 'active market participants', i.e. trading companies, banks and other corporations, is a 'regular phenomenon'[75]. In this wide sense the concept may have its merits in political economy but it is unsuitable as a criterion for the decision of contract cases. It is obscure and not appropriate as a basis for distinctions. I therefore reject the additional requirement of 'structural inferiority'.

Obviously, the suggested unconscionability test has to be elaborated and put into more concrete terms. The doctrinal basis in German Law could be § 138 (1) BGB concerning *bonae mores (gute Sitten).*   Criteria and arguments might be drawn from former cases concerning economic duress or *'Knebelungsverträge'* (strangling contracts).[76]   A difficult point is of course the borderline between a heavy but tolerable burden and an unconscionable overload. First of all I want to make it clear that a strict standard has to be applied. Unconscionability in this sense must be an exception limited to strong cases. It is impossible to fix a certain limit or a proportion to obligations and monthly income. The welfare mother who

---

[72] BVerfG NJW 1994, 36 (38), cf. supra IV.2 (n.38).
[73] NJW 1994, 2467.
[74] Reich, Markt und Recht, Neuwied 1977, esp. pp. 182 et seq.
[75] Reich, op. cit., n. 74, p. 181, and on the concept of structural inferiority pp. 182, 185.
[76] Cf. in German Law RGZ 147, 347, BGHZ 44, 161 and 83, 316; in English Law the already mentioned case King v. Michael Faraday & Partners Ltd., op. cit., n. 71.

had to struggle in order to feed her six children was overloaded by a debt of 12,000 DM for luxury bed linen, a sum which equalled her total net income per year. On the contrary, a surety limited to 12,000 DM and signed by a student who at present has no regular income, is something 'a man in his senses' could accept. If the bargain, however, has the character of a unserious speculation, a gamble,[77] the legal system should keep out; in most European legal systems gaming and betting obligations are unenforceable!

Banks will argue that they have a legitimate interest to prevent damage caused by the transfer of assets to members of the family. Firstly, it has to be stressed that this argument is only suitable in some of the cases, not even to all the surety cases.[78] Apart from that, I cannot agree with the BGH that this is a legitimate new type of surety. In my opinion it is a misuse of a legal form which must not be tolerated if it leads to the kind of result set out earlier in this paper.

V FINAL REMARKS

Is this suggestion a new step in the process of the demolition of contract? Is it perhaps shifting the emphasis from Contract Law to Constitutional Law or Social Law? I do not think so. The problem is a genuine problem of the Law of Contract, the standard applied is related to fair and reasonable contracting parties and the solution is based on the principles of private autonomy and self-determination, i.e. a further development of the inherent limits of contracts.

---

[77] A sort of gamble was the contract in the Earl of Chesterfield case, cited in n. 63: The obligor, at the age of 30 and not of good health, borrowed £5000 on bond to pay £10,000 if he survives his grandmother, but to repay nothing if she survives him.

[78] E.g. not in the 'Stuttgart mothers' case BGH NJW 1988, 2599.

2. Consent To Medical Treatment In English Law – A Critical Re-Examination

John A. Harrington – University of Warwick

INTRODUCTION

In the last twenty-five years consent has emerged as central to ethical and legal thinking on medical treatment. The meaning of consent and its importance and applicability in the medical context have been tested by scholars and judges in most western jurisdictions. This essay seeks to re-examine the role of consent in medical law, in England in particular, having regard to a recent series of cases concerning the refusal of treatment. By linking the law, such as it has emerged from these decisions, with that developed in the 1980's concerning the doctrine of informed consent it should be possible to draw some conclusions regarding the role of law and the courts in medicine. Throughout we shall be contrasting the supposedly traditional and outdated paternalism of the medical profession with the liberal, pro-autonomy strategies of (mainly) academic commentators. It will be suggested that the struggle of liberal critics of current medical law to overcome the disempowerment of patients through doctrines of informed consent and valid refusal are unlikely to meet with significant success for two reasons. First, in the light of such sociological evidence as exists, these commentators fail to have sufficient regard to the real features of medicine as practiced. Second, it may be said that they fail to appreciate the indeterminacy and scope for manipulation which concepts of consent and capacity to consent to or refuse treatment present to judges. It will be suggested that a liberal consent-based or contract model of medical relationships inevitably fails to do justice to the professed aims of patients' rights and that an alternative approach, based upon a fuller understanding of therapeutic relationships is required. Such an approach has been suggested in recent decisions of the Canadian Supreme Court.

A. Medical Paternalism

Medical paternalism has a long and venerable lineage. The teachings of the Hippocrates, which have stood at the centre of medical professional ethics in the West for centuries, not only tolerate, but in fact encourage decision-making by doctors on behalf of their patients. The model of doctor-patient interaction envisioned in the Hippocratic Oath and other writings is one of entrustment. The following exhortation to doctors from 'the father of medicine' is a good example of this paternalism:

Perform these duties calmly and adroitly, concealing most things from the patient while you are attending to him. Give necessary orders with cheerfulness and sincerity, turning his attention away from what is being done to him; sometimes reprove sharply and emphatically, and sometimes comfort with solicitude and attention, revealing nothing of the patient's future or present condition.[1]

Accordingly, the doctor is injuncted first and foremost not to do harm, *primum nil nocere*, then to act beneficently, in the best interests of his patient. Disclosure of information concerning risks or obtaining consent in detail to proposed treatment would be very likely to offend against both of these principles. Knowledge of risks and consequences would distress and thus harm the patient. It might also persuade him to forego therapy and, thus, frustrate the doctor's beneficent work.

Another significant factor in relation to medical paternalism concerns not so much its nature as its potential scope. Up to the middle of the nineteenth century the claims of medicine were modest indeed. Hospitals largely functioned as warehouses for the terminally ill and the impoverished and practitioners were not held in very high esteem. Thus, for example, the guild of barbers and surgeons, which was granted a royal charter in 1461, was not dissolved until 1745.[2] Formal control, if not direct licensing of the medical professions in England can be said to date only from the *Medical Act* of 1858. Since that period, however, most Western countries have experienced an increasing 'medicalization' of areas of personal and social life previously subjected to other forms of control or none at all. As *Thomas Szasz* has put it

Starting with such things as syphilis, tuberculosis, typhoid fever and carcinomas and fractures we have created the class, 'illness.' At first this

---

[1] Cf *Hippocrates*, Decorum, in Hippocrates (Harvard UP: Cambridge (Mass.] 2nd ed. 1967) quoted in *I Kennedy & A Grubb*, Medical Law: Cases and Materials (1st ed. Butterworths: London 1989) 229.

[2] *A M Carr-Saunders & P A Wilson*, The Professions (Frank Cass: London 2nd ed. 1964) 68-77.

class was composed of only a few small items all of which shared the common feature of reference to a state of disordered structure or function of the human body as a physical-chemical machine.   As time went on additional items were added to this class. They were not added, however, because they were newly discovered bodily disorders.   The physician's attention has been deflected from this criterion and has become focused instead on disability and suffering as new criteria for selection... with increasing zeal, physicians and especially psychiatrists began to call 'illness' ... anything and everything in which they could detect any sign of malfunctioning, based on no matter what the norm.[3]

Medicine has established itself as a science and its practitioners have won for themselves a large measure of collective autonomy in training, licensing and disciplining members of the profession.   Finally, medical technology has, as a matter of fact, opened up significant new possibilities at the beginning and end of human life.   From genetic screening and assisted conception to artificial prolongation of life, the scope of medical activity and, therefore, of medical paternalism has been steadily increasing. Medicine in the West, with the United States taking a lead, has come to be viewed as a social and consumer good with vast amounts of private and public resources spent on its production and acquisition.   Doctors, as suppliers of this commodity are also in the unusual position, through their diagnoses and recommendations, of determining the level of demand. This has resulted in the inflation both of health care expenditure and, more importantly for purposes of the present discussion, of medical science itself. In the almost apocalyptic vision of *Ivan Illich*, a medical colossus, vast and unaccountable, bestrides the land robbing human individuals and communities of liberty, authenticity and difference in their living and dying.[4]

B. Liberal Critique

Paternalism has been resisted, in theory at least, by claims rooted first in ethics, then in law that all authority in the therapeutic context proceeds not from the social and situational status of the medical professional, nor from any unquestioning entrustment, but from the freely expressed consent of the patient. The work of *Jay Katz* is pathbreaking in this regard in the United States, the jurisdiction which has given the lead for developments in

---

[3] *T S Szasz*, The Myth of Mental Illness (Harper & Row: New York 1974) 44-45.

[4] Cf. generally, *I Illich*, Limits to Medicine. Medical Nememsis: The Expropriation of Health (Penguin: Harmondsworth 1976).

Common Law countries at least.[5] It has, however, been in Germany that the liberal ordering of values in medicine has received most recognition at judicial level. In an often cited decision of 1958 the German Federal Supreme Court stated that 'the counsel of *Hippocrates* that as much as possible be concealed from the patient cannot be reconciled with the individual's right to self-determination'.[6] On this view it is the autonomous choice of the patient and not the Hippocratic principle of beneficence which justifies the medical intervention. In so far as this choice is not obtained or is obtained but not respected by the attending physician, the patient is (literally) treated as a mere means to the end of the doctor, be that end however beneficial or (medically) necessary.   Indeed the patient's autonomy interest is seen as categorically distinct from and lexically prior to his somatic well-being.   As may be apparent, Kantian notions of personhood and the self-governing, self-determining individual are central to these strategies.

Consent is, however, the cornerstone of much wider liberal theorising. It has been the central justificatory paradigm of liberal political philosophy and legal theory from John Locke onwards. The consent of the governed justifies government, the consent of the victim justifies and exonerates the criminal and the consent of the contracting parties justifies the intervention of the court to enforce remedies for breach of contract. In support of the movement for 'patients' rights' liberal theorists have identified this principle of self-determination as a central moral and political value, embodied in ethics and expressed as fundamental in the written and unwritten constitutions of Europe and North America. Such writers have argued from consistency that to the extent that medical paternalism persists in practice and is endorsed in court there is a fatal lack of 'fit' between particular legal doctrine and the background ethical and constitutional principles which give it legitimacy.[7] Again the relevant German law is

---

5 For a recent review of the success of the informed consent doctrine, cf. *J Katz*, 'Informed Consent – Must It Remain a Fairytale' , 10 Journal of Contemporary Health Law and Policy 69-91 [1994]. For further exposition of the liberal critique of medical law, In varying forms and from a variety of national perspectives, cf. *I Kennedy & A Grubb*, Medical Law Cases with Materials (2nd ed Butterworths: London, Dublin, Edinburgh 1994) 87-251; *S McLean*, A Patient's Right to Know. Information Disclosure, the Doctor and the Law (Dartmouth: Aldershot, Brookfield (Vermont) 1989); *D Giesen*, International Medical Malpractice Law (J C B Mohr, Martinus Nijhoff: Tübingen, Dordrecht, Boston, London 1988) paras 482-601.

6 BGH, 9 Dec 1958 VI ZR 203/57 BGHZ 29, 46 (49).

7 'Fit' in this connection might be taken to indicate principled consistency as between the interpretation and application of the concept of consent in different areas of substantive (criminal or private) law or 'horizontal fit'. It may, however, also indicate the consistent specification or derivation of particular rules on consent from constitutional,

instructive.[8] The Federal Constitution or Basic Law declares in Article 1 that the dignity of the individual human person is inviolable.[9] Article 2 expressly guarantees the right of citizens to the free development of their personality.[10] This has been interpreted to include inter alia the right to self-determination. The significance of this right as a background to litigation arising from disclosure malpractice has been highlighted by the German Federal Supreme Court in the following terms

The freedom and dignity of the human personality require that the patient's wishes be honoured. (In a case involving disclosure) it is evident that the judge, in protecting the right to self-determination, does not uphold some merely formal principle. On the contrary, he protects a constitutionally enshrined right which must be applied and respected just as much as the right to health.[11]

Thus, for judges in Germany, by contrast with their counterparts in England, as well as for liberal commentators, paternalism is seen as an anachronistic remainder from pre-modern, pre-liberal times, an unacceptable abuse of professional status and a blemish upon the law. Making a rhetorical appeal of this sort *Professor McLean* of Glasgow has written that

Just as consensual politics is deemed to represent the best form of government, so consensual medicine is the best form of that discipline.[12]

Commentators have found two of the most significant instances of conflict between self-determination and paternalism in the areas of informed consent and refusal of treatment. In each case the liberal model predicates the absolute freedom of the patient to decide whether to be

---

political and ethical first principles or 'vertical fit'. It is thus clear that the Dworkinian theory of rights and judicial decision-making has been influential in the rise of consent in medical law. Cf. *R Dworkin*, Taking Rights Seriously (Duckworth: London 1977) and *R Dworkin*, Law's Empire (Fontana: London 1984).

[8] In this context, it should be mentioned that most significant developments in German medical law have evolved from case law. The codification of law in continental Europe significantly predates the rise of informed consent and of medical law in general. Thus, In Germany, for example, broad provisions of the Criminal Code (Strafgesetzbuch) and the Civil Code (Bürgerliches Gesetzbuch) have been inventively applied by courts in the specific medical context in implementation of the fundamental consitutitonal and human rights provisions of the Federal Basic Law (Grundgesetz).

[9] Art 1 Grundgesetz.

[10] Art 2 Grundgesetz.

[11] BGH, 9 Dec 1958 VI ZR 203/57 BGHZ 29, 46 (54). A highly influential minority decision of three judges of the Federal Constitutional Court in its leading case on disclosure in medicine reinforces this position, cf. BVerfG, 25 July 1979 2 BvR 878/74 BVerfGE 52, 131, 171ff.

[12] Cf., A *S McLean* Patient's Right to Know. Information Disclosure, the Doctor and the Law (Dartmouth: Aldershot, Brookfield [Vermont] 1989) at 25.

treated and what form this treatment is to take. In each arguments from individual autonomy are used to urge courts to maximize the transfer of information and decision-making from physician to patient. Reformulation of the relevant legal tests is seen as one of the most effective means of reversing the overwhelming power imbalance which exists in favour of medical professionals. Increased civil liability for failure to respect the patient's right to self-determination will, it is hoped, restrain the unchecked and unaccounted for progress of medical science.

II. INFORMED CONSENT

A. The Limits of Battery

In the words of *Cardozo J* in a leading United States decision on consent to treatment

Every human being of adult years and sound mind has a right to determine what shall be done with his own body; and a surgeon who performs an operation without his patient's consent commits an assault for which he is liable in damages.[13]

While this famous statement of the unlawfulness of unconsented to medical treatment has been accepted and repeated around the common law world, its focus on the tort of trespass to the person is misleading. In fact trespass, in the form of battery, plays a relatively insignificant role in medical malpractice litigation. In order to escape liability in battery the doctor must simply show that the patient consented to the very procedure carried out. As *Bristow* J stated in the case of *Chatterton v Gerson*

(O)nce the patient is informed in broad terms of the nature of the procedure which is intended, and gives her consent, that consent is real, and the cause of action on which to base a claim for failure to go into the risks and implications is negligence, not trespass.[14]

Battery, with its connotations of violence and criminality is thus seen as an inappropriately stigmatic label for doctors erring in good faith as to the wishes of their patients. Instead a duty of disclosure is imposed upon physicians, breach of which sounds in negligence. This requires that the doctor have been at fault by falling below the level of care expected by the law of him as a medical professional.

---

[13] *Schloendorff v Society of New York Hospital*, 211 NY 125, 105 NE 92 (1914) per *Cardozo* J at 93.

[14] *Chatterton v Gerson* [1981] QB 432, [1980] 3 WLR 1003, [1981] 1 All ER 257 (*Bristow* J).

B. Liability in Negligence

In the case of *Bolam v Friern Hospital Management Committee*[15] it was established that the general level of care owed by a medical professional to his patients in the conduct of diagnosis and therapy was to be determined by the standard of 'an ordinary skilled man exercising and professing to have that special skill'. In adopting a particular procedure a doctor would not be negligent if he acted in accordance with a practice accepted at the time as proper by a responsible body of medical opinion. This responsible body of opinion doesn't have to constitute the whole or even a majority of practitioners in the field. Indeed in the leading Scottish case of *Hunter v Hanley*[16], which predates *Bolam* by two years, it was held that a doctor would only be found negligent where his actions were such that no responsible practitioner would have undertaken them. The significance of this test of general liability, as interpreted in subsequent cases, chiefly by the House of Lords in *Maynard v West Midlands Area Health Authority*[17], is that it embodies an empirical rather than a normative test of liability. In effect, once an impugned practice is shown to be common among a number of doctors, English (and Scottish) courts refuse to reserve to themselves a power to review it and condemn it, nonetheless as negligent.

The leading English decision on the doctor's duty of disclosure is that of the House of Lords in *Sidaway v Bethlem Royal Hospital Governors*[18]. The plaintiff in *Sidaway* sought recovery in negligence for the failure of her surgeon to inform her of a one to two percent risk of paralysis resulting from neuro-surgery. It was found as a matter of fact that a significant body of neuro-surgeons would not have disclosed the risk which in fact occurred. The House of Lords was, however, split as to the applicability of the test in the context of disclosure. Only *Lord Scarman* committed himself *Bolam* to what he called the 'transatlantic' doctrine of informed consent. Adopting the rights rhetoric of pro-patient commentators, he held that 'the patient's right to make his own decision ... may be seen as a basic human right protected by the common law'.[19] He drew a clear, categorical distinction between therapy and diagnosis on the one hand and advice on the other. 'The doctor's concern is with health and the relief of pain. These are medical objectives. But a patient may well have in mind circumstances,

---

[15] [1957] 1 WLR 582, [1957] 2 All ER 118 (*McNair.*J).
[16] 1955 SC 200, 1955 SLT 213.
[17] [1984] 1 WLR 634, 1985] 1 All ER 635 (HL)
[18] [1985] AC 871, [1985] 2 WLR 480, [1985] 1 All ER 643 (HL).
[19] *Sidaway v Bethlem Royal Hospital Governors* [1985] AC 871, [1985] 2 WLR 480, [1985] 1 All ER 643 (HL per *Lord Scarman* at 649b).

objectives, and values ... which may lead him to a different decision from
that suggested by purely medical opinion.'[20] *Ibi ius ubi remedium*: the
conceded right required that a remedy be crafted from available Common
Law materials. Accordingly a doctor should be obliged by the law of
negligence to disclose such information concerning the risks accompanying
treatment or diagnosis as would be required by a reasonable patient in the
particular patient's position, not by a substantial body of medical
practitioners.[21]

Although *Lord Scarman* was clearly in the minority in opting for a
patient-centred standard of disclosure, of the majority only *Lord Diplock*
favoured an unmodified use of the *Bolam* test in such cases. He held for a
'single, comprehensive duty covering all the ways in which a doctor is
called upon to exercise his skill and judgement'.[22]   Referring to the
considerable benefits which medical science has conferred on mankind and
the need for the law not to hinder this progress by undue imposition of
liability on practitioners, he in effect identified with the form of classical
paternalism outlined above. On this view, somatic well-being, as defined
by the doctor, sets the limits to the patient's exercise of his right to self-
determination. *Lords Templeman* and *Bridge* also accepted that the level of
disclosure required by law had to be set primarily by applying the *Bolam*
test. An exception should be made, however, in the case of special as
opposed to general risks attending upon the procedure proposed to be
carried out *(Lord Templeman)*[23] or where there was a 'substantial risk of
grave adverse consequences' *(Lord Bridge).*[24]

C. Sidaway: The Aftermath

Critics of medical paternalism greeted the decision in *Sidaway* with
disapproval.[25] Apart from *Lord Scarman*, all the Lords had privileged

[20] *Sidaway v Bethlem Royal Hospital Governors* [1985] AC 871, [1985] 2 WLR 480,
[1985] 1 All ER 643 (HL per *Lord Scarman* at 654b-c).
[21] This test of disclosure has been adopted by the Australian High Court, in *Rogers v
Whitaker* (1992) 109 ALR 625, (1992) 67 AJLR 47. In the same decision the Court
expressly dissaproved of the use of the Bolam test in relation to treatment as well as
disclosure malpractice.
[22] *Sidaway v Bethlem Royal Hospital Governors* [1985] AC 871, [1985] 2 WLR 480,
[1985] 1 All ER 643 (HL per Lord Diplock at 657i).
[23] *Sidaway v Bethlem Royal Hospital Governors* [1985] AC 871, [1985] 2 WLR 480,
[1985] 1 All ER 643 (HL per *Lord Templeman* at 665c).
[24] *Sidaway v Bethlem Royal Hospital Governors* [1985] AC 871, [1985] 2 WLR 480,
[1985] 1 All ER 643 (HL per *Lord Bridge* at 663c).
[25] *M Brazier*, 'Patient Autonomy and Consent to Treatment: the Role of the Law?' (1987)
7 LS 169-193.

beneficence over autonomy. Only the qualifications upon the *Bolam* test adumbrated by *Lords Templeman* and *Bridge* provided a measure of hope that patient decision-making would gain a foothold, however small, in the Common Law of England.[26] This hope proved unfounded when in the subsequent Court of Appeal decision in *Gold v Haringey Health Authority*[27] *Lloyd* LJ took the judgement of *Lord Diplock* in *Sidaway* as definitive of the obligations of the doctor to make disclosure. Subsequently, informed consent and disclosure of risks has not generated any considerable amount of litigation in England. It has, therefore, only remained to commentators to highlight the undesirability of judicial endorsements of paternalism and to compare *Sidaway* and *Gold* with the reasonable patient test applied in Canada, Australia and in several of the United States.[28]

D. Why the Critique Fails

It is submitted that the liberal critique of *Sidaway* fails for a number of reasons. First, the proposed alternative test of disclosure, that focusing upon the informational needs of the reasonable patient, leads to a substantial endorsement of medical decision-making in spite of its pro-patient purpose. The information as to risks required by the truly idiosyncratic patient is not likely to coincide with that demanded by his 'reasonable' counterpart. Yet, such patients are more likely than others to attempt to assert their right to decide on treatment both on the ward and, ultimately, in court. Furthermore, whilst the individual patient is obviously best placed to testify to the risks of which he particularly wished to be informed, it will be the attending doctors and their colleagues appearing as expert witnesses who can most convincingly predict the informational needs of the average, normal or reasonable patient. Admittedly, unlike in *Sidaway* and *Bolam*, this evidence would have to be reviewed critically by the trial judge. However, given that doctors, particularly specialists, deal with patients undergoing specific treatment regularly and over extended periods of time, their testimony will frequently be decisive of the extent of legally required disclosure. An alternative to the reasonable patient test, which predicates the level of disclosure upon the needs of the particular

---

[26] *I Kennedy*, 'The Patient on the Clapham Omnibus' in *I Kennedy*, Treat Me Right. Essays in Law and Medical Ethics (Clarendon: Oxford 1988) 175-212.

[27] [1988] QB 481, [1987] 3 WLR 649, [1987] 2 All ER 888 (CA).

[28] Cf. *J Keown*, 'Burying *Bolam*: Informed Consent Down Under' (1994) 53 CamLJ 16-19.

patient, has gained some acceptance in Germany.[29]   This subjective test obviously promotes the right of the patient to information as a matter of principle. Its effectiveness as a means of limiting medical paternalism is greatly diminished, however, at the subsequent stage of the court's inquiry, that concerning causation. Even if patients can show that they were not adequately informed of the risks accompanying treatment, having regard to their own idiosyncratic needs, it is still open to the defendant doctor to show that they would have submitted to the procedure in any case. The evidence of doctors experienced in the care of patients of the particular type in question and in observing the general behaviour of such patients will again be of significant influence in this analysis.[30] It is likely that such a subjective analysis would merely postpone rather than displace the reliance of courts upon medical evidence and with it their privileging of medical norms of patient behaviour.

Second and more generally in this regard, tests of informed consent, whether in the formulations of the courts or of their critics, attempt to compress the interactive process which is the therapeutic relationship into an isolated moment altering the legitimate balance of power between doctor and patient. In this regard they mimic tests for the formation of contracts as derived from classical, will-based theories of contract law.[31]   However, sociologists of medicine, building on *Talcott Parsons'* 'Sick Role' construct, have identified an asymmetry in relations between people and therapeutic agents, embodied in the form of an institutionalized hierarchy. This hierarchy, it is asserted, is due to the 'competence gap' between lay person and professional, but also results from the emotional and existential anxieties experienced by patients in relation to their illness and its attending circumstances.[32] In addition, it has been stated in this regard that '(a) physician's ability to preserve his or her own power over the doctor-patient relationship depends largely upon the ability to control the patient's

---

[29] For a detailed and comprehensively referenced comparative discussion of (objective and subjective) patient-centred standards of disclosure cf. *D Giesen*, International Medical Malpractice Law (J C B Mohr, Martinus Nijhoff:Tübingen, Dordrecht, Boston, London 1988) paras 560-601.

[30] Admittedly, German case law indicates that, in that jurisdiction, a subjective test will also be adopted at the causation stage of the consent issue, cf. BGH, 22 Jan 1980 VI ZR 263/78 NJW 1980, 1333. This position, based on the strong constitutional rights analysis outlined above, certainly represents a clear doctrinal break with medical paternalism. It remains open, however, to the familiar scepticism regarding the theoretical coherence and practical feasibility of subjective tests in general.

[31] For a contemporary formulation of the 'will theory', cf. *C Fried*, Contract as Promise (Harvard UP: Cambridge [Mass.] 1979).

[32] *R C Fox*, The Sociology of Medicine. A Participant Observer's View (Prentice Hall: New Jersey 1989) 25-26.

uncertainty'.[33] The work of the American sociologist *Candace West* has de monstrated that the dominance of the physician is accomplished by the conversational strategies of both parties to the therapeutic encounter.[34] Thus, in an analysis of doctor-patient conversations in the American state of Georgia she found that doctors, not patients, initiated most questions, that, when they did seek information, patients frequently stuttered and mumbled, undermining their requests and that while patients employed formal mode of address this was not true of their physicians. Most alarming for any legal measure attempting to stimulate patients to seek information, she concluded that more assertive patients were less likely to obtain answers to their questions than their passive and deferential counterparts. Finally, she found that the level of disclosure was also influenced by the social distance between the speakers and by the ethnic background and gender of the patient. Clearly a contract model of information disclosure and consent to treatment fails to take account of the complex construction of the power of the doctor and, thus, of the power of the medical norm which he is promoting. This power is established and maintained not in an instant, but over the course of the whole therapeutic relationship. It is furthermore bolstered by patterns of empowerment and disempowerment in the wider community. It is submitted that this power cannot be easily bargained around and that it cannot be adequately constrained by a one-off duty of disclosure.

III. REFUSAL OF TREATMENT

As has been indicated, since the decisions in *Sidaway* and *Gold*, the issue of informed consent arising from inadequate disclosure prior to treatment which subsequently proved to be unsuccessful has ceased to be the focus of judicial attention in England. Instead, most of the recent case law involving questions of consent has arisen out of refusals of treatment, usually where the life of the patient is threatened by the refusal. Generally, doctors and hospitals, fearing liability in battery or negligence, have sought declarations of lawfulness prior to treating patients against their wishes.

---

[33] *H Waitzkin & J Stoeckle*, Information Control and the Micropolitics of Health Care, 10 Soc. Sci. & Med 263-276 (1976) at 265.

[34] C West, Routine Complications. Troubles with talk between Doctors and Patients (Indiana UP: Bloomington 1984) esp. 148-161.

A. The Right

The right to refuse medical treatment, as a corollary of the requirement of consent to medical treatment, has been enunciated and repeated in a number of leading English decisions in recent years. Thus, in *Airedale NHS Trust v Bland Lord Goff* stated that

(I)t is established that the principle of self-determination requires that respect must be given to the wishes of the patient, so that if an adult patient of sound mind refuses, however unreasonably, to consent to treatment or care by which his life would or might be prolonged, the doctors responsible for his care must give effect to his wishes, even though they do not consider it to be in his best interests to do so.[35]

These dicta are relevant to our discussion in two ways. First, they generally contain a bold assertion that a patient may choose to reject treatment even where acceptance is dictated by the medical evaluation of his well-being and by the standards of an average member of the community. Unlike in their rulings on information disclosure prior to treatment, the courts appear, at first glance, to be considerably more solicitous of the idiosyncratic or difficult patient. Second, however, the right to refuse is predicated upon the patient having sufficient capacity or being of sound mind to enable him to do so. Clearly if the patient is incompetent in the relevant manner there can be no question of exercising the right to refuse or the right to self-determination. It is hoped to demonstrate that the right to refuse, conceded in such high terms as a matter of first principle, is frequently undermined by courts using available common law resources. It will be shown that this also diminishes the power of liberal theorists of medical law either to explain such decisions as the courts have reached or to maintain their autonomy-based critique over the rest of the law.

B. The Cases

The leading English case in this area is the decision of the Court of Appeal in *Re T (An Adult: Refusal of Treatment)*[36] of 1992. *Miss T*, in her 34th week of pregnancy was involved in a road accident. On hospitalization, pneumonia was diagnosed and antibiotics and narcotic drugs were administered. The patient refused blood transfusions after the visit of her

---

[35] [1993] AC 789, [1993] 2 WLR 316, [1993] 1 All ER 821 (HL per *Lord Goff* at 864C-D); cf. also *Re T (Adult: Refusal of Medical Treatment)* [1993] Fam 95, [1992] 3 WLR 782, [1992] 4 AllER 649 (CA per *Lord Donaldson* MR at 102D).

[36] [1993] Fam 95, [1992] 3 WLR 782, [1992] 4 All ER 649 (CA).

mother, a Jehovah's Witness with whom she had lived until the age of 17. Her condition deteriorated and the attending doctors decided that a Caesarean section was necessary. After this was performed the patient was kept in intensive care. The consultant anaesthetist would have administered a blood transfusion, given *Miss T's* critical condition, but felt inhibited from doing so by her refusal. Her father and boyfriend sought a declaration of lawfulness to cover the proposed blood transfusion. The order was granted and this was upheld by the Court of Appeal.

It was there held that the scope of the refusal was not such as to cover the particular situation which arose. Reference was made to the fact that *Miss T's* allegiance to the Jehovah's Witnesses had diminished considerably since leaving her mother. Her decision had been announced 'out of the blue'. In addition, medical staff had failed to inform her sufficiently of the risks of someone in her condition foregoing a blood transfusion. Thus, there was held to be a situation of emergency without an applicable treatment decision by the patient. The hospital staff were therefore free and in fact obliged on the basis of the House of Lords decision in *Airedale NHS Trust v Bland*[37] to act in her best interests and perform a blood transfusion. *Lord Donaldson* MR went further, however, and, agreeing with the opinion of the treating doctors rejected the finding of capacity made at first instance by *Ward* J. The accident, the medication, the advanced stage of pregnancy and her severe pneumonia all constituted abundant evidence of the patient's incapacity at the time of her purported refusal. It may be noted in passing that the level of information required to be disclosed before a patient's refusal is held to be valid seems to be considerably higher here than in cases of alleged disclosure malpractice of the *Sidaway* type. A further point of interest is the willingness of *Lord Donaldson* MR to attribute an impairment of consent to factors which in the context of a subsequently impugned acceptance of treatment would be accounted background data of no significance.

By contrast with the decision in *Re T*,[38] the patient's refusal of treatment in the subsequent case of *Re C (Adult: Refusal of Medical Treatment)* [39] was upheld by *Thorpe J* in the High Court. The man concerned was a 68 year old, of Jamaican origin, suffering from schizophrenia who was confined to Broadmoor prison. He developed gangrene in one of his feet. He was informed by doctors that there was a significant chance that he would die if his leg was not amputated below the knee. The patient not only refused to consent to such an operation, but sought an injunction preventing

---

[37] [1993] AC 789, [1993] 2 WLR 316, [1993] 1 All ER 821 (HL).

[38] [1993] Fam 95, [1992] 3 WLR 782, [1992] 4 All ER 649 (CA).

[39] [1994] 1 WLR 290, [1994] 1 All ER 819, (1993) NLJR 1642 (*Thorpe J*).

the doctors from carrying it out in the future. For the first time in such a case in England it was found that *C* was competent to refuse the treatment and the injunction was granted. It was held that to be competent the patient had to understand or at least be capable of understanding the nature and effects of the proposed treatment in broad terms.

The medical witnesses in the case were divided on the question of *C's* competence and the judge chose between them and, effectively, in favour of *C's* right to refuse. Such division among the medics is very rare however, and in spite of the test adumbrated by *Thorpe* J the practice of courts in the past has very much been to leave the question of competence to the exclusive determination of medical witnesses. Yet if capacity is essentially a medical question and if a decision that a patient has capacity is a precondition of any exercise of the right to refuse treatment, then we may say that the medical profession have been installed as gatekeepers at the threshold of patient self-determination. Finally, a well-known study of the quality of doctors' decisions as to competence shows that whichever of the several available tests are applied there is a significant pro-treatment bias particularly where the benefits of proceeding are significantly greater and the risks significantly fewer than would be the case were treatment withheld.[40] (This problem was also recognised by the English Law Commission in its recent, wide-ranging report on mental incapacity.)[41] Would it be unduly cynical to suggest that an unarticulated dispute as to the probable benefits of amputation and the risks of foregoing it produced the conflict in the medical evidence as to *C's* capacity? It might be worth adding that he has survived his refusal without any significant deterioration in health.[42]

The exception to this line of cases, in view of its unconcealed abrogation of the patient's right to self-determination, is the decision of the President of Family Court in *Re S (Adult: Refusal of Medical Treatment)*.[43] Doctors at a London hospital sought an order, effectively compelling one *Mrs S* to undergo an emergency Caesarean section against her expressed wishes. This resolve was rooted in her religious belief as a 'Born Again Christian'. In a judgement which had to be delivered as quickly as possible if the life of fetus and mother were, on the medical evidence, to be saved, *Sir Stephen*

---

[40] *L Roth, A Meisel & C Lidz*, Tests of Competency to Consent to Treatment, 134 AmJ Psychiatry 279-284 (1977).

[41] *Law Commission* , Report No. 129: Mental Incapacity (HMSO: London 1995) 32-42. Unfortunately, discussion of the report is beyond the scope of the present paper.

[42] Speech of Mr Mike Hinchliffe to British Medical Association conference 'Statements, Directives and Dialogue', London, 5th April 1995.

[43] [1993] Fam 123, [1992] 3 WLR 806, [1992] 4 All ER 671 *(Sir Stephen Brown P)*.

Brown granted the declaration. In doing so he relied on dicta of *Lord Donaldson* MR in *Re T* to the effect that a compulsory operation of this sort might be permissible if the patient's refusal of treatment could lead to the death of a viable fetus.[44] This decision has been strongly condemned on policy grounds and because of its misapplication of a recent American case which, contrary to the President's reading of it seems to have brought a decade of judge-ordered Caesarean sections in the United States to an end.[45] Indeed, the American experience of such orders has been used by critics of the decision to indicate the undesirability, as a matter of policy, of recognizing and respecting the rights of the fetus in this manner.[46] It is also instructive, however, to examine the similarities between Re S and the line of cases from which it was said to deviate. Sir Stephen Brown, in reaching his decision as expeditiously as possible, left open the question of Mrs S's competence. Such evidence as there was cast doubt on her capacity to refuse. It is evident from his brief judgement, however, that capacity was not required to resolve the matter in any case. He clearly favoured one norm, that in favour of the life of the foetus, as established ex parte by the medical witnesses, over another, that favouring the self-determination of the pregnant woman Mrs S. In addition, it may be said that he favoured the medically and (presumably) socially orthodox way of proceeding to the point where he was prepared to allow the forced subjection of the patient to invasive treatment. The repugnance of the decision in Re S to many commentators is perhaps due to the fact that it represents an open endorsement of medically sanctioned standards of behaviour which also occurs in other, less controversial cases, though behind a veil of incompetence.

C. Coercion and Concealment

With the exception of Re S,[47] the right of the patient to refuse is almost always conceded in treatment refusal cases. The outcome of cases of such legal conflict as have arisen in England can be read as sanctioning the medical norm behind a mask of consent. Courts generally strive to

---

[44] *Re T (Adult: Refusal of Medical Treatment)* [1993] Fam 95, [1992] 3 WLR 782, [1992] 4 AllER 649 (CA per *Lord Donaldson* MR at 102E).

[45] *Re AC*, 573 A2d 1235 (1990).

[46] *M Thomson*, After Re S (1994) 2 Med L Rev 127-148; *K Stern*, 'Court-Ordered Caesarian Sections: In Whose Interests?' (1993) 56 MLR 238-243; cf. further, *N K Rhoden*, The Judge in the Delivery Room: The Emergence of Court-Ordered Caesareans, 74 California L Rev 1951-2030 (1986).

[47] [1993] Fam 123, [1992] 3 WLR 806; [1992] 4 All ER 671, (1992) 9 BMLR 69 (*Sir Stephen Brown P*).

establish the consenting patient as paradigmatic in the abstract, being then able use the concrete facts of the case, as constructed largely by medical witnesses to characterize the actual patient as non-paradigmatic, outwith those cases where autonomy and the right to self-determination need to be respected. This is done by use of the very concept of consent itself. Because the patient lacks capacity, respect for autonomy ceases to be an issue. Consent as a central concept of justification seems to remain intact. It continues to function for the legal system, while the patient is in effect coerced by or made to submit to medical orthodoxy.

Of further interest is the reason why the right to self-determination has received such frequent and express attention from judges in treatment refusal cases, by contrast with their reluctance to invoke it in the informed consent case law which was discussed earlier. A possible explanation is that where treatment is about to be ordered there may frequently be actual violence done to the person concerned, though the Court of Appeal has only recently owned up to this brute fact.[48] Furthermore, clear violence will be done to the principles of autonomy and free choice, which, as has been seen, are at the centre of orthodox legal and political theorising. By contrast, the denial of compensation for inadequate disclosure of risks which is the result of Sidaway and Gold, involves, on consideration, a more abstracted and indirect disvaluing of the same principles. The highly visible conflict of coercive medical norms with liberal political principles is simply absent or at least obscured in the latter type of case. Where refusals are overridden, however, the violation of principle is clear yet autonomy must continue to be seen as the norm. It must remain the cornerstone of medical practice and judicial regulation of it, even while the law provides the exceptions and supplementary strategies which enable it to be overcome or set aside. It might be concluded that, by contrast with the law on disclosure of risks, the liberal conception of patients as autonomous, self-determining rights holders has been accepted as the paradigm in treatment refusal cases. However, it is hoped that we have gone some way to demonstrating the insubstantiality of such principles and their lack of 'bite' in cases of treatment refusal where the medical norm, in favour of treatment, exerts an irresistible pull on judges and indeed upon many liberal theorists.

---

[48] *Riverside Mental Health Trust v Fox* [1994] 1 FLR 614, (1994) 2 Med L Rev 93 (CA).

V. CONCLUSION

A. The Scope of Paternalism in Medicine and Law

As stated the liberal paradigm is that consent should be the foundation of the doctor's authority and that it thus underpins the great majority of therapeutic experiences. Only in peripheral cases, mental illness, emergency, and incapacity, for example, does this break down, necessitating the application of other, paternalistic norms. This may be getting things the wrong way around. It is submitted that the therapeutic experience is, to a greater or lesser extent, characteristically paternalistic. This is accepted and acquiesced in not only by most individual patients, but also by much of the wider society. Such acceptance might in turn be positively characterized as an implicit transfer of power to professional groups, in this case the medical profession. This transfer, as endorsed by judicial practice, represents a privileging of the medical norm. Only where patients challenge this norm does consent become an issue. Generally, challenge is constituted by retrospectively asserted demands for more information, rejection of treatment deemed necessary by the treating professionals and medical opinion generally or, more rarely, by demands for treatment deemed unnecessary by professionals or administrators having regard to available resources. As challenges to a profoundly anchored medical hierarchy these claims very often take on a legal form; they are framed around the issue of consent.

But we have seen that tests of valid consent have proved so malleable as to be of little use in advancing patients' interests. In fact, decided cases consistently privilege medical norms regarding patient behaviour in the therapeutic context, not in spite of the requirement of valid consent but by means of it. Patients seeking compensation on the basis of non-disclosure of risks which have occurred are faced with a minimalist test of consent, which predicates validity, more or less on the amount which a reasonable doctor would disclose. We saw that patient-centred tests hardly offered a useful alternative to this. On the other hand patients refusing treatment who have or seek to deviate from medical and social norms in favour of treatment are faced with maximalist tests of valid consent in the form of capacity requirements as outlined above.

Thus, it is contended that the weakness of the liberal critique lies in its formalistic attachment to traditional conceptions of consent and self-determination as a means of redressing or overcoming the power-imbalance between doctors and patients. Furthermore, an overwhelming focus on individual autonomy precludes an acknowledgement of the context or situation of both doctor and patient. In the concrete situation it may be claimed that the patient often seeks not merely or even chiefly to exercise an abstract right to self-determination, but to advance a substantial interest. In cases of the Sidaway type this is commonly the interest in compensation for injury resulting from medical mishap, the application of medical technology or the pursuit of spurious medical progress. Refusals of treatment frequently involve the desire of the patient to live in conformity with religious ideals or value choices which deviate from dominant social norms as reflected in medical and judicial practice. However, the twin aspects of compression and abstraction rob concepts of autonomy and their legal expression in the right to self-determination and the notion of valid consent of any significant use in influencing the struggle of patients against domination by the medical profession. The effect of using tests of consent has rather been to give legitimacy to the privileging of medical knowledge and to divert the focus of resulting criticism away from central questions of power and dominance in therapeutic relationships.

B. An Alternative to the Liberal Critique?

A crude history of law and medicine might identify two major stages of development. In the prior state, law may be conceived of purely as having licensed the practice of medicine by a self-constituting professional elite. Training, admission and direct accountability was controlled by the (virtually) autonomous organs of the profession. The present state might be described as a gradual seeping of legal regulation into the fabric of medicine as practiced. The most obvious example of this is the medical malpractice action in tort or delict, but the struggle to establish consent and the contest over decisions of birth and death may also be accounted phenomena typical of the contemporary era. Yet a description of law as simply colonizing a growing area of medical activity would be inadequate to an understanding of the field. Instead, borrowing from the methodology of Max Weber, it is suggested that a number of competing ideal-types are being promoted not only to represent doctor-patient interactions, but also to contribute to their normative reshaping.[49] At trial, data yielded by the

---

[49] '[An ideal type] is not a description of reality but it aims to give unambiguous means of expression to such a description. [It] is formed by the one-sided accentuation of one or more points of view and by the synthesis of a great many diffuse, discrete , more or less present or occasionally absent concrete individual phenonmena, which are arranged according to those one-sidedly emphasized viewpoints into a unified analytical construct (Gedankenbild). In its conceptual purity, this mental construct (Gedankenbild) cannot be found empirically anywhere in reality. It is a utopia': *M*

therapeutic relationship are presented to the court, and thus to subsequent commentators, by expert medical witnesses. As part of this process, not only individual data, but the whole relationship itself must be reconstituted in a form cognizable to the law. This form will depend on the ideal-type employed by the court or the particular commentator, but will generally have been appropriated from the stock of conceptions of human relationships available within the given legal system. The foregoing discussion has illustrated the clash of the two hithertofore most significant ideal-types of medical relationships employed by the law and its critics. The majority judgements of the House of Lords in Sidaway[50] were seen to embody a classically paternalist position. It is worth noting that the Sidaway decision and its progenitor, Bolam[51] do not represent an abandonment of the task of classification and categorisation by the English courts, but are also based upon a specific ideal-type of doctor-patient relationship established in law. In essence the defining characteristic of this legally-reconstructed relationship is the submission of the patient to the doctor. The dependence of the former is protected, partly by weak rules of tort liability, but chiefly by the competence and good faith of the individual doctor and by the vigilance of his peers. Doctors and patients are bound to one another in a status relationship, which, faithful to the etymology of 'paternalism', resembles nothing so much as that between parent and child. The rival ideal-type is that of contract. As a free and self-determining agent, the patient's consent is required to any and all treatment undergone. The relationship is founded upon an agreement which binds, in the sense of exempting the medic concerned from legal sanction and depriving the subsequently injured patient of remedies, as long as there is no misrepresentation or concealment of the terms or attendant risks. It is hoped that the inadequacy of this model in promoting patient's interests has been shown in the course of this work.

More recently a further, well-established legal or, more exactly, equitable conception of human relationships has gained currency in discussions of medical law prompted chiefly by certain jurisprudence of the Canadian Supreme Court. In the cases of Norberg v Wynrib[52] and McInerney v

---

Weber, The Methodology of the Social Sciences [Trans. *EA Shils & HA Finch*] (The Free Press: New York 1949) at 90 (emphasis in original).

[50] *Sidaway v Bethlem Royal Hospital Governors* [1985] AC 871, [1985] 2 WLR 480, [1985] 1 All ER 643 (HL).

[51] *Bolam v Friern Hospital Management Committee* [1957] 1 WLR 582, [1957] 2 All ER 118 *(McNair J)*.

[52] [1992] 2 SCR 226, (1992) 92 DLR (4th) 449 (SCC).

MacDonald [53] several justices of the Court have appeared to move away from the notion of the doctor-patient relationship as founded on free bargain and have instead identified it as giving rise to fiduciary obligations with appropriate remedies for breach thereof. In Norberg the defendant doctor had supplied the drug fiorinal, to which his patient the plaintiff was addicted, in return for sexual favours. She brought an action against him variously for battery, negligence and breach of fiduciary duty. While all the judges were agreed that the plaintiff should succeed, the majority held that owing to the inequality of power between the parties and the drug dependence of the plaintiff her consent could not be said to have been voluntary. The defendant was therefore liable for battery. Identifying the strained reasoning of the majority required to reach this conclusion, McLachlin J dissented as to the appropriate head of action. In her view, 'the most fundamental characteristic of the doctor-patient relationship is its fiduciary nature'.[54] Traditionally, fiduciary obligations have been of most significant application in the commercial field. There they function as equitable supplements to rules and principles based squarely upon the ideology of the free market and the notion of arms-length transactions. Her honour held, however, that fiduciary principles are 'of general application, translatable to different situations and the protection of different interests than those hitherto recognized (and) are capable of protecting not only narrow legal and economic interests, but can also serve to defend fundamental human and personal interests'.[55] Unlike contract or tort, the fiduciary approach explicitly recognizes the power imbalance inherent in a given relationship and imposes obligations on that basis. As has been shown, aspects of dependence, entrustment and social and situational dominance indicate an undeniable inequality in relationships between doctors and patients. On the facts of *Norberg*, the defendant was found to have breached these obligations by 'sexualizing' the therapeutic relationship. Most notably, doctrines based on consent and immoral conduct, otherwise applying in contract and tort, could not be raised against the plaintiff to defend the claim for breach of fiduciary duty.

---

[53] [1992] 2 SCR 138, (1992) 93 DLR (4th) 415 (SCC). For further discussion of this case, cf. *BM Dickens*, 'Medical Records – Patient's Right to Receive Copies - Physician's Fiduciary of Disclosure: *McInerney v MacDonald*' (1994) 73 Can Bar R 234-242.

[54] *Norberg v Wynrib* [1992] 2 SCR 138, (1992) 93 DLR (4th) 415 (SCC per *McLachlin* J at 486a) emphasis in original.

[55] [1992] 2 SCR 138, (1992) 93 DLR (4th) 415 (SCC per *McLachlin* J at 499c-d).

The innovative deployment of the fiduciary relationship as the ideal-type of medical interaction by *McLachlin* J in *Norberg v Wynrib*[56] and by *La Forest* J in *McInerney v MacDonald* [57] is, of course, limited to the circumstances of both cases. It may be asked, however, whether this has any application beyond the disclosure of medical records and the conduct of sexual relations with a patient. It is submitted that it has. The micro-sociological studies mentioned above clearly indicate that a shift away from contract models of medical relationships is required if the law is to have a prospect of redressing medical paternalism and the disempowerment of patients. The fiduciary concept is at once closer to the reality of clinical experience and more fruitful as a doctrinal strategy affording remedies to injured patients. More fundamentally it represents an admission of persistent imbalance and of the need for substantive value choices by courts confronted with contested issues of medical practice. In doing so it can assist analysis of the decision-making process in the treatment refusal cases outlined above. In those cases, by adopting *prima facie* a rights-based analysis, with the ultimate outcome seeming to hinge on consent and capacity thereto, the courts have concealed the substantive value choices involved. The politics of treatment refusal and the wider politics of health care are thereby excluded from the text of judicial decisions. The privileging of the medical norm, which accompanies this represents an effective remittal of the contentious decision to treat or not to treat from the curial to the medical sphere. Courts and commentators will have to go beyond a formal consent analysis if this is to change. They will have to admit to the real struggle which is involved in such cases and to make explicit their own position in this struggle. If the patient's wishes are to be disregarded it should be made clear that this is a matter of state policy, open to dispute, negotiation and rejection as any other.

---

[56] [1992] 2 SCR 138, (1992) 93 DLR (4th) 415 (SCC).
[57] [1992] 2 SCR 226, (1992) 92 DLR (4th) 449 (SCC).

3. Pioneering or Perverse? Social Security Policy in the UK

Linda Luckhaus – University of Warwick

This paper looks at UK social security policy from a comparative perspective. It examines developments in social security law in the UK and other EU Member States during the last 15 years or so. It reveals that Member States' social security systems have been subject to thorough-going changes during the period in question but argues that those in train in the UK, unlike those in other Member States, constitute a fundamental restructuring of the legal regime. The paper then briefly explores some of the economic and political arguments used to justify this restructuring and the alternative vision of society they entail.

I INTRODUCTION

Social security reform in EU member states during the 1980s and 1990s took place in the context of rapidly changing social and economic conditions. During that time EU businesses faced growing competition in overseas markets from other producer and trading blocks, such as the US and Pacific Rim countries. Competition between producers within the EU also intensified to some extent as more barriers to trade were dismantled in the run up to '1992'.[1] In parallel with these changes, Member States' economies shifted, falteringly, between recession, recovery and back to recession again.[2] In the labour market, the demand for 'flexible' forms of working from those in employment grew. The numbers out of employment

---

[1] Doubt has been cast on the extent to which 'mutual recognition' has succeeded in removing the non-tariff barriers obstructing creation of the Single Market: see eg Woolcock, S. The Single European Market: Centralization or Competition among National Rules? Royal Institute of International Affairs 1994.

[2] Some commentators on the basis of certain economic indicators predict that the 1990's recession is currently coming to an end.

across the Community also expanded rapidly and remained stubbornly high, even in the late 1980s when recovery was temporarily under way.[3]

Throughout the period, high levels of social security spending were recorded in all Member States.[4] Expenditure across the Community, rose rapidly during the 1970s and early 1980s. It then stabilised at around 25% to 26% of Community GDP. At the same time, revenue from taxation and social security contributions tended to fall as unemployment increased, although, as we shall see, some Member States sought new sources of income by raising contribution rates. This shortfall in the financing of social security led to a further expansion of the already large public deficits operated by many Member States.

One of the major factors responsible for high levels of social security expenditure was the rapid increase in unemployment from the 1970s onwards. Another was demographic change. The growing number of elderly people, for example, led to greater demand for pensions and health care. Single parenthood also increased with those falling within this category tending to look to the social security system for financial support. A final demographic development affecting social security systems was the decline in the birth rate in many countries.[5] This raised fears among policy makers that there would ultimately be insufficient people in work to support the growing number of elderly people drawing state pension schemes financed on a pay-as-you-go basis.[6]

In the light of all these pressures, containment rather than expansion of social security provision became the conventional wisdom across all Member States. Trimming budgets in one place to meet new demands in another became common practice. Then, in the 1990s, attention shifted more explicitly towards reducing benefits in order to prevent budget deficits

---

[3] The EU-12 unemployment rate rose from 5% in 1980 to 11% in 1987. It dropped to 8% during the recovery of the late 1980s, steadily rising again from 1990s to reach its pre-recovery level by 1993: Employment in Europe 1994 COM(94)381:29.

[4] Although there was some variation between them. For example, in 1991, the biggest-spending Member States in terms of share of national GDP, were the Netherlands (32.4%), Denmark (19.8%) and France (28.7%), with Germany not far behind (26.6%). UK spending (24.4%) was below the Community average, and below other Member States (apart from Ireland) operating developed systems similar to its own: Social Protection in Europe 1993:42 Commission of the European Communities, DGV.

[5] see eg the Commission Communication to Council 'Problems of Social Security – Areas of Common Interest' COM(86)410, July 24 1986, Social Protection in Europe 1993:8. Italy and Spain, it may be noted, have the lowest fertility rates.

[6] The statistics from which 'support ratios' are predicted are a source of considerable controversy, not least because they are used to support the case for a policy switch from state pension schemes financed on a pay-as-you-go basis to funded schemes set up and run by the private sector.

from 'getting out of control',[7] and to enable Member States to have some prospect of meeting the EMU convergence criteria by the 1996 deadline (as it then was). Arguably, the single most important factor dictating developments in social security in the EU was national Government concern about burgeoning public deficits. The one exception was the UK, where social security changes were designed both to contain costs and to radically restructure the system. We now examine the changes which took place in Member States as a whole, before looking in more detail at specific developments in the UK.

II TRIMMING SAILS AND MEETING NEEDS: SOCIAL SECURITY IN EU MEMBER STATES: 1980-1995

Social security systems in most Member States comprise two types of benefit: social insurance benefits in which entitlement is linked to having contributed to (or been a member of) an insurance fund, and social assistance or means tested benefits in which proof of poverty is the primary test. Sometimes, too, systems include a third category of non-contributory, non-means-tested benefits. This is the case, for instance, in Denmark and the UK. The contributory, insurance-based, system of benefits is the main focus in this part of the paper since it is in relation to these benefits that many of the most significant changes have been made. We look first at contributory benefits providing protection against unemployment, old age, disability, maternity and the need for health care. We then examine a number of techniques which have been applied to benefits of all kinds (contributory, non-contributory, means tested) as part of a strategy of cost reduction and control. Finally, in this part, we look at specific developments in EU Member States in relation to social assistance, and at the implications of these developments for social insurance schemes.

Social Insurance and Contributory Benefits

Unemployment benefit
Three types of changes have been made in respect of unemployment benefits.[8] The first involved a reduction in the rate of benefit (UK,

---

[7] Carvel J. 'Social security budgets fall prey to new realism', Guardian, November ll, 1992.

[8] The sources for much of the data provided in this and subsequent parts of the paper are: Social Protection in Europe 1993 and Clasen, J. 'Social Europe', Poverty 89, 13 (CPAG).

Netherlands, Germany, Spain). The second involved tightening the conditions of entitlement to benefit and hence restricting the number of people who could gain access to it (UK, Germany, Belgium). The third type involved altering the duration of entitlement. In the UK, unemployment benefit duration was altered by reducing it, whereas in the other Member States (Netherlands, Germany, Spain, France, Greece, Denmark) benefit duration was extended, albeit only for older workers. Reducing unemployment benefit rates, tightening eligibility conditions and restricting the period of entitlement were all cost-cutting measures aimed at containing social security expenditure at a time when it would otherwise be expanding due to the rising number of unemployed people seeking assistance from the benefit system. The UK was alone among Member States in having adopted all three cost-cutting measures.

The Member States who altered unemployment benefit duration by extending it did so in order to make provision for older workers who proved particularly vulnerable to changing labour market conditions. In the early 1980s, Member States tended to introduce early retirement schemes to help this particular group. There was a switch to extension of unemployment benefit later in the decade as fears for the viability of pension schemes grew. The adaptation of unemployment benefit was also regarded as a more efficient way of targeting unemployed older workers than early retirement schemes which would be available to all workers. The extension of unemployment benefit provides a nice illustration of how cost containment was not a uniform trend across all Member States at all times and of how some systems adjusted to meet new demands thrown up by changing social and economic conditions, even at the risk of expanding provision and increasing costs.

Although the emphasis in Member States' schemes in recent years has been on providing financial support for the unemployed, more active labour market policies such as training, leave-of-absence schemes and job creation have been pursued in some States. Denmark has been particularly adventurous in this respect.

Old age and retirement pensions
As noted above, early retirement schemes, including reduction of the pension age, were adopted by some Member States (Germany, Belgium, France) in the early 1980s. These schemes helped to free up jobs for younger people as well as to meet the needs of older unemployed workers. Early retirement schemes faded in popularity as concern over the rising costs of pensions grew. Member States have pursued a mix of policies since then. These include extending the duration of unemployment benefit,

raising the pension age and adjusting the formula for calculating earnings related benefit rates so that less generous benefits will ultimately be awarded. Greece is an example of a Member State in which an early retirement scheme introduced in the early 1980s was later replaced by extended duration of unemployment benefit. In Greece, Germany, Italy and UK the pension age was raised (although in some instances the implementation date has been postponed). Three of these countries (Germany, Italy, the UK) also revised their earnings-related formula for calculating benefits so as to reduce the amount of pension payable. France likewise adopted this approach. The two most popular methods then for pruning the costs of pension provision were raising the pension age and adjusting (downwards) the earnings-related formula for calculating benefit payments.

Sickness and disability benefits

Trends evident in relation to sickness and disability benefits were the reduction in rates (Netherlands, Ireland, UK), the tightening of eligibility and contributions conditions (Greece, Ireland, Netherlands, UK) and the shortening of duration of benefit entitlement (Netherlands).[9] The disability reforms in the Netherlands were particularly far-reaching and were driven, as in other Member States, by the need to reduce provision in order to contain costs. The changes to invalidity benefits in the EU took place against the background of an unexpectedly steep rise in the number of claims being made in some Member States.[10] In the UK, for example, the number of invalidity benefit claimants rose from 612,000 in 1978/79 to 1,580,000 in 1993/93.[11] The 'common sense' explanation that this increase in claims merely reflected an increase in the incidence of sickness and disability has been treated with considerable scepticism. One view is that the 'unemployed' have turned to invalidity benefit as access to unemployment benefit has become more difficult; another, is that individuals are using invalidity benefit schemes to fund their early retirement.[12] Either view enables invalidity benefits (and their cost) to be cut without appearing to disadvantage the 'genuinely' sick and disabled.

---

[9] DSS Containing the cost of social security – the international context HMSO 1993:19-20.

[10] The phenomenon is not restricted to the EU: see Lonsdale, S. and Seddon, J. 'The Growth of Disability Benefits: an International Comparison' in Baldwin, S. and Falkingham, J. eds Social Security and Social Change 1994:149-165.

[11] DSS Social Security Statistics 1994 HMSO 1994 Table D1.23:189

[12] This is the official UK explanation of rising invalidity claims: DSS Containing the cost of social security – the international context HMSO 1993:19.

Maternity benefits

Maternity benefits are one of the few areas of social security to be expanded rather than restricted during the period under review. One of the reasons for the improvements achieved in this area is the adoption by the Council of Ministers of a Directive requiring Member States to promote equal opportunities and safe working practices for pregnant women at work.[13]   Another, perhaps more important, consideration was the perception by Member States of the need to both encourage women to remain in the labour force and to have children (and so halt the decline in fertility).

Health care

Changes to health care systems, including restrictions on entitlement to treatment and the introduction or extension of charges, were instituted in a number of Member States from the late 1970s onward. Member States' chief concern in this area was to reign in the costs of meeting the ever-expanding needs of an ever-expanding population of older people.

Social insurance contributions

The above analysis of developments in relation to specific contributory benefits points to a general movement across the EU towards reductions in provision in order to contain costs and reduce budget deficits. There were one or two exceptions to this trend, most notably, the exended duration of unemployment benefit entitlement for older workers. Member States' policy in relation to social insurance contributions related to these developments in complex, sometimes contradictory, ways. On the one hand, in some States (France, Denmark, the UK), contribution rates were increased, making it possible for these States (should they wish) to raise revenue and to maintain or even expand existing benefit provision without increasing their public deficits. On the other hand, some States (Belgium and Italy, France) introduced lower contribution rates, thereby increasing the likelihood of falling revenue, worsening budget deficits and of the Government having to impose benefit-cutting measures.

From the claimants' perspective, this latter policy of reducing contribution rates, at a time of growing demand, appears a rather strange one for Member States to pursue. The policy could nonetheless be justified by Member States on the grounds that contributions are a key element in labour costs and that labour costs must be kept to a minimum in order to maximise productivity, competitiveness and economic growth. As we shall

---

[13] Council Directive 92/85/EEC.

see, these economic considerations underpin virtually every aspect of social security policy in the UK but, so far, they appear to have had less influence in other Member States. The fact that only a few Member States have reduced contributions is a possible indication of this. France, it may be noted, has both increased and reduced contribution rates during the period under review. The UK has not reduced rates but has increased them solely for employees. In this way, perhaps, it sought to both increase revenue and to contain employers' costs and thus to have the best of both worlds.

Techniques For Containing Benefit

This section describes a number of developments in Member States over the last 15 years which appear to have functioned as devices for cutting or containing social security costs. The first two, indexation and privatisation, applied to all types of benefits. The third concerned expansion of one type of benefit, namely, social assistance.

Indexation of benefit rates

Indexation is the procedure whereby social security benefits are uprated usually on an annual basis. Most social security systems incorporate a procedure of this kind although there are considerable differences as to their detail. One difference concerns the choice of index. Some Member States' systems specify prices as the relevant index. In the UK prior to 1980, legislation provided that pensions and other long-term benefits would be increased each year in line with prices or earnings, whichever was the greater. The application of this prices-or-earnings formula led in practice to the more generous uprating of benefits in line with earnings. In Germany, prior to 1992, benefits were uprated in line with gross wages.

Clearly, the adoption of different indices could result in different rates of increase and thus differences in the cost of uprating. Some Member States therefore took to reviewing their uprating procedures with a view to adjusting them to save costs. At least two Member States altered their procedures after such a review. In 1992, Germany altered the basis of its pension uprating from gross to net wages. In 1980, the UK revised its uprating formula, switching from earnings to prices. This led to considerable savings in benefit expenditure. It has been estimated that uprating the state retirement pension in line with prices rather than earnings between 1980-81 and 1994-95 saved £49.5 billions.[14]

---

[14] See Bradshaw, J and Lynes,T, 'Benefit Uprating Policy and Living Standards' in SPRU Social Policy Report No.1 1995:38 citing figures from Hansard, HC January 26 1994 col.265-6.

Privatisation of social security systems
The term privatisation has been used to describe a variety of developments in the social security context. These include shifting funding of benefit schemes from the public to the private sector, compelling employers or private bodies to administer state-funded schemes, enacting opt-out provisions to enable participants in state schemes to switch to private or employer-funded schemes and offering financial inducements through the tax or benefit system to encourage individuals to take up this option. The possibility of 'privatising' social security in these various ways has been the subject of considerable debate (for example in the UK, Netherlands, France, Ireland) in recent years. Rising benefit costs and the need to reduce public deficits has provided the backdrop to this debate, with privatisation being regarded by some as the best and indeed only solution to Member States' financial problems.[15]

Although privatisation has been much discussed, there is some dispute as to what extent such measures have been acutally implemented by Member States. One commentator claims that the role of the private sector in social security systems has increased in recent years.[16] Others have noted how difficult it is to find concrete examples of this.[17] Indeed, only a handful of examples have so far been identified. These include the transfer of industrial accident insurance to the private sector (Belgium), requiring the self-employed and elderly to take out private insurance to cover medical expenses (Netherlands), permitting high income earners to opt out of the national health service (Italy) and employees to opt-out of the State Earnings Related Pension (SERPS)(UK). The UK has used financial inducements through the contribution system to encourage employees to opt-out.[18] Other Member States have used tax-reliefs for similar purposes.

Expansion of social assistance
Social assistance, means tested, benefits link entitlement to proof of poverty rather than to payment of contributions while in paid work. They are yet to be established in some Member States (Greece and Portugal) and are poorly

---

[15] Some proponents of this view would go further and argue that privatisation of all sectors of the economy in public hands (not just social security) should be transferred to the private sector if public sector finance is to be brought under control and economic prosperity restored.

[16] Yfantopoulos, J. 'Financing of Social Security in the E.C.' in Social Security in Europe, Miscellanea of the Erasmus-programme Social Security in the E.C. Bruylant Brussels 1991:220.

[17] Social Protection in Europe 1993:28.

[18] The UK has also shifted all the administration and some of the funding of sickness and maternity benefit for employees from the state to employers: see below.

developed in others (Italy and Spain). During the 1980s and early 1990s, however, they expanded in number across the EU as a whole.[19]   A significant development in this respect was the introduction in 1988 of the French revenue minimum d'insertion (RMI). The RMI provides means tested financial assistance to unemployed claimants over 25 on condition they enter a contract of 're-insertion' with the authorities undertaking to make every effort to return to the labour market as speedily as possible. The UK's contribution to the expansion of means tested benefits will be considered in more detail in the next part of this paper. The justification commonly given in the UK in support of means testing, however, provides a nice illustration of the extent to which cost considerations have influenced the growth of social assistance benefits in the EU. Means tested benefits, it is argued, only go to those who can prove they have insufficient resources and hence are not wasted (as, for example, are contributory benefits) on those who do not have 'genuine needs'. On the Continent, the selective nature of social assistance benefits is justified more in terms of their ability to combat 'social exclusion' and poverty in an efficient (ie cost-saving) manner rather than in terms of their ability to target 'genuine needs'.

Summarising Social Security Developments in the EU

It is clear, then, that there has been some retrenchment in social security provision in Member States in the last 15 years or so and that this retrenchment has largely taken place within the sphere of contributory and insurance benefits. Social assistance benefits, on the other hand, have expanded rather than contracted. I have argued that the key to understanding both these processes is the priority given by Member States to the need to contain costs and budget deficits when determining the structure and scope of their benefit schemes. The process was nonetheless uneven. Member States were prepared to forego financial stringency on some occasions in order to meet, and therefore give priority to, claimants' needs. Extending contributory unemployment benefit for older workers was one example.

In the main, however, the trend has clearly been towards reduction of contributory benefits and expansion of means tested ones. One question is whether this trend simply represents a move by Member States to restrain public expenditure or whether it also represents a fundamental restructuring of the principles on which Member States' systems are based. The major

---

[19] Schell,J. 'European social security systems' in Social Security in Europe, Miscellanea of the Erasmus-Programme Social Security in the E.C. Bruylant Brussels 1991:125

feature of post-war systems, both Beveridgean and Bismarckian in kind, was the pivotal role played by the contributory or insurance principle. Within this scheme, social assistance based on means testing always assumed a subordinate residual role. Indeed, in some South European States, as we have seen, social assistance was unknown. Do the changes of the last 15 years identified in this paper suggest that there is a clear shift from reliance on contributory benefits to reliance on means tested benefits? If so, does this in turn suggest a fundamental restructuring of social security systems in the EU?

One commentator seems inclined towards the view that a shift in basic principles from insurance to means testing has taken place.[20]

Others take the view that social assistance is not about to displace social insurance and that the cuts in contributory benefits, though serious, do not constitute an erosion of the contributory principle itself.[21] Some would go further and argue that contributory benefits are changing positively in response to rapidly changing economic and social conditions.

Two developments used to illustrate this process are the introduction of a new contributory benefit in Germany in 1995, to provide protection against the need for long-term domiciliary care,[22] and the launch by Denmark a year earlier of an 'earmarked' tax to finance unemployment benefit and other labour market expenses. Other examples of benefits adapting to changing conditions have already been noted: the extension of unemployment benefit duration for older workers and the experiments by Member States with early retirement schemes. The growth of means tested benefits is not regarded as antithetical to this process of adapation in the contributory system. Rather, it is seen as complementary to it.[23]

There thus seems to be a strong case for concluding that, despite the far-reaching reforms to Member States' social security systems in the last 15 years, the traditional insurance principle remains largely intact and that a fundamental restructuring has not (so far at least) taken place.

---

[20] Schell, J. ibid:126-7.

[21] See eg Falkner,G.: and Talos, E. 'The Role of the State within Social Policy', West European Politics (1994) 17,3:52-76, at p.70. Falkner and Talos base their conclusions on an analysis of changes to selected benefits in a number of EU Member States, including Austria and Sweden; Clasen,J. 'Social Europe', Poverty 89:13,15 (CPAG).

[22] See Gotting, U., Haug K. and Hinrichs, K. 'The Long Road to Long-Term Care Insurance in Germany', Journal of Public Policy (1994) 14,3:285-309.

[23] It may be noted that Germany's new care insurance scheme replaced means tested provision.

Social Security in the UK: 1980 – 1995

We now look in greater detail at developments in the UK social system during the 1980s and 1990s in order to support the thesis that the UK system, unlike its EU counterparts, is undergoing fundamental change.

Unemployment benefit
Contributory unemployment benefit in the UK was systematically reduced in both level and scope during the 1980s. Various techniques were used to achieve this. Rates of benefit were eroded through abolition of an earnings related supplement and child dependency additions and through bringing the benefit into tax. Access was restricted through a tightening of contributions conditions, through imposition of a weekly earnings rule and (in principle) through the introduction of an 'actively seeking work' test. The ability of the latter test to exclude large numbers of claimants depended on the zeal with which it was applied by the authorities. Administrative practice in this respect varied over time and between localities. More generally, the authorities made periodic 'trawls' of claimant cases designed to tease out and remove from entitlement claimants considered to be voluntarily unemployed (the 'workshy') and those allegedly making fraudulent claims.

These changes culminated in 1995 in a complete revamping of the benefit, such that it bears little resemblance to its former self. Introduced in 1966, the new benefit was called job seeker's allowance (JSA); it is payable for six months instead of 12 and at reduced rates for different groups of claimants. The test of availability and 'actively seeking work' remains formally the same but is to be strictly applied. After six months' receipt of contributory JSA, claimants will move on to another benefit. This is again called a job seeker's allowance but is means tested and is conditional on claimants taking any job offered to them, rather than one that might be considered 'suitable'. This means tested version of JSA replicates income support, the UK's existing means tested benefit for people (or their partners) employed for less than 16 hours a week. Arguably, it is income support in all but name. These latest changes to unemployment benefit clearly represent a considerable diminution in the level and scope of provision made for the unemployed through the contributory system and hence constitute a decline in the relevance of the contributory principle itself.

Sickness benefit and invalidity pension
Until the end of the 1970s, contributory benefits provided the main source
of protection in the UK system against against short term and long term
illness. These were sickness benefit and invalidity pension. In the early
1980s, the scope of sickness benefit was drastically reduced with the
introduction of a new non-contributory benefit called statutory sick pay
(SSP). Provision was made for SSP to be administered by employers rather
than (as with sickness and invalidity benefits) by the state. The scope of
SSP was restricted to certain categories of employees. Initially, employers
were reimbursed in full for SSP payments made by them. As a result of
these changes, contributory sickness benefit ceased to be the principal
benefit providing employees with protection against short term sickness.[24]
The benefit was further eroded through abolition of an earnings related
supplement and child dependency additions.

In 1995, both sickness benefit and invalidity pension were subjected to
further change. The two benefits were replaced by a single incapacity
benefit, comprising a short-term and long-term element. The rates for the
new benefit were generally lower than those applicable to the benefits it
replaced and and the test of incapacity was made considerably more
difficult to satisfy. As a result, both the number of people able to gain
access to the new benefit and amount of benefit awarded has dropped
significantly. These combined changes to sickness and invalidity benefit
constituted yet a further whittling away of the scope and level of protection
afforded by contributory benefits in the UK.

Statutory sick pay and statutory maternity pay
As already noted, the introduction of SSP marked a further shift away from
reliance on contributory benefits in the UK. Its introduction was also seen
as indicative of a trend towards privatisation. This was because
responsibility for administering the new benefit was imposed upon
employers rather than upon the state (as was the case with sickness benefit)
and because this was regarded by some (especially employers) as a
preliminary step towards transferring the cost of provision to them as well.
This fear proved well grounded. Reimbursement of expenditure by
employers on SSP was gradually withdrawn during the 1980s and the early
1990s so that by 1995 SSP was financed almost entirely by employers.[25]

Contributory maternity benefit has developed along similar 'privatised'
lines. In the mid-1980s, it was transformed into a non-contributory benefit

---

[24] Although it continued to play an important role in providing protection for the self-
employed and for some categories of employees.
[25] Small employers continued to receive partial reimbursement.

for employees and called statutory maternity pay (SMP). Employers were made responsible for administering the benefit and were reimbursed in full for payments made. The first step towards transferring the cost as well as the administration of provision to employers occurred in 1994, when improvements were made to SMP rates in order to comply with EU law[26] and employers were required to shoulder the costs. As a result, employers were only partially reimbursed for any payments of SMP they make. The suspicion is that all reimbursements will be ultimately withdrawn.

The basic retirement pension and SERPS

In the mid-1980s, the UK Government announced its proposal to abolish SERPS. There was also speculation on a number of occasions that the basic retirement pension was to be taken out of the contributory system and means tested. In the event, the speculation proved unfounded and the Government did not proceed with its SERPS proposal because of the strong opposition it provoked. The Government did however institute a system of financial inducements to SERPS contributors to opt-out of SERPS and into private provision.

Three other major reforms affecting state pensions were made. First, as already noted, indexation of pensions was switched from earnings to prices. In consequence, the basic pension was worth £17.50 less to recipients in 1994.[27] Secondly, the earnings-related formula for calculating SERPS entitlement was altered twice, once in 1986 and again in 1995. The consequence of both revisions was a reduction in the level of benefit available to SERPS recipients. Thirdly, the age of entitlement to the basic state pension and to SERPS was raised for women contributors from 60 to 65. This reform will be phased in over a ten year period beginning in 2010. It will result in a delay in payment and hence loss of benefit to women reaching 60 in 2010. Research also indicates that it will result in lower SERPS benefits in real terms.[28] The decision to equalise pension age was made in the name of equality. The decision to raise it for women rather than to reduce it for men was justified on grounds of the need to reduce costs, as were all the UK reforms referred to in this part of the paper.[29]

---

[26] Council Directive 92/85/EEC.

[27] See Bradshaw J and Lynes, T, 'Benefit Uprating Policy and Living Standards' in SPRU Social Policy Report No.1 1995:38 citing figures from Hansard, HC January 26 1994 col.265.

[28] Hutton, S et al, Equalisation of State Pension Ages: the Gender Impact, Equal Opportunities Commission/Social Policy Research Unit York, 1995:80-84.

[29] As to savings to be made, it has been estimated that the new JSA and incapacity benefit will help cut £8bn. off projected spending in the year 2000 while equalising pension

Though perhaps not as serious as the changes made to unemployment and invalidity benefits, these reforms to the basic pension and to SERPS constitute yet a further erosion of the contributory principle.

Means tested benefits
The last set of changes to be considered concern means tested benefits. In the early 1980s, there were three main sets of means tested benefits, supplementary benefit, rent and rate rebates, and family income supplement. All three have been subjected to considerable change during the 1980s and 1990s.

Supplementary benefit was completely restructured in 1980 and then replaced in 1988 by two new benefits, income support and the social fund. The social fund was an overtly cost-cutting measure, with limits being placed on the amount of benefit which could be awarded. Awards took the form of loans as well as grants and were made largely on a discretionary basis. Income support was withheld from 16 and 17 year-olds when it replaced supplementary benefit. Other changes have been made to income support since then. In 1995, for example, help with mortgage interest payments was severely cut. This effectively reduced the rate of benefit to which people with mortgages were entitled. Rent and rate rebates which gave means tested assistance to people on low incomes paying rent and rates were abolished in 1982 and replaced by a complex structure called housing benefit. This, too, has been changed a number of times since then.[30] Family income supplement, a means tested benefit for people in low-paid work with at least one child, was revamped and relaunched in 1988 under the name of family credit.

The 1980s and the early 1990s was therefore a period of rapid change for means tested benefits, the effect of which, in general, was to secure their position as a prominent and permanent feature of the UK benefit system. Two developments towards the end of the period, however, indicate the extent to which means testing in the UK not merely consolidated its position but extended its hold. The first development was the introduction in 1992 of disability working allowance. This form this benefit took was significant both because it was the first benefit for the disabled to be means tested and because it made entitlement conditional on claimants being in paid work (of 16 or more hours a week). Since 1992, the benefit has been further improved by enabling claimants to take child care expenses into

---

ages at 65 could reduce expenditure by £41bn. a year in the longer term: Secretary of State for Social Security, Mr Peter Lilley, quoted in the Financial Times, July 18 1995.

[30] A council tax benefit provides assistance with payment of the council tax which replaced local authority rates and their successor, the community charge.

account in the means test and by granting an additional allowance of £10 to those working 30 or more hours a week.

The second development pointing to expansion of means tested benefits, was the introduction in 1996 of a new benefit called 'earnings top-up'.[31] Introduced on a trial basis,[32] it was made available to all adults in paid work of 16 or more hours a week and with insufficient means, irrespective of whether they had children, were disabled, or whatever. Earnings top-up, then, together with disability working allowance, represent a considerable extension of means testing in the UK. As additions to the existing range of means tested benefits, they have the potential for increasing rather than reducing social security costs.[33] What then is their rationale? In official quarters they have been justified principally in terms of work incentives. The idea behind both, it is said, is to ensure that people are better off in work than out of it.[34]

Britain's Pioneering Work

It was argued earlier that social security changes in EU Member States over the last 15 years, in particular, the contraction of contributory benefits and the growth of means testing, had not fatally undermined the insurance principle in those States and had not therefore led to radical restructuring of their social security systems. It was also suggested that this proposition could not be sustained with respect to the UK. The argument to be made out here, then, is that while the social security changes in the UK have given rise to trends similar to those occuring in other EU States (the contraction of contributory benefits, the expansion of means tested ones), they nonetheless amount to a radical restructuring of the UK social security system.[35]

---

[31] DSS Piloting change in social security, helping people into work 1995.

[32] Eight pilot schemes were launched in 1996 to test whether availability of the new benefit would lead to 'unexpected effects, for example on employers' recruitment strategies and on employees' decisions about their choice and hours of work: ibid. 2.

[33] The potential may not materialise if they lead to savings elsewhere in the benefit system, by, for example, the disabled switching from income support or incapacity benefit to disability working allowance. The potentially expensive nature of the earnings top-up was acknowledged by the DSS in its discussion paper: ibid.

[34] DSS ibid.3; The Way Ahead: Benefits for the Disabled (1990) Cm 917 HMSO: para 5.8. More precisely, one might add, the benefits are intended to ensure that people are better off on benefits and in-work than on benefits and out of it.

[35] Albeit that the process is far from complete. For a contrary interpretation of developments in the UK see Bradshaw,J. 'Developments in social security policy', Jones, C. ed. New perspectives on the welfare state in Europe:43.

The first ground for this claim is the extent to which UK contributory benefits, especially unemployment, sickness and invalidity benefits, have been seriously and systematically eroded over the last 15 years. The second ground focuses on the two new means tested benefits, disability working allowance and earnings top-up, and the extent to which these benefits are structured on principles and policies antithetical to those on which the UK system has traditionally been based. It may be objected that these benefits are of little importance in terms of benefit expenditure and numbers of recipients and hence little significance should be attached to them. The view taken here, however, is that their present low profile within the UK system should be seen within the context of the UK Government's incremental approach to social security reform[36] and that the fact that they are one of the few areas of expansion within the benefit system is more significant than the relatively small amount of money (as yet) being expended on them. The novelty of these benefits lies, principally, in their insistence on claimants being in paid work in order to establish entitlement. The UK has pioneered the use of this in-work principle[37] through its introduction in the 1970s of family income supplement. Family income supplement as we have seen was replaced in 1988 by family credit which subsequently provided the model for the new benefits. These three in-work, means tested benefits are not only an expanding area of benefits; they also represent a significant conceptual and political challenge to traditional contributory benefit principles.

The conceptual challenge consists of a denial of the relevance of the out-of-work principle around which key contributory benefit concepts, such as unemployment, incapacity and retirement, have been constructed.[38] It also consists, of course, in a denial of the relevance of the contributory principle

---

36 According to one commentator, this incremental approach is 'yielding radical change without – as yet – any serious backlash', Adonis, A. 'Concern for the Nation's Welfare' Financial Times July 17 1995.

37 The UK Government itself makes this claim: DSS Piloting change in social security, helping people into work 1995:3.

38 The rules embodying these concepts tended to impose an all-or-nothing test: claimants had to be either totally out of work or in it. There were exceptions to these rules, eg, the earnings rules permitting 'retired' people to undertake some paid work. In addition, anachronistic features of the benefit system, eg, the linking of entitlement to days rather than weeks of unemployment, enabled people to work some days of the week and claim unemployment benefit for the others. The notorious 'full extent normal' rule attempted, unsuccessfully, to put a stop to this practice. The problem has now been resolved by the abolition of unemployment benefit and its replacement by JSA. See further, Luckhaus, L. 'The Regulation of A typical Work: Social Security and Emploment Law', paper given at the EOC-IER Seminar on 'Labour Market Structures and Prospects for Women' University of Warwick, March 29,30 1993.

itself. Both these principles were prerequisites of a benefit system, the purpose of which, according to Beveridge, was to compensate workers, who had made contributions while in paid work, for loss of earnings when out of work. The denial of the principles structuring the contributory benefit system would seem to imply a rejection of its purpose. What then is the purpose implied by the in-work and means testing principles on which the two new benefits and family credit are based? Because the benefits are paid only when claimants are in work and can satisfy a means test, the purpose could be said to be supplementation of low-paid work. However, as is clear from the discussion above, the rationale of these benefits is not usually presented by officials in quite these terms. Officials tend to justify them instead on the basis that they ensure people are 'better off in work than out of it' and that people's incentive to work is thereby maintained.

The issue of work incentives raises in acute form the political challenge presented by these new benefits. Arguably, the switch to in-work, means tested benefits represents a policy shift in which maintaining people's incentives to take and retain low-paid work is accorded greater priority than ensuring satisfaction of their financial needs. If so, this represents a departure from traditional UK post-war policy in which work incentives tended to take secondary place to the satisfaction of need. This shift in policy is discernible (it cannot be put higher than that) in official documents justifying the introduction of the new benefits. The Government made no reference, for example, to social security's traditional function of meeting the financial needs of the disabled in its White Paper discussion of the new disability working allowance.[39] Even more telling, perhaps, was the DSS's statement in its document announcing the earnings top-up that a means tested, in-work, benefit paid by the state was preferable to a minimum wage since the latter 'would destroy jobs by forcing employers to pay unrealistic rates above what the job is worth to them'.[40]

This privileging of what employers are prepared to pay over what workers (and others) might consider to be adequate money to live on lies at the heart of the Government's objection to a minimum wage. It also lies at the heart of what it considers to be the appropriate criteria for measuring the adequacy of benefit rates and hence the level of financial protection to be afforded by the social security system.[41] The social implications of this are

---

[39] The Way Ahead: Benefits for the Disabled (1990) Cm 917 HMSO:para 5.8; see also Luckhaus,L. 'New Disability Benefits: Beveridge Turned Upside Down', Industrial Law Journal (1992) vol. 23 no. 3 237, 240-44.

[40] DSS Piloting change in social security, helping people into work 1995:10.

[41] The UK Government since 1985 has rejected the possibility of an 'objective' notion of poverty or of minimum income standards, preferring instead an approach based on 'the

severe. Social security benefit rates must shadow wage rates, however far wages fall. Though not a necessary feature of a system based on in-work means tested benefits, the pegging of benefit rates to wage rates would appear to be an efficient way of enforcing work incentives. The same applies with equal force to the requirement that claimants be in-work in order to receive benefit.

How can this pioneering of an in-work, means tested benefit system be justified? The answer would seem to lie in the UK Government's insistence that the social security system operate in support of its wider economic policies.[42] These policies are in turn derived from neo-liberal economic principles which regard 'flexible labour' as the solution to unemployment and as the key to achieving greater competition, productivity and economic growth. Flexible labour in this context means workers able and willing to meet demand for their labour wherever and at whatever price employers are prepared to offer. On this view the function of the social security system is not to ensure adequacy of income or the satisfaction of financial need according to independently set critieria but to provide residual financial assistance at or below the rate at which the lowest wages are paid. If and when wages fall, benefit rates must follow.[43] The social system implied by these principles is one in which the market is the sole determinant of how resources are to be distributed, however unequal that division may be. If this neo-liberal theoretical and normative framework does in fact underpin the UK's policy shift towards in-work, means tested benefits in the last 15 years, then it is a policy shift that may rightly be regarded as both pioneering and perverse.

---

relationship between benefit levels and the reward available to those in work, and the total resources available for public spending' DHSS Reform of Social Security 1985 Cmnd, 9517 HMSO:para 5.3, discussed in Brádshaw, J. and Lynes, T. 'Benefit Uprating Policy and Living Standards' in SPRU Social Policy Report No.1 1995:29.

[42] See Social Security Departmental Report 1994 Cm 2813 1995 HMSO:2 for a statement of current UK social security policy. In addition to supporting the Government's wider economic policies, UK social security policy aims are: to focus benefits on those most in need, to maximise incentives to work, to encourage personal responsibility, to prevent fraud and abuse and to simplify the benefit system wherever possible.

[43] This application of the 'less eligibility principle' to benefits comprising an in-work requirement distinguishes these benefits from the Speenhamland system under which benefit levels were determined according to criteria independent of the wage system.

4. Advice and Information in Social Security Law, In Particular Restoration and Indemnification In Case of Misinformation

Professor Eberhard Jung – University of Giessen

I INTRODUCTION

In Social Security Law about thirty years ago the Federal Social Court (Bundessozialgericht / BSG) developed an entitlement which since then has not yet been included in the written law, called 'claim to restoration in Social Security Law' (sozialrechtlicher Herstellungsanspruch).[1]

This claim especially is relevant, in particular, when an insurer or a governmental or official local Social Security agency gives false or insufficient advice, and relying on this advice, a citizen or an insured person is prevented from applying within a prescribed period or fails to make an extra contribution as a special condition for a pension. The injured person will then be treated as if the wrong advice had not have given; the delayed application will be deemed to be timely and the extra contributions will be subsequently allowed.

---

[1] For details see the report on the conference of Deutscher Sozialrechtsverband (German Social Security Federation) in Bayreuth, 1994, published by Chmielorz Verlag, Wiesbaden 1994.

II ADVICE AND INFORMATION: RIGHTS AND OBLIGATIONS (GROUNDS IN LAW AND LEGAL PRINCIPLES)

Before discussing the administrative liability for a failure to give advice or the giving of false advice and information, the legal grounds and legal principles must be looked at.

1. Secondary Obligations Arising Out of the Relationship Between the Administration and the Citizen/Insured Person

The legal principle of equity (Treu und Glauben : § 242 BGB) can be regarded as a starting-point for secondary obligations in public law. In the German Civil Code (BGB) we have many regulations concerning information, clarification, notice, announcement, indication, confidentiality or advice. When such secondary obligations are disregarded, a claim for damages will follow (positive Vertragsverletzung : breach of contract).

A right to information can also be derived from general principles of constitutional and administrative law, being based on the position of the citizen as an individual (Art. 1 and 2 of the German 'Grundgesetz') or justified by the rules of legality in administration.

Looking at the decisions of the German Supreme Administrative Court (Bundesverwaltungsgericht/BVerwG) we find a special principle showing the influence of the ideas of § 162 BGB (German Civil Code) in public law, that is, when the occurrence of an event puts a party at a disadvantage and he is prevented from taking a course of action, equity will regard the event as though it had not occurred. In a decision of this Court for example in 1959[2] an applicant had visited a civil servant in his office. This minor official refused to accept the application which was written in an antiquated form, despite the fact that time was running out. The Federal Administrative Court considered the official not only to be a servant of the state but also a help for the citizen. Authorities therefore, had the obligation to help applicants to achieve their rights within the bounds of law. In this present case the civil servant had prevented the application within the specified time, in breach of his duties and contrary to equity in the sense of § 162 BGB. As a result of this the application was regarded as submitted in time.

---

[2] BVerwGE 9, 89 (91 et seq.).

2. Principal Entitlements

Since 1976, when the German Social Code was brought into force, the Federal Social Court (Bundessozialgericht) has derived the 'claim to restoration in Social Security law' not only from secondary obligations arising out of the general relationship between administration and citizen, but also from decisions based on the principal provisions of §§ 13 to 15 Social Code Part I (SGB I).

2a. Clarification

All insurers, their federations and other social authorities are bound by § 13 SGB I within the scope of their competence to enlighten and to educate, all persons about their rights and duties under the Social Code. The authorities are required to inform everybody but individuals do not obtain entitlements from these general obligations except in the case of incomplete, false or misleading explanations. Explanations are made and instructions are given, in leaflets, pamphlets, gazettes, papers, radio and television.

2b. Individual Advice

In § 14 SGB I we find an express provision of the right 'for everybody' to obtain advice about his rights and duties from the competent authority. To get advice a citizen or an insured person must contact this authority directly. In addition to this express provision, the secondary obligations arising out of the relationship between citizen and administration also exist, and must be fulfilled as well, without any specific application being made. In obvious cases, for example, the authority must act on its own initiative, when an intelligent and reasonable citizen or insured person selects an inappropriate arrangement or when a chosen arrangement has turned out in fact to be inappropriate.

2c. Information

The local authorities responsible for Health Insurance and Long-term care Insurance are bound by § 15 SGB I to give information about all social matters under the Social Code. Every citizen seeking advice may use this information as a directive to the competent authority. § 15 SGB I thus gives citizens seeking advice an express entitlement.

2d. Special regulations

Special requirements regarding information for persons concerned are also to be found in the Labour Promotion Act (AFG), in the Federal Social Assistance Act (BSHG) and in the Rehabilitation Adjustment Act

(RehaAnglG).   Since 1989 the Health Insurance authorities have had to inform insured persons about dangers to health and how to organise successful prevention (§ 20 Social Code Part V).

2e. European Dimensions

On July 27, 1994, the European Commission[3] announced that, to improve transparency and certainty in European Law, it would produce a survey of all the European social regulations, a guide concerning the national steps required to transfer social European applications, and a summary of Social Security Law. Such a publication would inform the individuals about their rights and duties and about the possible results if it were necessary to go to court.

III LIABILITY FOR OMITTED OR FALSE ADVICE AND INFORMATION

In the case of failure to provide information it is not only a 'claim to restoration' that has to be considered. A citizen may also make use of an action for damages on the ground of violation of administrative duties.

1. The Action For Damages on Account of Violation of Administrative Duties

This entitlement according to Art. 34 of the German 'Grundgesetz' together with § 839 BGB has the following features :
– violation of an administrative duty to an applicant by a failure to give advice or information or the giving of false advice and information,
– a wilful or negligent act by the employee or civil servant,
– damage to the applicant as a result of the violation of this administrative duty,
– pecuniary compensation,
– the claim is made in the civil courts.
In order better to understand the following remarks it is necessary to give an example.   Since 1969 an insured person had been receiving a Social Security pension on account of occupational invalidity ('Erwerbsunfähigkeitsrente').   In 1972, at the age of 65, she made a claim to transform this pension into an old age pension ('Altersrente'). But to get a retirement pension in this special case, she should have paid an extra

---

3   White Paper, KOM (94) 33. (German edition).

contribution, and this would have been possible only in the years form 1972 to 1975. The appropriate insurance authority, having failed to inform the insured person about this time limit, in 1981 refused to pay a retirement pension. The Federal Social Court in 1984 held:[4] That the insurer was bound to grant a retirement pension, as the 'claim to restoration in Social Security Law' puts the insured person in such a position as if she had duly paid the extra contribution in the years from 1972 to 1975. So the insured person reached her goal, and got her retirement pension.

Because in this case duties in regard to administrative inquiries were also broken (a mistake in reading a microfilm led to a false wedding date), an action for damages would also have been possible, provided that an employee or civil servant had acted negligently (or wilfully). But such a claim for damages would lead only to a financial compensation. The performance of the original administrative duties – even belatedly – could not have been achieved in this way.

2. The 'Claim to Restoration' in Social Security Law

The 'claim to restoration' with the object of subsequent performance of the original administrative duties, has the following 'case-law' features:

– omitted or false advice and information in performing an administrative duty towards an applicant or in the course of other administrative activities,
– unlawful act of an employee or civil servant, but not necessarily a negligent or wilful act,
– the illegal act must have caused loss to the citizen,
– the restoration leads not to a pecuniary indemnification, but the applicant instead is put in the position that he would have been in if the wrong advice had not been given,
– the restoration is back-dated four years, analogous to § 44 Social Code Part X (withdrawal of an unlawful act),
– the claim is made in the social courts.

---

4   BSG, Decision of 28.02.1984, SGb 1985, 295.

IV DOCTRINAL ARGUMENTS IN LEGAL SCHOLARSHIP AND JURISDICTION CONCERNING THE ENTITLEMENTS TO INFORMATION AND RESTORATION

1. Different Views

Since the elaboration of the 'claim to restoration in Social Security Law' both legal scholars and the courts have tried to find dogmatic arguments for this entitlement. These activities cannot be seen simply as a typical example of German 'case law', with the intention not only of solving a case, but to find a rule which will fit harmoniously into the legal system as a whole. A good basis is also necessary for a description of the extent and the limitations of the administrative duties to advise, to inform and to enlighten the citizen (§§ 13 to 15 Social Code Part I). In the following part the different views occurring in the courts and legal scholarship will be set out.[5]

2. The Principle of Equity

The violation of the obligations to advise and inform which arise out of the relationship between the administration and the citizen, rests on the example of the civil law (§ 242 BGB; positive Vertragsverletzung : breach of contract).

3. The 'Claim to Set Aside the Results of Illegal Administrative Activities' (Folgenbeseitigungsanpruch)

For some decades the Supreme Administrative Court has had jurisdiction to enforce this claim and the effects of illegal administrative activities can be revoked, e.g. an invasion of somebody's property rights will be redressed by re-establishing the original ownership, not by payment of damages. Here it is also of some interest, that the 'claim to set aside' was first developed by legal scholars and was afterwards taken up by the Supreme Administrative Court, whereas the reverse was true for the 'claim to restoration'. Here the entitlement was developed by the Federal Social Court and then accepted gradually by legal scholars.

---

[5]   See Ossenbühl and Wallerath, conference report, op. cit., n. 1; Seewald, Kasseler, Kommentar zum Sozialversicherungsrecht, Rz. 38, vor §§ 38 – 47 SGB I; Schmidt-De Caluwe, Der sozialrechtliche Herstellungsanspruch, Berlin 1992.

4. Constitutional Basis

From the perspective of the German 'Grundgesetz' the 'claim to restoration' can be derived from the principles of administrative lawfulness (Art. 20 par. 3 Grundgesetz), from the confidence in a lawful public administration, and from the effectiveness of legal protection (Art. 19 par. 4 Grundgesetz).

5. The Prohibition of Contradictory Behaviour

Further arguments rest on the prohibition of contradictory behaviour (venire contra factum proprium). It will be an abuse of a citizen's rights, if the administration deviates from previously established particular facts, or when there are other particular circumstances in connection with an administrative act which would result in a breach of the citizen's right of confidence in lawful administration.

6. Restoration to the Previous State of Proceedings

Some people look upon the 'claim to restoration' as a further development of the special restoration available under the German Civil Procedure Code in cases in which a specified time limit in proceedings has been missed through no fault on the part of the applicant.

7. All-Embracing Arguments

Repeatedly in legal scholarship some people have taken the view that it would be better not to rely on one argument only. The 'claim to restoration' has proved its worth, we should not seek a single 'truth', and all arguments include a part of the 'truth'. We should not hinder the possibility of further development by uni-dimensional arguments in the case of unforeseeable events or conflicts.[6] On the other hand we cannot ignore one particular rule in the Social Code itself, which in fact may provide grounds for the 'claim to restoration': § 2 sentence 2 of the Social Code Part I.

---

[6] See Ossenbühl, conference report, op. cit., n. 1.

8. § 2 Sentence 2 Social Code Part I

In the first place, it is explicitly declared in § 2 Social Code Part I, that the 'social rights' in §§ 3 to 10 Social Code Part I (e.g. § 4 : the right to social security) are entitlements only as far as the requirements of the regulations in the particular parts of the Social Code are fulfilled. Sentence 2 of § 2 further declares that the following social rights must be observed when interpreting all regulations of the Social Code and all discretionary decisions. In this process it must be guaranteed that the social rights will be granted as far as possible.

According to a judgement of the Federal Social Court in 1980[7] the administration has the general duty to realise as far as possible the objectives of the Social Code. This means in particular that an applicant who can choose between several alternatives must be put in the position actually to do so. He or she must be enabled to make an 'informed' decision. Information should enable an applicant to make a decision corresponding to his personal needs and to be aware of all the important circumstances. This means that all regulations should be interpreted in such a way that a citizen should not be held to statements, which were reached on the basis of misinformation. In 1984 the Federal Social Court pointed out,[8] that the public interest must be taken into consideration too. Social benefits intended by law must be granted and anybody fulfilling the requirements to an entitlement must obtain the appropriate benefits. These are elementary duties to ensure a comprehensive realisation of the law according to the principles of the 'Rechtsstaat' and of equality.

Taking into account these ideas of the Federal Social Court the 'claim to restoration in Social Security Law' can be based on § 2 sentence 2 Social Code Part I, where confidence in the administration of the law as a part of the principles of the Rechtsstaat, and of equality, has been put in concrete terms. Each applicant is entitled to assume that the administration will take the necessary steps to guarantee a comprehensive realisation of his individual rights under the Social Security Law. In this way the social rights in §§ 3 to 10 Social Code Part I will be realised as far as possible.

---

7   BSGE 51, 81.
8   BSG, op. cit., n. 4.

V EXTENT AND LIMITS OF INFORMATION AND RESTORATION

1. Actual Limits

The 'claim to restoration in Social Security Law' was originally developed to solve the problems of late applications resulting from misinformation. The applicant was entitled to the benefit, and he received the legal benefit, but later than he should have. The first difficulties in using the 'claim to restoration' arose under the Employment Promotion Act, when requirements had to be fulfilled which were no longer possible, e.g. an 'application in person' to draw unemployment benefit (§ 105 AFG).[9] When an applicant has asked at the Employment Office about the requirements for unemployment benefit, before leaving his employment, and receives wrong advice that leads him to quit his job prematurely, then it is impossible for him to fulfil the requirement of 'completion of a qualifying period of insured employment' by using a 'claim to restoration'. An applicant will be eligible for unemployment benefit only when he has filled the missing 'qualifying period' with actual employment. The court has made it clear that only requirements within the relationship between administration and citizen are regarded as fulfilled by means of the 'claim to restoration', not requirements outside of this relationship.[10]

Quite recently there have been repeated attempts to use the 'claim to restoration' as an 'open sesame!' in confused legal situations,[11] but it must be clearly seen, that with this special claim, only legitimate benefits can be obtained, not non-existing entitlements. That seems to be obvious, but frequently there is a lack of understanding on the part of the persons concerned. An employer, for example for some years paid contributions to an unauthorised insurer under the Industrial Injuries Insurance scheme because the relevant authority had not referred this firm in time to the competent insurance institute. Since the contributions to an authorised insurer were lower than to an unauthorised insurer, the employer demanded a refund of the higher contributions relying on the 'claim to restoration'. In a decision in 1992[12] it was held, that by law (§ 667 RVO-Reichs insurance regulations) there was no claim in relation to questions arising in relation to a referral between insurers of Industrial Injuries Insurance and also that a

---

[9] See Kreßel, Der Herstellungsanspruch in Vorsorgesystemen, NZS 1994, 395 et seq.

[10] Bezirksgericht Erfurt (Senat für Sozialrecht), SGB 1993, 43.

[11] Bezirksgericht Erfurt, op. cit., n. 10.

[12] LSG Baden-Württemberg 01.10.1992, L 7 U 366/89 (see Jung, Die Berufs-genossenschaft 1994, 503 et seq. , 506).

'claim to restoration' could not succeed here either. Apart from these limitations on the legal scope of the claim the following requirements of the 'claim to restoration' have to be considered too.[13]

2. Behaviour of the Insured Person

It is a requirement for a 'claim to restoration', that the administrative misinformation is the only essential cause of the disadvantage to the person concerned. When a claimant has brought about the cause of administrative misinformation himself - in particular with false representations – then the necessary ground for a 'claim to restoration' will be lacking.

An insured person is not protected from relying on false administrative advice, when he himself is responsible for gross negligence.

In the case of an applicant having obtained insufficient information himself otherwise than from the appropriate authority, the duties of the administration to advise and to inform are not cancelled, but they are reduced. A 'claim to restoration' will be excluded, when a citizen notwithstanding that he himself has gathered correct information, does not follow it.

3. Information on the Basis of an Administrative Initiative

There are not only duties to give advice and information to an applicant, but an authority has also to act on its own initiative, when it has an existing relationship with a citizen and
– in an obvious case an intelligent and reasonable citizen selects an inappropriate arrangement, or
– the arrangement chosen has turned out to be actually unsuitable.[14]

In such a case the authority has to consider all the facts available. Supplementary inquiries are not necessary, unless the previous inquiries were insufficient or misdirected.

In an area of large scale administration – as for example in the case of Invalidity and Retirement Insurance – an authority will not actually be in a position to give each one of the insured persons individual advice as to how to arrange optimal conditions for insurance. Nor is the authority required to

---

[13] See e.g. Dörr, Grenzen der 'Herstellung', DAngVers 1993, 182 et seq.; Eisenreich, Ludwig, Der sozialrechtliche Herstellungsanspruch, Die Sozialversicherung 1995, 1 et seq.

[14] BSG 6. 5. 1992, Breithaupt 1993, 283.

give information about possible and beneficial loopholes in the law or alternative arrangements which are not actually forbidden.[15]

In a decision in 1994 for example[16] the 'claim to restoration' was denied in the case of an agricultural employer who had applied for an additional pension. The Invalidity and Retirement Insurance insurer had not informed this man who received a retirement pension at the age of 65, that he could have used a provision in the law which involved giving up his status as an employer 3 months before his 65th birthday and worked as an employee. He would then have obtained an additional pension – contrary to the true purpose of the law, which had in mind improvement in the pensions of persons who had lost the economic basis of their status as an agricultural employer and had become employees as a result.

An illegal administrative act can also arise from a change in the interpretation of the law, when an interpretation is later changed, so that the authority earlier had acted incorrectly. An authority which has not acted in accordance with the ruling or current opinion in a particular case, has to point this out to the claimant. When an expert's opinion is given as to the state of health of an applicant and as a result benefits have not been granted, the authority must mention in its refusal any differing opinion of other experts as there is a possibility that an insured person could have reacted differently if he had known of all the experts' opinions, especially when his application for a pension failed.

This extensive information must be considered in view of the narrow basis of the 'claim to restoration'in § 2 sentence 2 Social Code Part I. There it is laid down, that the 'social rights'must be realised as far as possible and that a claimant can rely on the administration. The competent authority will take the necessary steps to guarantee each citizen his individual legal rights.

4. Joint Administrative Action

The Federal Social Court has declared that the competent authority may also be liable for the unlawful acts of another authority in the case of joint administrative actions.[17]

In this connection the term 'unity of action or function' ('Funktionseinheit') has been developed. Accordingly, for example, an Invalidity and Retirement Insurance insurer is included within the procedure for admission of an old age pensioner to a Local Health

---

[15] See Krause, Sattler, Jahrbuch des Sozialrechts 1993, 73 et seq. (74).
[16] LSG Niedersachsen, Breithaupt 1995, 222.
[17] BSGE 51, 89; 71, 217.

Insurance Fund scheme.[18] The Local Insurance Office (Versicherungsamt) gives advice to applicants on Invalidity and Retirement Insurance insurers as part of what is seen as a 'division of labour'[19] But payment of child benefit by the Employment Office (Arbeitsamt) and the provision of financial assistance for education by the competent office (BAFöG-Amt)[20] was not seen as part of a single activity or function in this sense. And misinformation from a local government office (Ordnungsamt) concerning the insurance of an employer was not attributed to the competent Industrial Injuries Insurance authority.[21]

The Federal Social Court has pursued a middle course in relation to the notion of 'unity in action' The advocates of a restrictive view[22] would only accept the 'claim to restoration' in cases of misinformation from the competent authotity. When another authority has given wrong advice a 'claim to restoration' would be out of the question, and only an action for damages on account of the breach of administrative duty (wilful or negligent) would be possible. It is not difficult, to reject this restrictive view. Joint actions of different authorities are used to simplify and to standardise administrative procedures, but this should not lead to disadvantages for citizens. A contrary opinion[23] rests on the constitutional principles of the rule of law and the unity of all public administration, and would regard each authority as being liable for the errors of all others, the only one exception being where an authority obviously has no competence. This extreme opinion has to be rejected too. The ultimately competent authority cannot be expected to accept liability for almost every mistake in public administration. A preliminary legal decision concerning such a liability, for example evidenced by a 'unity in action', is essential.[24]

The position of the citizen as an individual, responsible for his own actions,[25] has to be considered too. The citizen's right to confidence in the activities of the administration cannot be protected infinitely. In all spheres of life the individual has to collect information himself about the competences of other individuals and institutions, not only in the case of an evident incompetence.

---

[18] BSGE 51, 89.
[19] BSGES 29.10.1991, – 13/5 RJ 38/89.
[20] BSGE 71, 217.
[21] BSG, NZS 1994, 275.
[22] See e.g. Benz, Die Berufsgenossenschaft 1987, 31 et seq. (40); Bley, Gesamtkommentar zum SGB I, Anm. 5 et seq., vor §§ 13 – 15 SGB I, Anm. 8 and 9 on § 15 SGB I.
[23] See Kreßel, conference report, op. cit., n. 1, p. 49.
[24] See Wallerath, conference report, op. cit., n. 1, p. 82.
[25] See Jung, Das Recht auf Gesundheit, München 1982, pp. 103 et seq., 249 et seq.

The interests of the authority made liable must also be considered. There is a possibility that the ultimately responsible authority has some influence on the 'affiliated' administrative body, for example, in the supply of information and in the training of the employees of the administrative departments concerned. Therefore we have to agree with the Federal Social Court, that a 'claim to restoration' requires something more in such cases, a 'unity in function' between two (or more) authorities.

VI CONCLUSION

For quite some time now we can observe the existence of very detailed legislation all over Europe, together with ever increasing electronic data processing. At the same time great efforts are being made in the fields of public relations and consumer protection. In Social Security there has been a call for more protection for the insured person against his own mistakes. There must be harmonisation and the convergence of the European Social Systems. All this requires regular clarification, advice and information. It is for this reason that special regulations such as §§ 13 – 15 Social Code Part I are necessary. But these laws have to be accepted by a people-orientated administration. In this respect it is a benefit, that the German Federal Social Court has developed the 'claim to restoration'. Administrative mistakes may not only be subsequently remedied within limits, but the existence of this entitlement should have a preventive effect as well, in achieving more and better administrative information.

5. Games Without Frontiers:- Free Movement in Sport

Ken Foster – University of Warwick

I INTRODUCTION

One of the highlights of the sporting year of 1995 was the dramatic victory of the European golf team over the USA in the Ryder Cup. What was almost unique about this victory was that it was gained by a genuine pan-European team containing Spanish, German, British, Swedish and Italian players. The blue flag of the European Union was carried by the fans without any artificiality. There are few if any other occasions on which a sporting enthusiast feels 'European'. Most of the time he or she supports a national or a local team. If European integration is to signify anything to the average person, it needs this kind of transference into popular culture. Football is a common cultural heritage within Europe and for it to be de-nationalised in the mind of Europeans could be the most important way of rethinking the nation-state. An important recent case in the European Court may accelerate this process of sporting integration. The outcome of the case of Bosman, a Belgian footballer, has brought closer the day when the football supporter finds it normal to see 'European' players rather than 'English' or 'German' players.

In this paper, I want to use the case of Bosman to ask a number of questions. One, can sportspeople be granted exactly the same rights of free movement as other workers or are there justifications for treating the employment contracts of professional sportspeople as sufficiently different to warrant separate legal treatment? Two, is sport an economic activity that can be treated as a business so that the normal framework of European law, especially in relation to monopoly and the regulation of workers, applies without modification? Or is it just a game or an entertainment in which the pursuit of profit is incidental? Three, can the restrictive internal regulations of most professional sports be defended, even if they trespass on individual rights or the right of enterprises to conduct their business as they see fit?

And finally, as the implications of Bosman suggest that sport in general, and football in particular, is becoming a global market with a corresponding move to a global labour market, what does this mean for the creation of local and cultural identities? Sport mediates but also creates the links between the sporting fan, the European citizen and the nation state.

Free Movement Within Europe

The free movement of workers within the community has been one of the key pillars of the European Union since its inception. This principle is enshrined in the original Treaty of Rome by Article 48, which states that 'freedom of movement for workers shall be secured within the Community'. It is one of the four fundamental freedoms. The principle implies that workers must not be impeded in moving from an employer in one member state to another employer in a different state. But it also embodies the wider concept that workers should not have unreasonable restrictions contractually placed upon them by employers that hinder or restrict their ability to move freely and take a job with any other employer. These restraints can take various forms, and in particular labour markets can be a significant limitation on the worker's right to work for whomsoever they choose. In English law, workers have some protection because the doctrine of 'restraint of trade' can be used to render unenforceable clauses in contracts that are unreasonable and not in the public interest.

However, one area where the principle of free movement of workers has never fully been implemented is sport, especially in team sports such as football. The ruling authorities of football, at both national level and at international level, have placed restrictions upon players moving freely from one club to another. These typically involve the payment of a transfer fee by the new club to the old club, nominally to represent the transfer of the player's registration with the football authorities, or provisions that prevent a player from moving to any other club even when no longer under contract to his old club. As football associations and federations are usually the sole supplier of professional football within their own territory these restrictions can have the economic effect of tying a player to one club.

History of Bosman

These restrictions are currently been challenged by Jean-Marc Bosman. Bosman was a professional footballer with RFC Liege playing in the Belgian League. When his contract with the club expired in 1990, he was 'retained' by his club. This meant he could not move to another club without his ex-employer's permission. The club offered him a new contract at a quarter of his previous salary. He refused it. He was put on the transfer list at a fee four times what Liege had paid for him. This unrealistic fee meant that after two years no other club had shown any interest in buying him. When finally a French club, Dunkerque, made a lower offer for him, Liege refused to sell him. Bosman sued his club, the national association the Belgian FA, and UEFA, the European governing body. Effectively, he has been prevented from playing professional football anywhere within Europe for the last five years. His challenge in the European Court of Justice attacked the legality of two fundamental aspects of European football, the transfer system and the 'foreigners' rule that restricts the number of overseas players that a football club can use in a game. He argued that the rules should prohibit a club requiring or receiving a fee for players who are out of contract. He also argued that national and international federations should not have regulations and provisions that restrict foreign players as this discriminates against players from within the European Union. Bosman's case relies on two main legal arguments; that the restrictions placed upon him by RFC Liege were in breach of Article 48 by denying him free movement to work anywhere in the European Union and that UEFA, who holds a monopoly on the organisation of professional football within Europe, was abusing its dominant position and thereby in breach of Articles 85 and 86. In September 1995, the Advocate-General issued an opinion in his favour. If this is confirmed by the Court itself the implications for football in particular and professional sports generally could be profound.

Conflicting Concepts of Space

This case and the problems that it exposes have geographical implications. Football has traditionally been an expression of local identity. People supported their local team. Cities with more than one team produced fierce local rivalries, often based on an expression of communal or religious identity as with Glasgow Rangers and Celtic. Players were often born in the town for which they played. The commercialisation of football has weakened these local bonds. Fans are now more mobile, less likely to support their local team especially if it is unsuccessful, and more likely to transfer their support to a large successful team. A recent survey showed that English Premier League clubs are supported by fans from all parts of the country. This support can also be indirect. Fans can follow top teams on television and through the newspapers rather than in person. Loyalty is displayed by wearing replica kits or buying other club merchandise.

Football does not have eligibility rules for players based on birth or residence for a period in the locality of the club, unlike cricket or Australian rules football. Players are recruited from anywhere in the British Isles, and for the top teams, anywhere in the world. The English Premier League in the 1995-6 has players from 35 different nations. The richest clubs tend to be large town clubs as they attract the biggest crowds. Football is traditionally an urban sport, but the successful teams are increasingly from metropolitan areas or large conurbations.

The increasing global market for football players has lead to a massive flow of players from the poorer footballing countries, which find it difficult to support a thriving domestic professional league, to the richer leagues in Italy, Spain and England. But there are restrictions on the number of foreign players that can be used by any one side. Typically, the major leagues now impose a limit of three foreigners in any game, and often a higher limit on the number of foreigners that a club may employ. UEFA has a rule of three foreigners plus two 'assimilated'[1] players for its own European cups. The justifications for these restrictions are to prevent the richest clubs buying up all the best players and monopolising the market and to allow the development of home players so that the interests of the national team are preserved. Such rules raise legal problems. The rules talk only of 'foreigners' and make no discrimination, as European law would, between nationals of a member state and nationals from outside the Union.

At the European level, not being able to buy and play the best players from anywhere can limit a club's potential in the European competitions, which are now commercially very important. A successful run to the final of the European Champions Cup has been estimated as worth £75 million to a club. In a world where the largest European clubs are treating themselves as transnational businesses such limitations on the free labour market can also be a hindrance for the employers as well as the workers.

Sport As Business In A Global Market

Sport as a business has some distinctive features. It is unusual in that sporting success not financial profit is the aim. A football team does not exist to make money. It rarely has a corporate form in Britain and investors are often local business people uninterested in a return on their money. For the most successful clubs, their financial base however increasingly depends on sponsorship and marketing the club as a name in a global

---

[1] These are players who have learnt the game in the country by playing there for 5 years including 3 in a youth team.

market place. The product is no longer just the game on a Saturday afternoon. The club is a brand image and has a corporate identity as distinctive as Disney or Macdonalds. Take as an example, Manchester United plc. Their annual report for the year ending July 1995 reported a pre-tax profit of £20 million on a turnover of £60.6 million. Of that turnover, £23.5 million came from merchandising such as the sales of replica kits.[2]

But sport is also part of a wider trend in post-modern businesses. Business is not just about making commodities or selling services. Many enterprises today are in the 'hits' business. What they are seeking is the 'big hit', whether in music, film, fashion, book publishing, or sport. These post-modern businesses have distinctive features. They are prepared to subsidise a number of losses for the one big hit that can recover these losses. This can lead businesses to gamble for the 'big hit' in ways that would be considered irrational in conventional enterprises. They deal in people rather than making or providing things. Their raw material is talent. They are prepared to scout for, and nurture new talent who may be the next big star to give them a string of hits. Their assets are often intellectual property rather than physical commodities. Enterprises are about marketing the star product. Success is transient and has to be continually renewed.

These 'hits' industries also have peculiar labour markets, where the stars who can guarantee success are the key to the business and are likely to be poached by rivals, discarded quickly if no longer likely to produce the 'hits' and often need good personal relationships to give their best performances so that management is of a special kind. They also have labour markets in which the effective working life of even the star performer is often a short one; and where the supply of hopeful star-struck entrants far exceeds demand thus leading to exploitation of young workers and oppressive contracts signed by workers desperate for a chance of the 'big time'.

A further distinctive feature of sport is that it is a curious kind of cartel in which clubs have a mutual interest in each others business health. Each club plays each other. In team sports the product to be marketed, the commodity to be sold, is the game itself. But games have to be interesting enough to attract the fans to the ground or be an exciting spectacle for the television cameras. It takes two to tango, and for this reason no single team can sell the product by itself. It has to be marketed as a competition, a league or a cup. Each team needs the other teams in the league to produce the end product. So whilst football clubs may be fierce competitors on the field, they are mutually dependent partners in economic terms to a much

---

2 Financial Times 4/10/95, p.22.

greater extent than normal businesses. This has a number of odd consequences. Sports need to ensure that free market principles do not lead to the richest clubs buying up all the best players. The predictable result will be less equal competition on the field and therefore a less attractive product and the possibility that the weaker clubs will go out of business to the detriment of the overall product – the league itself. There can be few economic enterprises where the aim is not total control of the market – playing with yourself is no fun, where enterprises are prevented from making a profit, as happens with Italian football clubs, and where redistribution of income to keep one's rivals in business is a normal practice.

In a global market, team sports are redefining the nexus between the players and the team. In most traditional team sports, such as football and cricket, this has been geographical; town-based in professional football reflecting its roots in Victorian cities and county-based in cricket to reflect its earlier origins in agricultural society. These spatial links can assist in creating a loyalty to roots in both players and spectators. But the money nexus of modern sport driven by the finances of television has weakened these links to the locality. American team sports have operated on the franchise principle, whereby a right to operate a team in a specified geographical area is sold. This can lead to the odd consequence, at least to European eyes, of teams suddenly moving from one city to another with all the theoretical mobility of capital in any economic arena. This is partly explained by American team sports having a single competition without promotion and relegation from lower leagues, and this inflexibility makes it difficult to adjust to changing demographics. Moving franchises in American sports over the last forty years has mainly reflected the population shift from the Eastern rust-belt to the Western and Southern sun-belt.

These confusion as to the nature of the link between place and team are linked to the regulation of the sport. They are graphically illustrated by the financial and legal arguments involved in international rugby union's attempt to professionalise itself, and the conceptual confusion of what the 'product' of sport is. On one hand, the traditional controllers of the sport have been the amateur administrators who organise international rugby on the basis of national teams and domestic rugby on the basis of clubs organised into leagues. They have 'sold' these competitions to Rupert Murdoch's television organisations for ten years. The assumption here is that the 'product' that has value in the sports marketplace is the competition, that for example New Zealand v. South Africa 'sells', whoever represents these labels. A challenge was mounted by Kerry Packer's television interests which involved buying the players as the 'stars' and thus the 'product' that will sell the television package. In his proposal the 'teams' appear as secondary and not always representing traditional localities. A similar battle is being waged in rugby league with traditional teams, often based on very local communities in the North of England, being replaced with bastard combinations and new artificial entities in order to make the 'product'more suitable for television. Although this kind of mutual self interest is emphasised in team sports, it not entirely absent from individual sports. Professional sport is ultimately about competition between players; few fans get much pleasure from watching the star player doing a solo exhibition performance. Tennis and golf players need tournaments to play in, athletics needs the best runners to run against each other. So some overall organisation or governing body to produce the best competition is needed. However, for the top athletes and golfers prize money alone may not be sufficient to ensure their appearance. In order to preserve the appeal of a tournament to spectators and television the 'star' players with proven ability to attract fans can and do get 'appearance money' for their participation. The 'product' in such cases is not solely the competition itself but the opportunity to watch and admire the 'big name'.

Allocating Talent And Wealth

For many, the key issue in the Bosman case is that football players should have the same rights as other workers. Indeed, to allow them to be bought and sold as if they were serfs or commodities is morally wrong. To deny them basic human rights of free movement means more money for the clubs who can reap the financial rewards from transfer fees. Why sportspeople should be treated differently from normal employees who can move freely to a new employer at the end of their employment is a difficult question to answer. The most frequently used arguments against free agency and free movement in sport are twofold. One is that such freedom allows the best players to be bought by the richest clubs so that ultimately sporting success becomes a function of money. It hardly needs emphasising that there are some unproven causal links in this proposition. Nevertheless it remains true enough in most major professional sports to be perceived as a real danger. Secondly, it is argued that the essence of sport as a competition is the uncertainty of outcome. If one player or one team dominates a sport to the extent of making the result a formality, then it is believed that the public will lose interest and be less likely to support it. The long-term economic health of the sport is seen to rest on equalising competition. This means either equalising talent and, as money can buy talent in a free labour market, requiring that income has to be redistributed within the sport or by interfering with the labour market to get an even spread of the available talent.

There are several potential strategies that a governing body of sport can use to try to redistribute money or players within team sports. One possibility is to treat the sport, at least at professional level, as a single commercial entity and develop methods of approaching equal resources. Most sports leagues assume a need for a minimum number of teams to make the sport viable and that therefore it is in the communal interest that weaker or poorer clubs survive and indeed are strengthened so that a sporting monopoly does not develop to the detriment of the sport as a whole. Talent, and the resources to buy it or develop it without fear of it being poached by richer clubs without proper compensation, needs to be spread as evenly as possible. It is only by this process of equalisation that more competitive and uncertain contests can be achieved. There seems to be a crude relation that the more predictable the result in a particular sport (given one team being superior to the other) the more the sporting authorities feel the need to evolve tactics to fix the labour market and equalise teams. High scoring sports, such as basketball and rugby, are prone to this effect whilst low scoring sports, such as football, are more likely to get unexpected results and 'giant-killing' feats. To prevent wealth becoming concentrated or monopolised, therefore, many sports have rules to prevent the best supported teams, spectators until recently being the major source of income for most sports teams, keeping all their wealth. One such rule is that income from gate receipts be shared in some proportion and not go solely to the home team. Such a rule means that the teams from smaller towns who are less well supported at the gate are more likely to have resources redistributed towards them. Another is to insist that all other sources of income are the property of the league and not the clubs. Thus income from sponsorship, the legal rights to logos, badges and team colours are retained by the league not the individual club. Similarly, there may be rules that the income from broadcasting games goes to the league rather than the clubs by the league retaining or taking the right to sell the broadcasting rights. These rules assume that the exploitation and marketing of these ancillary sources of income is to be undertaken by the league for the collective benefit of all and will be redistributed by the league, often in equal shares. English football, however, has overall not perused these tactics. It has allowed clubs to retain all gate receipts in most competitions, especially the Premier League, and let clubs sell their own merchandise. On the other hand, the broadcasting revenues from the sale of television rights has gone to the League.

One reason for this reluctance to share all incomes has been what might be termed 'overlapping geographies'. To make all clubs more equal within the national league means, it is argued, that the top clubs are less able to compete successfully in European competitions. It is even asserted that the national team requires talent to be concentrated in a smaller number of clubs. It is noticeable that American sports, which have developed these 'rules of equal and fair competition' more than most other countries, are dominated by four sports[3] in which meaningful international events are absent.

The main alternative to equalising wealth is for governing bodies of sport to have rules that attempt to equalise talent and thereby prevent clubs monopolising success in the sport. The legal difficulty with all these rules is that they will to some extent limit freedom for the players because they restrain the players from working for whomever and wherever they choose, and thus restrict the players' ability to earn a living or at least to maximise their earnings. So governing bodies may literally redistribute the players each season by assigning the players to new teams, for example on the basis of their performance over the previous season. This can be done legally by the governing body signing contracts directly with the players so that it employs the players rather than the individual clubs. It also requires a monopoly of professional competition by the governing body and the players signing exclusive contracts, otherwise the stability of the sport is potentially at risk from a rival organisation. Another method aims to allow new talent into the sport only on a rota basis, with the weakest team, usually in sporting rather than financial terms, getting first choice and thus preventing the best teams getting the best young players and so reinforcing their hold on the sporting honours. This has been historically the preferred method of American sports, where it is known as the 'draft' system, but it assumes a single source of recruitment and a single route into the game. It also requires voluntary restraint on the part of other teams as the ultimate sanction against a player who refuses the single offer that he can legitimately receive under this system is that no other team will employ him; in other words a collective boycott by the employers. A third method is to create a system of qualification or eligibility to play for a particular club so that a player has only one choice of potential employer. Such eligibility rules are usually territorial in character so that a player can only qualify for the area of their birth or long residence. The rules of 'county' cricket in England are still ultimately based on these criteria. The extreme example of such geographical rules has been Australian rules football

---

[3] Baseball, American football, basketball and ice-hockey.

which historically was based almost exclusively on Melbourne, and the players' eligibility depended on which part of the city they had been born in[4]. The consequence of these geographical rules is that there is no market for players to move at all as they are ineligible to be employed by any other team. An international version of this is to restrict eligibility to play for a team on grounds of nationality. This can be achieved by rules prohibiting or restricting the number of overseas players that can be employed or used by any single team. This has been used extensively in many sports, for example in English cricket, where climate and history mean that it is the only place in the world where professional cricket is played for four months of the year. Thus in principle English teams could employ any of the world's best players[5]. In football as the 'three foreigners' rule it has been one of the two grounds of Bosman's case. These rules of national eligibility can be reinforced by the laws of a particular country which allow nationality to be easily claimed so that sportspeople can effectively play under a 'flag of convenience'.[6] Furthermore, laws relating to work permits can make it difficult for sports clubs to employ foreign workers in preference to domestic labour.[7]

Finally, there are some restraints that have been used by sports governing bodies that try to maintain nominal freedom of movement for players but also try to equalise sporting chances in competition. One intriguing example is the device known as a 'salary cap'. Under this system teams are allowed a maximum figure that may be spent each season on players' salaries. This figure may be different for different teams so that weaker teams can be permitted to spend more. But within the 'cap' clubs can allocate their money as they think fit, perhaps gambling on one or two highly paid stars. Such a system was tried in Australian rugby league, where, however, the courts have declared it to be illegal.

All these devices so far described aim to limit the concentration of wealth and talent, in part by trying to redistribute resources. Other ways of achieving the same objectives centre on limiting players' freedom to move. One blunt instrument for stopping players moving to whatever club they

---

[4] The system is described in the case of *Hall v. Victorian Football League* [1982] V.R. 64 where it was challenged as a restraint of trade.

[5] This market and the fear that rich clubs would exploit it was part of the background to the case of *Greig v. Insole* [1978] 3 All E.R. 449.

[6] See Fiona Miller, Profession: UK Footballer, Nationality: Unclear, Sport and the Law Journal (1994) vol. 2, p.10.

[7] English practice, as interpreted by the Department of Education and Employment, requires non-European Union players to be established internationals. See James McKinnell, Work Permits: The Professional Footballer, Sport and the Law Journal (1994) vol. 2, p.11.

wish is to prevent them moving even at the end of their contracts, by legal devices that give the club first option to renew the contract. Such is baseball's reserve clause, described thus by the leading work: 'It is an ingenious device which gives the club a continuing option on the services of the player and protects its property rights in him. When a player signs his first contract in Organized Baseball, he is in reality signing for the duration of his career, because he not only agrees to perform for the period specified (usually one season), but allows the club to "reserve" him for the subsequent season. Since each succeeding contract which he signs contains the same provision, he cannot escape.[8]' Another is the retaining rule used against Bosman which in essence allowed the old club to retain the player's registration, effectively his licence to play the game in that league, until they wished to release it.[9] However the transfer system itself, where players move whilst still under contract and their old club receive a transfer fee is often defended on the grounds that it is a crude but effective device for redistributing wealth within a sport. This has been the claim of the English football governing bodies. It protected them in 1964 when the High Court on flimsy evidence, accepted it as a major element in the successful argument that the transfer system was legal.[10] There is still little systematic evidence. Less remarked upon is that the transfer system can allow an unsuccessful team to buy rapid advancement if they can find disproportionate sources of outside funding not available to other clubs, as the recent success of clubs such as Blackburn Rovers has shown.

One reason why these apparently indefensible restrictions have survived is that the international governing bodies of sport have regulations that allow them to suspend clubs and national federations from competitions if they challenge these restraints in the courts. The legality of these rules is in itself dubious, but there are jurisdictional difficulties as to who can challenge the rules.

Consequences of Bosman

The consequences of a successful result for Bosman are difficult to judge, both for the future of European football specifically and professional sport generally. Let me begin an assessment by concentrating in the effects on

---

[8] H. Seymour, Baseball: the Early Years Oxford University Press, New York, [1989] p.107.

[9] It was this 'retain' element of the then existing transfer system in English football that was declared void as a restraint of trade in the landmark case of *Eastham v. Newcastle United F.C.* [1964] Ch. 461.

[10] See Eastham's case, supra.

football. The initial reaction in the British media was pessimistic[11] but this may have been an over reaction for three main reasons. Much of the initial reaction assumed that the current transfer system in English football was threatened and would need revising.   But Bosman only applies to restrictions placed on players after their contracts have ended. The Belgian system that Bosman was challenging was at the extreme end of the range of possible restrictions.   The current system within British football is that players are registered with a club. If they wish to move clubs during their contracts, they need their club's permission. The two clubs will agree a fee; supposedly for the technical transfer of the player's registration. But at the end of his contract a player is free to move. If his old club offers a new contract as good as the previous one, then a player who moves nevertheless will incur a liability for his new club to pay a fee. If the two clubs cannot agree a fee, then the case must be taken to an independent tribunal that fixes a fee. If his old club offers worse terms or none whatsoever, the player is entirely free to move without his old club being able to claim any compensation at all.[12] Thus the only restrictions on free movement that this system has for the player out of contract is that the tribunal fee may be a disincentive. If a prospective club still has to pay a fee to another club to employ a player no longer under contract this could limit the number of prospective clubs that could 'buy' him. Just why a new employer should pay any compensation to a worker's previous employer when their contractual relationship has finished is hard to justify.

A second reason for being cautious about the implication of Bosman is that it appears only to apply to cross-border transfers, and so its implications for domestic transfers within national leagues could be limited. This is apparently because part of the opinion rests on Article 85 rather than Article 48 and this Article only applies in so far as inter-state trade is involved. A third reason for caution is that the Advocate-General's opinion is not decisive. Although such advice is normally followed, to assume that it will be automatically in this case may underestimate the political lobbying power of UEFA, the governing body of football in Europe. UEFA has a long history of negotiation and compromise with the Commission that has allowed them to keep these restrictions that have always clearly breached the treaty, especially Article 48.   Since at least 1978,' the Commission has had numerous contacts with the national associations and

---

[11] Not untypical newspaper articles were John Williams, A kick up the 90's, Guardian 21/9/95, p. 17: Jimmy Hill, Recipe for Disaster, Observer sport, 24/9/95, p. 10: Paul Wilson, Whole new ball games, Observer sport, 24/9/95, p. 5: Peter Berlin, They think it's all over, Financial Times Weekend, 30/9/95, p.7.

[12] Older players, over 32, must be allowed a free transfer in all circumstances.

UEFA in order to obtain commitments from the national federations with a view to eliminating discrimination'.[13] It was an agreement between the Commission and UEFA in 1991 that introduced the compromise under which the national associations of UEFA must have rules that state three non-nationals as a maximum in the teams in the top division of the national championship.[14]

Although it this very agreement that in part has been advised to be illegal in the Bosman case, the previous long-lived success of UEFA in getting football treated as a special case should not be forgotten.

But given these reservations, what might be the likely consequences? The easier of the two elements in the Bosman case is the 'foreigners' rule. There is little obvious case for this especially as it is a direct discrimination that makes no attempt to distinguish between citizens of European Union countries and those outside, so it is likely that the rule will go. Players from other E.U. countries will move freely, attracted by the best available terms and conditions as governed by the logic of the internal market. English clubs will no longer find that Scottish, Irish or Welsh players count as foreigners. It may be however that the increased freedom of movement within the Union provokes a backlash that increases the restrictions on players from outside the Union so that players from the ex-Soviet bloc or Africa find it more difficult to join clubs.

As the richest football leagues in the world are within the European Union, it is likely that the world's best players will be attracted both financially and competitively to these leagues. So the development of a global labour market in footballers will continue. In this global market, some countries will act as developers of talent and exporters of players; the core metropolitan counties will be net importers. As national, never mind local links disappear, the top European teams will become truly international and football will be de-nationalised so that inter-national games will suffer. The World Cup may become less important and undermined by these developments.

Other consequences for English football will depend on exactly what alterations to the transfer system, if any, are made or forced upon the football authorities. It may be that no changes are deemed legally necessary so that the present tribunal fixing mechanism stays. At the other extreme,

---

[13] O.J. (92/C 102/92). Written answer No.2346/91.

[14] The agreement was to apply to all professional leagues by the end of the 1996-7 season. It also allowed two extra 'assimilated' players: O.J. (92/C 102/106) Written answer No.2692/91. See also previously O.J. 90/C 233/67 and the Janseen van Raay report, and generally Fiona Miller, Free Market Football, Sport and the Law Journal (1993) vol. 1, p. 13.

the transfer system could disappear completely and total free agency emerge as in any normal labour market. Or most likely, a midway house might emerge that removes any compensation at the end of a contract but allows clubs to agree a fee when a player under contract moves. The principal difficulty with this midway house is that it assumes consensus among the three parties or an effective internal regulatory system by the governing bodies. If a player under contract really wants to move, English law does not allow his employer to insist on specific performance; although there is authority[15] that an injunction can be granted to prevent him playing for a rival club.

Assuming for the sake of illustration, no transfer fees whatsoever, what can be said of the likely outcomes? Most commentators assume that this will result in fewer clubs in the long term. At present, there are 92 full-time professional football clubs in England organised over four divisions. This is more than any major rival league in Europe. Free movement of players without compensation will, it is argued, lead to fewer clubs, the remaining clubs getting richer i.e. a centralisation of the industry, and players becoming richer as the money now passed on to other clubs in transfer fees will be used to attract the best players via higher salaries and signing-on fees.

The financially weaker clubs could try to protect themselves by putting players, particularly those likely to be poached by richer clubs, on longer contracts, so that some compensation could be claimed if the player moves as damages for the breach of contract by the player or for the inducement by the other club. But would players sign such contracts? Rationally, no player with ambitions beyond his present club would sign a long contract thereby limiting his own freedom of movement and also increasing his price in the labour market by attaching a buy-out tag around his neck. However, football is a short career; injury or loss of form can ruin a player's chances of moving and some players may prefer the security of a long contract to guard against such contingencies. But for young star-struck players this is not a rational economic market. Young players will sign on unfavourable terms on long and even oppressive contracts when attracted by the glamour of the club or the chance of the 'big time'. In a sport where the top salaries are already over £1,000,000 per annum, getting a foot on the ladder is not likely to be spurned by potential entrants over issues such as the length of the contract.[16]

---

[15] *Warner Brothers v. Nelson* [1937] 1 K.B. 209.

[16] cf. the contracts in *Watson v. Prager* [1991] 3 All E.R. 487 and in *Panayiotou v. Sony Music Entertainment (UK) Ltd* [1994] Ch. 142.

Generally, clubs may become divided into those who eschew long contracts for players because they fear that they could be lumbered with a huge wage bill and fewer financial resources to meet that bill if they are unsuccessful and relegated, and those clubs whose financial or playing success makes them immune to such considerations.

Clubs who want to attract the best players will be able to do so not by buying expensively in the transfer market and thereby benefiting their rivals but by offering the best personal terms to players. The top players at least will bargain individually rather than accept the club's collective terms. Clubs may consequently find it more difficult to have fair and equitable wage structures. The use of agents by players to negotiate the best possible terms is likely to increase and this will intensify the demands for agents to be registered and their activities to be regulated by the governing bodies of football. Overall, the economic effect is likely to benefit players at the expense of the smaller clubs.

There are comparative lessons that can be deduced from the experience of other countries. In the USA professional sport has been forced towards free agency by the courts applying the anti-trust laws. One major result is that teams have found it harder to maintain consistency or to develop teams and squads. With a greater flux and movement of players, there has been less loyalty from players and from fans. Whether the greater mobility has allowed more rotation of honours and winning teams is an open question. Initial indications in American football, where the process is most advanced, suggest no great levelling of results.

One of the strongest arguments in favour of retaining transfer fees has always been that is allows a 'trickle-down' effect whereby smaller clubs can develop and train young players who are then sold on to the top clubs. The fees received for these players are claimed to be a vital element in the finances of smaller clubs that saves them from bankruptcy. Without this incentive to recoup their developments costs or to receive a windfall from a transfer, the smaller clubs will no longer invest any time or money in finding new talent. This argument was strong enough for the Advocate-General to address it in his opinion. There have been several mechanisms suggested to allow the real training costs to be compensated. One would be to allow a player to be transferred once so that his first club could be properly compensated for the development costs but subsequent employers do not receive unwarranted windfalls. This argument assumes that players develop only at the start of their career and top clubs are incapable of improving a player. Another would be to allow the original club a 'tracer' fee or royalty on each move by the player as a percentage of his salary. Similar clauses are commonly inserted in transfer deals at present so that a club receives part of the 'profit' when a player is resold or receives bonus payments dependent on the player's performance.[17]

An alternative to this emphasis on the development of new young talent by smaller clubs is that the richer clubs would develop their own players via full-time coaching and scouting networks. By attempting to buy up lots of promising young players, the richer clubs could corner the market. This may lead to the development of 'nursery' or 'farm' teams, as has happened in American baseball or Spanish football. The elite clubs buy another club or pay the club to allow themselves to be used as breeding grounds for young players. The players are still employed by the elite club and then loaned out to the 'farm' team. Such arrangements are not allowed in most professional sports, including English football, because of rules prohibiting multiple ownership. The attraction for the smaller host team is financial security; the parent club needs continuity in this process. The major disadvantage is that the 'farm' team cannot compete against the 'parent' team, thus placing a limit on their progress and ambition. 'Farm' teams cannot be promoted to a higher division if their parent team is already there; indeed if the parent team is relegated, then automatic relegation follows for the 'farm' team. It tends to increase the centralisation of elite clubs as smaller teams cannot break through either because they are forced into such an arrangement or because they find themselves in sporting competition with better 'farm' teams filled with the players of an elite parent club.

II CONCLUSION

Bosman's case is likely to hasten the process of change within the European football industry. The rules of national federations will need to be changed so that players out of contract can move freely. UEFA will need to reconsider their 'foreigners' rule to ensure non-discrimination against players from the European Union. English football may be less effected than initial reaction suggests, but whether the system that requires some fee for an out of contract player is legal is now questionable. But overall Bosman may mark the point at which the regulation of football within Europe was no longer able to argue that the sporting needs of equal competition were paramount over the basic human rights of free movement and equal treatment for workers. The positive side of the decision could be that it integrates 'Europe' as an idea in popular culture in a way that

---

[17] Such as goals scored, games played, international honours gained.

institutional and legal harmonisation could never do. When football fans accept Dutch players in an English team as 'one of us' or cheer on the European golf team, the day when 'we are all Europeans now' comes closer.

6. Do We Need a European Competition Agency?

Professor Meinrad Dreher – University of Mainz[1]

I INTRODUCTION

For a couple of years, there has been a discussion about the desirability of a European Competition Agency, independent of the Commission. The background to this discussion is above all the fact that European competition law is becoming more and more significant and, furthermore, the consideration that the application of EU competition law should be independent of changing political influences.[2] The reason for this latter consideration is the common opinion that the commissioners are often attached to the industrial-political ideas of the Member States from which they are sent.[3] Furthermore a variety of duties has been conferred on the European Commission by the Maastricht treaty recently – duties which are not always compatible with European competition law. There are many incompatibilities which lead to purely political decisions. The establishment of an independent European Competition Agency would hopefully diminish this de lege lata strong influence of the politics on the implementation of the competition law of the EU Treaty.

Furthermore, the establishment of a European Competition Agency would bring more transparency to the decision-making process. As far as decisions are politically influenced, those motives and procedures within the Commission are hardly transparent to the persons concerned. For example, there is the serious question whether 'comfort letters' do have disadvantages in spite of their efficiency and informal character. That is so because the Commission has the possibility not to make formal decisions,

---

1 I would like to thank Frank Wamser for valuable research assistance.

2 Groger, Janicki, Weiterentwicklung des Europäischen Wettbewerbsrechts (Further Development of the European Competition Law), WuW 1992, 991, 998.

3 See Schwenn, Zwischen Markt und Politik – Wettbewerbsbehörden (Between Market and Policy – Competition Agencies), FAZ Nr. 52 of March 2, 1995, p. 15.

by simply using 'comfort letters'. This slight transparency may result in the circumstance that, consciously or unconsciously, political considerations become part of the final decisions. A European Competition Agency might lead to a much greater transparency in the competition procedures. Above all it could fulfill the urgent desire of the business community to be able to act according to formal and foreseeable criteria. It is the companies, which are often global players, which need efficacious and supranational criteria, which are foreseeable for them, so that they can take them into account. As nowadays political considerations are, for institutional reasons, necessarily taken into account by the Commission when it decides anti-trust cases, not only is the acceptance of the decisions of the Commission significantly diminished, but it becomes harder and harder for the European enterprises, which face an increased competition from businesses from the NAFTA-States from South-East Asia and from Japan, to plan their future intentions according to the European competition law as applied by the Commission.

An alternative which might come easily to the mind, might consist of having European competition law applied more and more by the national competition agencies of the Member States. Yet such a reform would have disadvantages. Above all, the uniformity of the interpretation and application of European cartel law would be in danger, in spite of the existence of the European Court. This diversity of interpretation and implementation of competition law would lead to a diminution in justice.

The different treatment of corporations – according to the Member States which have to apply the law – would be unbearable and contradictory to a EU-wide acceptance of official acts from single Member States. Finally, this would be an open invititation for forum shopping.

Although there are, as shown, significant arguments for an independent European Competition Agency, the Commission and probably most of the Member States are sceptical about this idea or reject it.[4] Up to now, it has apparently been only the government of Germany which is interested in the creation of such a European cartel agency.[5] Not before the government conference 1996 the European Union will discuss the idea of a European Competition Agency again. Nevertheless there are more and more

---

[4] See Commissioner van Miert, Wirtschaftswoche Nr. 44, October 27, 1994, p. 23.

[5] For example Federal Government of Germany, Statement on the report of the Bundeskartellamt (Federal Cartel Office), 1991/92, official document of the Bundestag 12/5200, p. I and IV; Federal Government of Germany, Annual economic report 1995, official document of the Bundestag 13/370, p. 25.

competition experts and officials who demand a European Competition Agency[6] or who would welcome it in the long run.[7]

II THE NEED FOR A EUROPEAN COMPETITION AGENCY

1. Structural Disadvantages of the Powers of the Commission

In order to discuss the desirability of a European Competition Agency in a way which is as matter-of-fact as possible, it must be stressed at this point, that the desirability of a European Competition Agency does not result from a dissatisfaction in the practices of the Commission. There is no reproach on the Commission, against the individual commissioners or the DG IV. There is only the conviction that the Commission has to labour under some institutional or structural disadvantages, which may make an appropriate application and implementation of European competition law in some cases doubtful.

This begins with the fact that the Commission is committed not only to competition but also to a broad variety of goals which are in part contradictory to the goal 'competition'. For example there is the reproach made against the Commission that it has the inclination to assume the existence of supranational markets even where there are only national markets, just in order to realize the single market.[8] Also, it is still open, how the goal of environmental protection which has to be considered while implementing other policies of the EU (Article 130 r EU Treaty) can be made compatible with the goal of competition. Furthermore, it is sometimes argued, that the catalogue of the duties of the Commission shows that the Commission is competent only for the central questions of the Union.[9] However, out of the hundreds of cases, which are annually

---

[6] For example, the Director General of the UK Office of Fair Trading, Gordon Borrie, Time for a Euro-MMC, Financial Times, November 11, 1994, p. 16: 'Perhaps now is the time to reconsider whether a 'European Competition Agency' would be better able than the Commission itself to apply competition principles to mergers.'

[7] See for example, Director-General Ehlermann, who was responsible for competition within the European Union until spring 1995: Zur Wettbewerbspolitik und zum Wettbewerbsrecht der Europäischen Union (Some remarks on the competition policy and the competition law of the European Union), 1994, p. 43.

[8] See the former President of the German Federal Cartel Office, Wolfgang Kartte, Zur institutionellen Absicherung der EG-Fusionskontrolle (The institutional framework of EC merger control), ORDO 43 (1992), 405, 409.

[9] Kartte, op. cit., n. 8, p. 410.

considered by the Commission, only a few really concern central questions of the European Union.

Due to the heavy work load of the Commission, most decisions in competition matters rely on preparatory work of the DG IV. It prepares the actual competition cases in regard to both legal and factual points, so that the Commission has only to make the final decision, which often means simply to choose one of the suggestions. It is common knowledge that the merger task-force submits three alternatives to the Commission in all complex merger cases: allowing the project, prohibiting the merger or granting permission under certain conditions. Two things can be seen from the shift of the essential procedural steps from the Commission to the DG IV which becomes more and more self assured because of its powers. On the one hand, it must be a disadvantage in relation to the work load that there is not one single agency competent for the whole competition procedure, but that the final decision is with the Commission which has to consider the case with its legal and factual aspects within a very limited period of time. In contrast, a European Competition Agency would be obliged to apply the law and only the law, unlike the Commission also takes into account political considerations.

From this it follows also that the final decisions in anti-trust cases are often not in the hands of competition lawyers or economists, as with the DG IV, but in the hands of the Commissioners, who are neither by their other duties nor by their professional education prepared to fulfill this task. Hence there is the danger that decisions in anti-trust cases are made on the basis of non-legal considerations which means a loss of legal security and the ignoring of the very ideas of competition law. The president of the German Federal Cartel Office, Dieter Wolf, is for example, as regards the decisions of the Commission in anti-trust matters, of the opinion: 'There are 17 Commissioners who talk about it. Whatever reasons had been decisive, in the end they are unknown to anybody in Brussels once the decision has been made.[10]' The decisions of the Commission, he argues, are like a collection of motivations and considerations, which have in fact nothing to do with competition, but are nevertheless put into competition terms in the end.[11] Even if one does not feel inclined to agree with this sarcastic evaluation by Mr. Wolf, it is clear that a European Competition Agency with the right to make final decisions would result in an enforcement of the competitive elements, in the decision-making process.

---

[10] Wolf, Deshalb muß ein Europäisches Kartellamt her (That is why we need a European Cartel Office), FAZ Nr. 234 of October 8, 1992, p. 17.

[11] Wolf, Eine europäische Behörde für den Wettbewerb (A European Agency for Competition), FAZ Nr. 258 of November 5, 1994, p. 15.

At the same time, the decisions of the European Competition Agency would be more transparent. It is just this aspect of legal security which is of vital importance to enterprises. That is so because the planning of joint ventures needs a huge amount of manpower and other business resources which would be better placed if the project is – unexpectedly – forbidden by European competition law. Above all, and what is more important, an increase in the professionality of the decisions in European competition cases would result in an increased quality of the decisions. It goes without saying that especially in the field of the competition law, wrong decisions are of grave consequence.

In contrast to the civil servants of a European Competition Agency, who would be strictly limited to the application of the competition law of the EU Treaty, the commissioners are exposed to a variety of political influences. Firstly, the attachments must be taken into account, which the commissioners bring with them, consciously or unconsciously, from their own Member States. An increasingly significant disadvantage, for example, is the inclination of perhaps British and French competition law to take into account industrial-political goals. This results in the effect that in competition cases it is not anymore the competition which is the final goal of competition procedures, but the public interest or the bilan économique. It is argued that these two economic powers increasingly decide on the basis of single cases, how much competition there may be.[12] But also Germany must face some critical remarks because of its still existing exemption areas in the federal competition law. Add to this that the Federal Cartel Office has, in some cases, shown the inclination to be open to political considerations when deciding whether to examine a case or not. It is obvious therefore, that commissioners who are more ready to further competition according to industrial-political or other non-competitive criteria bring with them these ideological prejudices into the decision-making practice of the Commission, as long as the Commission allows political considerations being taken into account in competition cases.[13] Even if the competition law of the European Union cannot be examined in detail in this essay, the note is made that industrial-political considerations, which are based on the competition which comes from the United States or NAFTA, South-East Asia or Japan, is not well-founded in the long run. A

[12] That is the opinion of the president of the German Federal Cartel Office Dieter Wolf, *Eine europäische Behörde für den Wettbewerb* (A European Authority for Competition), FAZ Nr. 258 of November 5, 1994, p. 15.

[13] The German Monopoly Commission, in its main report 1992/93, annotation 619, states that in single cases of merger decisions the Commission has shown to be open to political considerations.

competition order like that of the European Union is based on the assumption that workable competition is the best guarantee for the competitiveness of enterprises. A Competition Agency which is free of industrial-political considerations would at first glance be better for the business world than a Commission making politically motivated decisions. Even if the Commission sometimes is rather generous when treating uncompetitive acts, it will fail to protect the European business world from the international competition in the long run, if the undertakings are not strong enough to survive in a competitive atmosphere.

The introduction of a European Competition Agency independent of the Commission would finally lead to an acceleration of the decision-making process. That is so because a Competition Agency, which would be able to concentrate solely on the implementation of competition law and which would be prepared to do so, could make much quicker decisions than an agency which is, like the Commission, loaded with many other duties.

2. Further Advantages of an Independent European Competition Agency

It has become clear when discussing the disadvantages of implementation of competition law by the Commission, that the creation of an independent European Competition Agency would diminish the risk that non-competitive interests could influence the application of competition law. Above all, a Competition Agency which would be led by European civil servants, would be less open to the influences of policy, be it actual or industrial-political.[14] As already shown, because of this there would develop a greater transparency in the decision-making process.

Such a transparency of the decision-making process would not only be helpful for companies who could plan their projects better in accordance with expected decisions in the field of competition law, but would also be of significance, because there is no uniform public opinion in Europe. Such a uniform European public opinion, which would be an advocate for competition, would strongly demand a greater transparency in the decision-making process in the field of competition law. Since this public opinion will come into being only slowly, the transparency must be made by legal means. It is exactly the existence of a controlling instance which results as a consequence, that the steps made in a decision-making process in competition cases are clear. The persons concerned are able to see whether their rights or whether procedural rights have been breached and

---

[14] This is also the opinion of the Monopoly Commission, op. cit., n. 12, p. 620.

furthermore, the slowly developing European public opinion can formulate its critic more clearly. The result will be that the idea of competition will not only be known to the Commissioner in charge for competition and some European civil servants, but to the whole European public.

In addition it would be within the framework of the institutional guarantee of correct competition decisions, if there were a clear separation of legislative and administrative duties, if an independent European Competition Agency is established in future.[15] In this way, the right to suggest European secondary law and also the group exemptions would stay with the Commission. This separation of powers, with its checks and balances, would guarantee appropriate decisions. By establishing a European Competition Agency with the right to make final decisions in individual cases, the problem of the work load of the Commission would also be partly solved – otherwise there is the danger that the Commission will be too generous in anti-trust cases because of the many cases it has to decide each year.

Last but not least, the increasing convergence of the competition laws of the Member States as regards European competition law is also leading to the establishment of the European Competition Agency.[16] There are more and more Member States which are about to establish their own independent competition agencies.[17] That is why the idea of a European Competition Agency is a necessary part of a uniform competition order in the Single European Market.[18] On the other hand a European Competition Agency would do away with the existing institutional deficits of the European competition order. It would be a model for those Member States who have not yet a real competition agency and would thereby enhance the creation of a structurally uniform competition order in Europe.

---

[15] Groger, Janicki, op. cit., n.1, p. 998; Official Document of the Bundestag 12/5589 of August 27, 1993, p. 27.

[16] A detailed discussion of this point can be found in Dreher, Kartellrechtsvielfalt oder Kartellrechtseinheit in Europa? – Harmonisierungsbedarf und Harmonisierungsgrenzen für nationale Kartellrechte (Variety or Uniformity of European Cartel Laws? – The Need and the Limits to Harmonize the National Cartel Laws), AG 1993, 437 et seq.

[17] See Article 20 Spanish Cartel Law, Art. 10 II Italian Cartel Law, Art. 2 et seq. French Cartel Law as well as the rules of the Belgian Cartel Law as regards the Competition Council.

[18] See also Dreher, Gemeinsamer Europäischer Markt – Einheitliche Wettbewerbsordnung? (Single European Market - Single Competition Order?), in: FIW (Edit.), Umbruch der Wettbewerbsordnung in Europa (Changes in European Competition Policy), 1995, pp. 1, 12 et seq.

III THE NECESSITY OF A TWO-STEP PROCEDURE

The German Federal Government demands the creation of a European Cartel Office, against whose decisions there would be an appeal to the Commission which could formally review the decision. The argument for this one-stage procedure is the fear that a full second decision by the Commission would be open to non-competitive influences. Nevertheless there is much in favour of a two-step procedure. But this does not mean a new decision of the Commission in all the legal and factual aspects of the case. In the first stage the European Competition Agency would apply the competition rules of the EU treaty and make a final decision. The second stage would involve the competence of the Commission to set aside these decisions because of serious non-competitive reasons.

Only by means of such a two-step procedure would it be guaranteed that the aim to make non-competitive influences transparent and thereby to reduce them would be reached. The one-step proposal of the Federal Government goes further insofar as it intends to eliminate any political influence on the decision. However, this is a goal which cannot be reached, because the formal exclusion of all such influences does not take into account that these influences exist and that they will try to be taken to court – as can be seen in many of the famous European competition cases. Our proposal intends to make these influences transparent and to give them a legal framework. This proposal will eliminate the danger that such influences will find their way into the formal review-procedure in a covert way; thereby there will be a clear and secure competitive decision in the first step and the Commission would be only rarely inclined to set aside this decision because of general public interest.

The fear that the possibility of the Commission regarding the general public interest to be more important than competition and as such will make the public interest more important in the future, can be easily allayed. First of all such a decision would require a well reasoned justification because it cannot hide itself behind alleged competitive considerations. It is this obligation clearly to state that secondary interests were decisive, which will in many cases make such a decision less likely. Another reason for the reluctance of the Commission to set aside decisions of the European Competition Agency would be the surveillance of the Commission by the European Parliament and other institutions, as well as European public opinion which would begin to develop. Furthermore one must take into account with our proposal that the Commission would be obliged to ask the European Competition Commission for its opinion before setting aside a decision of the European Competition Agency.[19] Finally the competence to set aside the decisions of the first instance could be further limited by stating that these reversals would be only made on grounds concerning public interest which are in the EU Treaty, for example Article 85 III and Article 130 r II 3 EU Treaty.

IV THE STRUCTURE OF THE EUROPEAN COMPETITION AGENCY

1. The Staff

On its decision level the European Competition Agency should be staffed by lawyers and economists; on the investigation level further professional groups should be employed who would be specially trained in co-operation with the national investigation authorities.

Decisive for the appointment of a civil servant in the European Competition Agency must be nothing else than the professional qualification of the applicant. The applicant should dispose of legal or economic knowledge because only then is it guaranteed that competition cases will be decided according to abstract general rules and in accordance with common legal principles.

There should be a further guarantee that the applicant will not get be appointed because of his or her being part of a certain group in society, an advocate of certain interests or because he or she is nominated by a Member State. That is so because the Agency should decide its cases solely on the legal and factual issues of the case. Furthermore it seems to be not very helpful to have laymen or laywomen, for example managers or trade union secretaries, in these decision bodies. There would be the danger that these laymen and laywomen would not only bring with them their professional knowledge to the decision of a case – which would be quite desirable –, but that they would also turn out to become the advocates of the specific interests of their group, which is exactly what we want to eliminate in the handling of competition cases. There is a guarantee that our interests, above all those of the consumers and the employees, will be taken into account because the Competition Agency will be supervised by the European Parliament, the Economic and Social Committee and the European Competition Commission (which will be discussed below). Where the consideration of consumer interests, for example, was thought to

---

[19] As to the European Competition Commission see below at VI.3.

have been of importance, it was written down in the EU Treaty, see, for example, Article 85 III EU Treaty. Finally it is exactly our suggested two-step-procedure which will give the Commission in clear cases the possibility to consider contradictory, serious non-competitive interests.

The decision-makers in the European Competition Agency should be as independent as possible and be European civil servants. The decision makers should not be civil servants of the Member States who work only for a limited period of time in the European Competition Agency. That would mean that the decision-making process would be open to national influences, prejudices and ideologies. The national cartel offices should have the opportunity or obligation to cooperate in so far as this is already now the case (for example by means of committees) where it is necessary to investigate the facts of the case. Above all the European Competition Agency will need the help of national authorities to execute the decisions.

2. The Decision Bodies

The European Competition Agency should consist of decision-making bodies. Only then will it be guaranteed that the decision makers are sufficiently informed about all the details of the individual case, and above all the situation in the relevant market. Furthermore it has to be taken into account that, especially in the field of competition law, a close knowledge of the relevant market is necessary. Often quite difficult prognoses will have been to be made, which can only be made if the decision maker has known the market for many years. Therefore it would be sensible for the decision makers to specialize in some markets. This is even more important on the European level than on the national one – as for example in Germany where there are decision chambers in the Federal Cartel Office – because the European markets are bigger, less homogeneous and more difficult to understand than any national market. Yet, after a couple of years, the civil servants of the European Competition Agency should change their allotted market in order to avoid the effects of the well known "capture" theory. Since not each decision body can be comprised of persons from all Member States it will be necessary to accept that there will be bodies which are composed only of members of other Member States, which decide a case which concerns one Member State in particular. Such a development has already taken place within European institutions which are active in the field of intellectual property law in Europe and will continue to take place because of the fact that the European Union consists of more and more Member States and that those Member States have to cooperate. Furthermore it must not be forgotten that the EU competition rules will only be applied if trade between Member States is affected or large mergers are concerned so that normally at least two Member States are involved.

3. The European Competition Commission

Whereas in the Member States of the European Union there is a quite differentiated public opinion formed by the media, the newspapers and the academia, there is no such thing in the European Community up to now. While a national cartel authority can base its decision on the public – or at least published – opinion in its country in order to have its decisions accepted, there is no equivalent to that on the European level. In contrast to the situation in the Member States where there are national think tanks, conferences and seminars in which the national competition law is discussed, the European competition law is still a matter for experts only. In order to compensate for this lack of a European public opinion it seems it would be helpful to create a European Competition Commission. This would have to give its opinion on both general and concrete competition issues as well as on competition cases and make periodic reports on the development of competition law and competition policy in the European Union.

As regards the staff, it must be taken into account that this body has a serious responsibility because it shall serve as a not yet existing European public opinion. Therefore the body should be composed of persons from whom there can be expected well founded and unbiased statements in the complex field of competition law and policy. The members of the European Competition Commission should therefore have had a commercial, legal, technical or socio-political professional training. In the Commission there should be no advocates of group interests. The task of this Commission to observe and to advise the European Competition Agency and the European Commission in a neutral way would not be in harmony with the specific group interests of such advocates.

The Competition Commission should have no more than ten members because otherwise, it would not be able to work quickly and efficiently. That means that not each of the 15 Member States can have its own representative on the Commission. Yet, this is an advantage, because otherwise there will always be the danger that the members of the Commission will feel obliged to support the interests of their state of origin. In the long run, however, that would mean that, for example, by means of limiting the time in office to two periods, a certain rotation among the Member States would be possible, if not necessary. The members of the

Commission should be in office for at least five to seven years. With respect to the small circle of members and its important function the members should be nominated by the Council of Ministers. It is only the professional qualifications and the bona fides of the candidates which should be taken into account in the appointment. It is only thereby that the Competition Commission would be able to make substantial contributions to the competitive order of the European Union, and have its opinions accepted.

4. Regional Offices

A close knowledge of the relevant market is decisive in anti-trust law. Therefore it might seem helpful to have a couple of decision bodies of the European Competition Agency situated in the Member States – a model which is known in the United States where there are field offices of the US-Department of Justice. These regional offices should be an integral part of the European Competition Agency. The decisions of the field offices should be decisions in the name of the European Competition Agency. An independence of the regional offices which would be greater than those bodies which are in the European Competition Agency itself, would not be justified.

The European competition law will be applied, in principle, only if there are at least two Member States affected, but because of the broad interpretation of the so-called interstate trade clause, there are less important cases which could nevertheless be decided by the European Union. For example, a minor case which involves the misuse of market power and concerns only Finland and Sweden or Greece and Southern Italy needs not to be investigated in Brussels – in such cases the establishment of regional offices would be helpful. Through regional offices, investigative methods could be performed quicker and more easily; the need for translations would be diminished, which is desirable because translations always include the danger of a loss of meaning. The regional offices should have the competence not only to investigate but also to make decisions, because otherwise the motivation of their employees would not be great. The regional offices would be decision bodies of the European Competition Agency and the only difference would be that their offices were not in Brussels but somewhere else. The more that further states become members of the European Union, the greater will be the need for decentralization in European competition matters.

5. Amicus Curiae

In the procedural laws of the United States there exists the so-called amicus curiae. By becoming an amicus curiae the anti-trust division can make its point clear in private anti-trust cases and thereby help to interprete the US anti-trust law in a uniform way and develop it in a sense which the government thinks to be appropriate.[20] Such an amicus curiae participation is also possible in German competition cases (section 90 GWB) for the Federal Cartel Office although it seldom really participates in private cases, limiting itself to be informed about the cases by the courts.

Such an amicus curiae, who should be a civil servant of the European Competition Agency, should also have a right of audience before national courts in which European competition law is applied. Up to now there is no legal basis for the participation of such an amicus curiae in the national competition procedures. To avoid the complications of altering the EU treaty, a guideline should be made. For Germany that would mean that section 90 GWB would be extended as regards the European Competition Agency.

V LEGAL BASIS FOR A EUROPEAN COMPETITION AGENCY

In order to establish a European Competition Agency the EU treaty has to be altered according to Article N of the treaty of the European Union from February 7, 1992. That is so because such an independent agency would dispose of quite far reaching rights which might severely interfere with the rights and the economic freedom of commercial enterprises. Such far reaching powers can not be given by the Minister Council or the Commission out of their own competence, but must be made by the parties to the EU treaty. As early as 1958 the European Court noted that the transfer of discretionary powers to institutions other than those nominated in the specific section of the EU treaty would not be compatible with the EU treaty.[21] Such a major transfer of powers as would be the result of the creation of a European Competition Agency, is not covered by the general

---

[20] See Wamser, Enforcement of Anti-trust Law, A Comparison of the Legal and Factual Situation in Germany, the EEC, and the USA, Frankfurt 1994, 1, p. 30.

[21] EuGHE (European Court Reports) 1958, 9, 44.

authorization of Article 235 of the EU treaty - although there are different opinions here.[22]

VI THE POSSIBILITY OF IMPLEMENTATION

In the Member States of the European Union there is only little interest in the creation of a European Competition Agency at the moment. The only exeption so far is Germany. As long as some states remain attached to industrial-political ideas in their competition policy it is unlikely that those states will plead in favour of a European Competition Agency, because such an independent agency, which would be free from political influences, would be contradictory to the interests of those Member States. Much has to be done in order to convince those states of the importance of a competitive order which is independent of industrial-political considerations. As long as there is no consensus on this point – and at the moment there is no such consensus – it will be quite difficult to convince a majority of Member States to establish a European Competition Agency. But as soon as it has become general knowledge that a competitive order orientated solely by legal and economic criteria will serve the best interests of all the enterprises and nations concerned, the more the creation of an independent European Competition Agency will be welcomed by Member States. It is realistic then, that our proposals to organize the Competition Agency into decision making bodies will find its supporters. Out of the twelve Member States of the European Union in 1994 there are already such decision making bodies, or equivalents to them, in the competition related authorities in Germany, Belgium, France and Spain; and the Italian president of the anti-trust authority is very much in favour of establishing such decision making bodies, because for the heavy work load of his authority it is increasingly unable to decide all cases in open court. Therefore the government conference on Maastricht II in 1996 might give rise to new thinking on the need for a European Competition Agency.

---

[22] For a survey of the discussion see Merz, Bedarf die Errichtung eines Europäischen Kartellamtes der Änderung des EWG-Vertrages? (Does the establishment of a European Cartel Office require an amendment of the EEC Treaty?), EuZW 1990, 405, 406; and extensively Bartodziej, Reform der EG-Wettbewerbsaufsicht und Gemeinschaftsrecht (Reform of the European Control of Competition and Community Law) 1994, 1, pp. 242 et seq., 266 et seq.

7. A Traders' Charter?: Free Movement of Goods and the Sunday Dilemma

Imelda Maher* – University of London

I INTRODUCTION

The free movement of goods rules are viewed as uncertain.[1] Because the tensions within the Community as it progresses from an internal market to something closer to political union are reflected in Article 30, its interpretation is a fraught process. On the one hand, the European Court is keen to push forward the creation of an internal market and to prohibit barriers to trade. On the other hand, as the most conspicuous barriers to trade have disappeared, it has become more difficult to balance the needs of the internal market with the sovereignty of the Member States to set down standards either in areas outside the competence of the Community entirely or where harmonisation has not yet occurred.[2]

This balance reflects a broader issue throughout the Community which is the absence of any definitive demarcation of competence between the Community and the Member States, particularly where cultural and economic imperatives clash. This fluidity has made it easier for the Community to expand its competence over time.[3] However, with the

---

[1] See Chalmers, 'Repackaging the Internal Market – the ramifications of the *Keck* judgment', 19 EL Rev. (1994), 385; Gormley, 'Some Reflections on the Internal Market and Free Movement of Goods', LIEI (1989), 9-20; Mortelmans, 'Article 30 of the EEC treaty and legislation relating to market circumstances: time to consider a new definition?', 28 CML Rev. (1991), 115-136; Steiner, 'Drawing the line: uses and abuses of Article 30 EEC', 29 CML Rev. (1992), 749-774; White, 'In search of the limits to Article 30 of the EEC treaty', 26 CML Rev. (1989), 235-280.

[2] See Reich, 'The "November Revolution" of the European Court of Justice: Keck, Meng and Audi revisited', 31 CML Rev. (1994), 459 at 473.

[3] Barents, 'The Internal Market unlimited: some observations on the legal basis of Community legislation', 30 CML Rev. (1993) 85-109; Majone, 'Market integration and regulation: Europe after 1992', 43 Metroeconomica (1992), 131 at 138 and Tschofen, 'Article 235 of the Treaty establishing the European Economic Community: potential conflicts between the dynamics of lawmaking and the Community and

introduction of the principle of subsidiarity in Article 3b EC it is clear that there is some concern among Member States over the extension of Community competence.[4]   The Commission has called for a clear indication of where competence lies in the Community but none has been provided.[5] Until there is some attempt made to delineate competences, the European Court will continue to balance Member States and Community powers within the confines of the Treaties themselves, including disputes about the balance of power within Article 30.[6] The Court thus decides cases where the balance of power between Member States and the Community are in dispute in a political climate where there is much concern about the democratic deficit of the Community;[7] where there is a link between the decisions of the Court and the legislative competence of the Community;[8] and where the role of national courts as Community courts enforcing EC law is vital to the effectiveness of that law.[9]

Within this context, the Court has had to balance the needs of the internal market with the powers of the Member States to regulate their own domestic markets.   In early cases, it was possible to achieve a balance without great difficulty as the obstructive effect on integration outweighed the valued regulatory contribution of the measure in issue.[10] As the internal

---

national constitutional principles', 12 Michigan Journal of International Law (1990), 471-509.

[4] For differing analyses of the principle see Emiliou, 'Subsidiarity: an effective barrier against the "Enterprises of Ambition"?', 17 EL Rev. (1992), 383 at 392; Toth, 'The Principle of Subsidiarity in the Maastricht treaty', 29 CML Rev. (1992), 1079-1105.

[5] In its Communication on the Principle of Subsidiarity presented to the Council and Parliament Bull. EC 10/92 at 119 the Commission calls for a list of national powers so that the public perception of the Community as having no precise limits and being able to meddle almost at will would be countered. This would also meet some of the demands of the German Länder who are keen to see a clear delineation of powers at the different levels of the Community see Emiliou, fn. 4 at 388.

[6] See Weiler, 'Journey to an unknown destination: a retrospective and prospective of the European Court of Justice in the arena of political integration', 31 JCMS. (1993), 417, 435-436; 439.

[7] See Curtin, 'The constitutional structure of the Union: a Europe of bits and pieces', 30 CML Rev. (1993), 17, 34-44; Featherstone, 'Jean Monnet and the "democratic deficit" in the European Union', 32 JCMS (1994), 149-171; Neunreither, 'The democratic deficit of the European Union: towards closer cooperation between the European Parliament and the national parliaments', 29 Government and Opposition (1994), 299-314. For an alternative view of the democratic deficit see von Bogdandy, 'The contours of integrated Europe', Futures (1993), 22, 29-30.

[8] Reich, fn. 2 at 482-484.

[9] Maher, 'National courts as European Community courts', 14 Legal Studies (1994), 226-243; Weiler, fn. 6 421-424.

[10] Wils, 'The search for the rule in Article 30 EEC: much ado about nothing?', 18 EL Rev. (1993), 475 at 478.

market has developed, the sorts of cases arising before the Court have become more diverse and raised issues closer to the boundaries of Member States and Community competence than in the early years.[11] With increased integration, national measures are more restricted and hence have to be of substantial value to survive in an internal market. Thus the Court may be required to evaluate the regulatory effect of a national measure which is brought before it. However, it is questionable whether the Court is competent to evaluate the regulatory benefits of national measures, a limitation that was apparent in the Sunday trading cases.

The Court has been faced with litigation where the impact on inter-state trade seems marginal but is concerned to ensure that state regulations are not used to impede on the integration agenda. Thus the jurisprudence of the Court has become more strained as it seeks to make sense of Article 30 where the structural objective of the completion of the internal market has to be balanced with the power of the Member States to regulate their domestic markets. The concerted Sunday trading litigation eventually placed such a strain on the rule of law[12] and the operation of Article 30 that the Court ultimately changed its position reducing the scope of Community regulation of domestic marketing rules.

The aim of this paper is to examine recent developments in the free movement of goods in the light of national experience, in particular, the debacle of the Sunday trading litigation in England and Wales. It analyses the way Article 30 was invoked as a trader's charter guaranteeing unrestricted trade and how, as a result, EC law was used to undermine the rule of law and was itself undermined in the process. Having located recent developments in the jurisprudence on Article 30 in the light of this experience the paper concludes that despite criticisms that these developments fail to provide certainty and may reduce regulation of Member States measures controlling domestic markets, the changes can restore faith in the rule of EC law and the integration process at the national level. In other words, the integration process cannot simply be seen in terms of the completion of the internal market. Instead, regard must be had to how EC law is perceived at the national level and its effectiveness at that

---

[11] Ibid. at 485 et seg.

[12] For the purpose of this paper, I am adopting a formalist approach in relation to the rule of law i.e. that there be a lawful exercise of public authority which allows individuals to organise their behaviour because that authority provides clear, open and enforceable laws see e.g. Raz, 'The rule of law and its virtue', 93 LQR (1977), 195-211.

level.[13]   If EC law is not being effective at national level and in fact is undermining the operation of the rule of law, rolling back the scope of Community regulation where there is little impact on inter-state trade is a small price to pay for restoring public confidence in the Community and its laws.

II SUNDAY TRADING: A PECULIARLY ENGLISH DISPUTE?

The Sunday trading stage in the European Court was dominated by players from England and Wales with significant cases also emanating from Belgium, France and most recently, Italy. Why did this issue become such a live one in England and Wales[14] where Sunday does not hold any particular religious significance for the vast majority of the population?[15] A number of factors converged to create a climate allowing for a change in Sunday trading regulation in England and Wales. Since the original legislation had been passed consumption and shopping patterns had changed dramatically. The development of refrigeration, the growth in car use and a liberalisation of planning laws had all led to the growth of large self-service shopping stores situated outside town centres.[16]   Similar changes in consumption were to be found throughout the Community but other factors had a role to play in England.

Trade union membership in Britain had been falling through the eighties and with the collapse of the traditional manufacturing sectors unions were looking to the retail sector to maintain membership levels.[17] Unions would traditionally have opposed Sunday opening seeing it as a means of

---

[13] Snyder, 'The Effectiveness of European Community Law: Institutions, Processes, Tools and Techniques', 56 MLR (1993), 19-54; Rawlings, 'The Euro-law Game: Some Deductions from a Saga', 20 JLS (1993) 309 at 334.

[14] The law in Scotland is different and the relevant legislation only applied to England and Wales.

[15] Current adult active enroled membership of Trinitarian religions is 15% of people over 16 years see 24 Social Trends (1994), at 145.

[16] See generally *Reforming the Law on Sunday Trading: a Guide to the Options for Reform*, cm 2300 (1993); Marwick, *British Society Since 1945*, 2nd ed., (1990), ch 7. For changes in planning laws see Montgomery, 'Counter revolution: out-of-town shopping and the future of town centres', in Montgomery and Thornley, *Radical Planning Initiatives* (1990).

[17] See 24 Social Trends (1994), 147. For a case study on one of the most important British unions in the retail sector see Upchurch and Donnelly, 'Membership patterns in USDAW 1980-1990: survival as success?', 23 Industrial Relations J. (1992), 60-68.

employment protection but with the growth in part-time work and the number of people willing to work on Sundays, they changed their position and eventually supported Sunday trading.[18] The number of women in the work force was also a factor in promoting change.[19] In the Community of twelve, there were more British women in the work force than in any other Member State except Denmark.[20] Women are more likely to bear the burden of family shopping but because of their work could no longer shop at the usual opening times.[21] This can be compared with the experience of other Member States where union memberships remain high and there are not as many women in the work force.[22] Sunday trading is strictly controlled in Germany and a campaign for reform of the French rules has been led by a British company.[23] In both countries, fewer women are part of the labour market and unions are stronger than their British counterparts.[24]

The legislation that regulated Sunday trading, the Shops Act 1950, was a crude consolidation of earlier legislation and was not well drafted.[25] Riddled with anomalies, it did not prohibit Sunday trading completely, but

---

[18] See generally, Price and Yandle, 'Labour markets and Sunday closing laws', Journal of Labour Research (1987), 407-414. For a discussion of the approach of the unions to the English Sunday Trading Act 1994 see Maher, 'The new Sunday: reregulating Sunday trading', 58 MLR (1995), 72-87. Two surveys carried out showed that the majority of workers in multiples were women and many worked part-time. Over half were in favour of working on Sunday, the main reason being given was additional income. See generally Freathy & Sparks, *Sunday Working in the Retail Trade*, Institute for Retail Studies, University of Stirling and Deakin & Wilkinson, *Employment Protection and the Reform of Sunday Trading*, Small Business Research Centre, University of Cambridge.

[19] The importance of women entering the work force as a factor leading to reform in Sunday trading rules has been borne out by research in the US see Yandle and Price ibid.

[20] 24 (1994) Social Trends 58.

[21] See House of Commons Research Division *Sunday Trading Report* no. 281 (1992) at 15.

[22] For a survey of Sunday trading rules in all Member States see Askham, Burke and Ramsden, *EC Sunday Trading Rules* (1990). For a more recent discussion of the French and German positions see London Economics *The Economic Impact of Alternative Sunday Trading Regulations*, a report for the Home Office Research and Planning Unit (1993) at 44 and 46.

[23] Virgin opened its Paris store in defiance of the law see Dwyer, 'Shop till you drop hits Europe' International Business 29 November 1993 at 38.

[24] In Portugal there are liberal rules towards Sunday trading but there is a strong shop workers union and strict regulation of working time for workers see Askham, Burke and Ramsden, fn. 22 at 55.

[25] It was subject to many attempts at reform see Rawlings, fn. 13 at 311.

simply the sale of certain goods on Sundays.[26] Initially, retailers sought to exploit these anomalies and exceptions. For example the Act allowed Jews who conscientiously objected to opening on Saturday to open on Sundays instead.[27] Retailers started to appoint sleeping Jewish partners who would register as conscientious objectors so the shop could open on Sundays. This loophole was later blocked by statutory instrument.[28] One of the most ridiculous but temporarily successful contentions under the Act was that everything in a Do-It-Yourself store could be sold because it could be used in a caravan and therefore fell within the motor accessory exception.[29]

Finally, there was a well financed and sufficiently motivated group of large retail traders,[30] who sought to exploit the weaknesses in the Act to undermine its efficacy and ultimately to seek its removal from the statute book. The objective of deregulation spoke the language of the Thatcher government which introduced a Bill deregulating Sunday trading in 1986.[31] Those against deregulation, an unlikely but effective combination of religious and trade union interests, set about organising opposition to the Bill at grass roots level and a huge letter writing campaign was embarked upon. As a result, the Bill was far more controversial than the government had expected, especially as Parliament was faced with a stark choice of continuing the unsatisfactory 1950 Act or completely deregulating Sunday

---

[26] Section 47 of the Act prohibits shops from trading on Sunday, subject to the exceptions contained in the 5th Schedule to the Act. This is where the infamous anomalies were to be found. A shop could sell magazines on Sundays but not books: this allowed the purchase of Penthouse but not the Bible.

[27] Section 53. The exception remains in the Sunday Trading Act 1994 for those whose Sabbath falls on another day of the week see schedule 2 part II.

[28] See G. Alderman, Jews and Sunday trading: the Use and Abuse of Delegated Legislation (1982) Public Administration 99-104.

[29] *Hadley* v. *Texas Homecare* (1989) 152 JP 268 see Diamond, 'Sunday Service: Trading Restrictions' (1991) 135 SJ 564-565.

[30] The retailers sought deregulation through legislative reform but when that failed, they established the Shopping Hours Reform Council. Many large food and DIY stores were supporters of the Council e.g. B&Q, Tesco and Asda see Diamond, 'Dishonourable defences: the use of injunctions and the EEC Treaty – case study of the Shops Act 1950', 54 MLR (1991), 73 at 74.

[31] A committee had been appointed to review the 1950 Act in 1983 and it had recommended complete deregulation see Home Office, *Report of the Committee of Inquiry into Proposals to Amend the Shops Act* Cm 9376 (1984) (the Auld Committee). The Institute of Fiscal Studies was also asked to review the economic effects of changes to Sunday trading rules see House of Commons Library research Division, *Sunday Trading* Background Paper 281 (1992) at 15.

trading. The Bill was defeated: the only Parliamentary defeat of the Thatcher government and the country was left with an anachronistic law.[32]

III LITIGATION

1. An Unenforceable Law

With the avenue of legislative reform closed off, those large retail stores in favour of deregulation chose to return to the previous forum of attack: the courts. They had the resources to acquire expert legal advice and to maintain a sustained attack on the Act. Because local authorities, who were responsible for enforcement, could injunct those who persistently breached the Act, they could enforce the law effectively. However, if doubt could be cast on the validity of the Act then local authorities would be deterred from bringing enforcement actions because of the potential legal costs involved.[33] If the Act were not enforced for a period of time, then shops could open with impunity and once the public became accustomed to Sunday shopping, there would be the necessary change in social climate to allow for legislative reform.[34] Hence the litigation strategy was two-fold: to challenge the validity of the Act in light of EC law and to challenge enforcement of the Act until any uncertainty about the relationship between EC law and the Shops Act was resolved.

Trading on Sundays in goods not listed in the schedule of the Act was a criminal offence for which the fine was £1000 and later raised to £2500.[35] The issue was tried at the lowest level of the criminal courts, the Magistrates courts. These courts are staffed mainly by part-time non-lawyer magistrates, assisted by law clerks. Legal costs were small but local authorities with limited resources tended to fine only larger shops.[36] For some large retailers the amount of turnover that could be generated on a Sunday was considerable and the Sunday trading fine simply became a small business cost. When it had become clear that the fine was no longer a deterrent, some local authorities had sought to impose an injunction to

---

[32] For an illuminating account of the life of the 1986 Bill see P. Regan, 'The 1986 Shops Bill', 41 Parliamentary Affairs (1988), 218-235.

[33] Rawlings fn. 13 at 311; Diamond fn. 30 at 82.

[34] See Rawlings (1993) fn. 13 at 332.

[35] In the Criminal Justice Act 1991.

[36] Blomley, 'The Shops Act 1950: the politics and the policing', 17 Area (1985), 25 at 31. Local authorities are still responsible for the enforcement of the Sunday Trading Act 1994 see schedule 2 part I.

ensure shops traded within the law.[37] This approach was confirmed by the House of Lords in *Stoke-on-Trent* v. *B&Q*[38] where an injunction was awarded against B&Q which had repeatedly opened on Sundays and refused to give an undertaking that it would not do so.[39]

If there had been no EC law angle to the case law, the question of whether or not the Act was enforceable would have ended here, before the 1986 Bill was defeated. Instead, the retailers against whom interlocutory injunctions were sought claimed cross-undertakings in damages from local authorities on the basis that the Shops Act was being challenged under EC law and could be held invalid. If it were invalid then the retailer could have lawfully traded while the injunction was in place and would want compensation for lost trade. Those retailers being injuncted and seeking such undertakings were those who raised substantial revenues on Sundays. Most local authorities could not afford the risk of having to pay such compensation and stopped seeking injunctions until the question of cross-undertakings in damages was resolved in the courts.

The cases where the issue of cross-undertakings in damages was discussed centred around one key issue: what was the effect of EC law on the enforcement of the Shops Act? Or, from another perspective, did Article 30 confer rights on traders which the courts had to protect? Those cases where Article 30 was seen as conferring rights on traders led to a refusal to award an injunction without a cross-undertaking in damages. Thus in *Rochdale* v. *Anders* Caulfield J. viewed favourably the likelihood of a successful challenge to the Act on the basis of Article 30 and refused to award an injunction without a cross-undertaking in damages.[40] The Court

---

[37] See Blomley, ibid., Diamond fn. 30 at 83 et seg. and Rawlings note 13 at 323 et seg. In *Stafford BC* v. *Elkenford Ltd*. (1977) 1 WLR 324 (CA) it was held that local authorities could apply for injunctions even though they had not exhausted other remedies. An injunction would only be granted if the criminal law had been broken and there had been a flagrant violation of the law see Section 222 Local Government Act 1972.

[38] [1984] AC 754 at 767 per Lord Roskill. This 1984 case shows how soon B&Q became involved in challenging the Act. It was B&Q who was the defendant in four of the cases referred to the European Court from the English courts: see cases C-306/88 *Rochdale BC*, C-304/90 *Reading BC*, C-169/91 *Stoke-on-Trent* [1993] 1 All ER 481 and 145/88 *Torfaen BC* [1989] ECR 3851, judgment being given in the last two cases. See C. Barnard, 'Sunday trading: a drama in five acts', 57 MLR (1994), 449-460 at 449.

[39] The local authority has also received complaints from other retailers who threatened to open on Sundays if the defendant was not prevented from doing so.

[40] [1988] 3 All ER 490. A preliminary reference was sent to the European Court but the questions were substantially answered by the decisions of the Court in 145/88 *Torfaen* and C-169/91 *Stoke-on-Trent* and none of the question therefore had to be answered. See C-306/88 *Rochdale BC* v. *Anders* [1993] 1 All ER 520.

of Appeal in *Kirklees* also insisted on cross-undertakings in damages being given if an injunction was awarded to the local authority.[41] By the time of this appeal, the House of Lords had applied the decision of the European Court in *Factortame* and held that a statute could be suspended where the EC law challenge to its validity was firmly based.[42] Relying on this decision, the Court of Appeal held that if Article 30 applied in this instance, the defendant would have had the right to trade and should be compensated if denied the opportunity to exercise that right while the issue was being decided. EC law was given priority over the enforcement of the domestic law in both these cases,[43] an approach that can be contrasted with that of the first instance decisions in *Kirklees*[44] and *Mendip*[45] and most importantly, the decision of the House of Lords in *Kirklees*.[46]

The High Court in *Kirklees*[47] granted an injunction without any cross-undertaking in damages. It doubted that the substantive EC law argument would succeed and more controversially, the judge also reasoned that even if it did, it might only be applied prospectively and the defendant would not be eligible for damages in any event. This is obviously a mistaken view as European Court decisions are only very rarely limited prospectively.[48] By the time the House of Lords came to consider the issue in *Kirklees*, the European Court had handed down its decision in *Francovich*.[49] The House

---

[41] [1991] 4 All ER 240. This was a joint appeal from *Kirklees* v. *Wickes Building Supplies Ltd* [1990] 1 WLR 1237 and *Mendip BC* v. *B&Q* [1991] 1 CMLR 113 where injunctions had been awarded without cross-undertakings in damages. At the time of the decision over 100 interim injunctions without cross-undertakings in damages had already been granted by the High Court see the judgment of Mann LJ. These decisions were now cast in doubt so it was unsurprising that the decision was further appealed to the House of Lords.

[42] *Factortame Ltd.* v. *Secretary of State for Transport (No. 2)* [1991] AC 603.

[43] In both cases the local authority had also claimed that it was to be equated with the Crown for the purposes of enforcement. The Crown would not have to give an undertaking in damages and therefore the local authority should not have to either. In both instances, the court refused to accept this argument.

[44] *Kirklees* v. *Wickes Building Supplies Ltd* [1990] 1 WLR 1237.

[45] *Mendip BC* v. *B&Q* [1991] 1 CMLR 113.

[46] [1992] 3 All ER 717.

[47] [1990] 1 WLR 1237. This decisions was handed down before the European Court decisions in case C-213/89 *R.* v. *Secretary of State for Transport, ex p. Factortame* [1990] ECR I-2433.

[48] In *Mendip* [1991] 1 CMLR 113 Mummery J. in the High Court followed the first instance decision in *Kirklees*. In both these cases the local authority was equated with the Crown for enforcement purposes.

[49] Case C-6 & 9/90 *Francovich* v. *Italian State* [1993] 2 CMLR 66 where the European Court held that damages could be awarded against a Member State for failure to implement a directive. Three conditions had to be met: (1) the result laid down by the directive must involve rights conferred on individuals; (2) the content of those rights

held that as a result of this decision, the State was liable to an individual who suffered loss as a result of the non-enforcement of EC law. The state in this instance meant central government and because there would be a remedy against the government if the Act was contrary to EC law, there was no need for a cross-undertaking from the local authority also.[50]

The case highlights the problem of the court seeking to enforce the 'law' when that law is not a single entity but arises out of two legal systems which overlap. The doctrine of supremacy resolves the issue of which rule applies when the two systems conflict. However, because of the absence of a clear demarcation of competences between the Member States and the Community (in this instance in relation to Article 30), there can be a period of time when there is doubt as to whether the Community rule will ultimately apply or not and in the meantime the national law has to be suspended. By interpreting state liability as the liability of central government, the House sought to reconcile the supremacy of EC law and the suspension of domestic law pending an Article 177 reference with the perceived need to prevent wilful disregard of the domestic law. The case thus straddles the two approaches of the lower courts: by enforcing the Act while also seeking to give effect to EC law. The difficulty is that such a reconciliation was impossible. There is nothing in the *Francovich* judgment to imply that the State was to be limited to central government and such a conclusion flies in the face of other decisions of the Court which indicate that the loyalty clause in Article 5 applies to all organs of the state and not just the government narrowly defined.[51]

The result of the House of Lords decision was that injunctions could be awarded to local authorities without cross-undertakings being given. However, the lower courts were by now justifiably nervous of the Sunday trading cases and when Kirklees went to the local court in search of its

---

must be identifiable by reference to the provisions of the directive itself; (3) a causal link must be shown between the failure of the Member State to carry out its obligations and the damage suffered by the individual. Noted by Bebr, 29 CML Rev. (1992), 557-584.

[50] The local authority was also equated with the Crown for the purpose of enforcement of the Act.

[51] For example case 77/69 *Commission* v. *Belgium* [1970] ECR 237 where a draft law to bring Belgium into line with its obligations under Article 95 EEC had been delayed in the legislature. The government could do nothing about the delay and sought to use this as a defence. The European Court rejected the defence because the obligation to comply with Community law fell on the whole state and not just on the government. In fact, local authorities are required to give effect to directly effective Community rules, even if these conflict with national law see case 108/88 *Constanzo* v. *Commune di Milano* [1989] ECR 1839.

injunction with its House of Lords decision in hand, it was turned away pending an outstanding Sunday trading case before the European Court.[52]

The retailers who challenged the Act were able to render it unenforceable partly because of the refusal of central government to get involved. Central government did not assume an enforcement role throughout this time in the national courts, insisting that it was a matter for local authorities only. It has been criticised for its reticence which appears suspect in the light of the close links between the main pressure group advocating reform and the Conservative party.[53] It could have intervened and sought injunctions itself as guardian of the public interest but the Attorney General decided not to and there is no redress against such a refusal in English law.[54] In one forum at least central government did defend the law, Luxembourg. Even the Attorney General himself went to defend the law in the final reference on the issue from the English courts.[55] Thus the government was defending a law in the European Court that it would not or could not enforce in its own domestic courts.

2. The Euro-Defence

The validity of the statute could only be challenged directly in the light of EC law[56] because the only British constitutional principle permitting judicial review of the validity of a statute is the supremacy of EC law.[57] However, rather than mount a direct challenge against the Act before the High Court, the retailers instead raised Article 30 as a defence when prosecuted in the Magistrates Courts. The EC law argument was not a very strong one and if the challenge had been raised directly in the High Court, there was a greater risk that no reference would be made to the European

---

[52] See Rawlings fn. 13 at 329.

[53] Diamond, fn. 30 at 75 and 87.

[54] See Poole, 'Sunday Trading: The Shops Bills 1992-1993', Parliament: Economic Affairs Section at 12. He cites from a statement made in the House of Commons by the Attorney General see HC Deb 27 November 1991 cc 913-4.

[55] Case C-169/91 *Stoke-on-Trent* v. *B&Q* [1993] 1 All ER 481; Rawlings fn. 13 at 315.

[56] See generally, Craig, *Administrative Law*, 3rd ed., (1994), 188-209. This can be compared with the Canadian experience where Sunday trading rules were challenged directly on constitutional grounds see Bakan, 'Constitutional arguments: interpretation and legitimacy in Canadian constitutional thought', Osgoode Hall LJ. (1989), 123-193.

[57] See the House of Lords decision in *Factortame (No. 2)* [1991] AC 603 and the more recent *Equal Opportunities Commission* v *Secretary of State for Employment* [1994] 1 All ER 910 where the House of Lords held that a statute was inconsistent with EC law.

Court and the Act would continue to be enforced uninterrupted.[58] At the other end of the judicial spectrum, it would only be a matter of time before Magistrates, unaccustomed to arguments of EC law, would refer the issue to the European Court.

The aim of the retailers was to render the Act unenforceable so they could open their shops on Sunday and bring about the necessary change in social attitudes.[59] Thus the strength of their EC law argument was not that important. What was important was to secure an Article 177 reference and to ensure that the law remained in a state of uncertainty so that it would be difficult or impossible to enforce. In short, they sought to exploit one of the most complex aspects of Article 30 which is the question of allocation of competences between the Community and the Member States in particular in relation to marketing rules. By simply questioning who should regulate Sunday trading, they created a regulatory gap. The combination of vague boundaries of competence in Article 30 and the suspension of national law pending an Article 177 reference created a regulatory vacuum. Domestic law was suspended and yet it was not clear that EC law applied.[60]

The extent to which EC law applied to marketing rules such as those found in the 1950 Act was unclear. The European Court, in adopting a broad definition of measures capable of falling within Article 30, had to decide to what extent the internal market required regulation of domestic measures capable of indirectly affecting inter-state trade. There is no de minimis rule in Article 30 and theoretically, if a measure could be shown to have an effect on inter-state trade, then it would fall within the Article.[61] Thus in a series of cases broadly concerned with marketing rules, the Court had developed a confusing and somewhat contradictory case law. Some marketing rules did fall within Article 30 e.g. rules requiring licences for

---

[58] For a discussion of the difference between the way the law is administered in the Magistrates Courts and the higher courts see Cotterrell, *The Sociology of Law*, 2nd ed., (1992), 157-161.

[59] See generally, Rawlings, fn. 13.

[60] See London Economics, *The Economic Impact of Alternative Sunday Trading Regulations* (1993), at 8 where a survey for late 1992 and early 1993 indicated 38% of shops opened on Sundays - and these figures excluded pre-Christmas opening.

[61] Mortelmans suggests that Advocate General Van Gervan's approach in *Conforama* and *Marchandaise* of examining a measure to see if it affects the pattern of trade introduces a de minimis test. He criticises this approach as being difficult for national courts to apply, see fn. 1 at 127 and 131. Gormley is also critical of this approach and he is concerned that although the Court did not adopt this approach in *Keck*, its decision might be seen as introducing a de minimis test, even though he does not think that this is how the decision should be read see Gormley, 'Reasoning Renounced? The remarkable judgment in *Keck* and *Mithouard*', EBL Rev. (1994), 63 at 66.

sex shops.[62] There was a parallel line of cases where the Court held that the marketing rules in issue fell outside Article 30, without fully considering the effect on inter-state trade.[63] Finally, in the *Cinetheque* case,[64] the Court developed what seemed to be a new approach to domestic rules regulating the domestic market.[65] It held that French restrictions on release of film videos could fall within Article 30 but did not because they pursued an objective justified in relation to EC law and they did not exceed the means necessary to achieve that objective. In other words, if a national measure affected domestic and imported goods equally and was not intended to affect inter-state trade, it would not be contrary to Article 30 provided its objective was one justified under EC law and it was proportionate in light of that objective.[66]

In the first reference on the Shops Act, the Court chose to follow the approach it had adopted in *Cinetheque*.[67] The Act did have an affect on inter-state trade[68] but that effect would be lawful if its objective were ensuring that working and non-working hours were so arranged as to accord with national or regional socio-cultural characteristics. The Act also had to be proportionate as to the means it used to achieve its objective. However, it was for the English and Welsh courts to apply both parts of this tests.[69] The judgment is sparse and offers no criteria according to which the English magistrates could apply this new test, controversial even within EC law academic circles, let alone among the part-time judiciary of the English and Welsh courts.[70]

It seems the court was wary of treading on national toes,[71] and hence did not identify criteria as it would have had to move into potentially sensitive

---

[62] Case 23/89 *Quietlynn Ltd.* v. *Southend BC* [1990] ER I-3054.

[63] *Oebel* [1981] ECR 1993; *Blesgen* [1982] ECR 1211.

[64] [1985] ECR 2605.

[65] Chalmers, fn. 1 at 288 et seg.

[66] The Court's reliance on the intention of the legislation has been criticised see Gormley fn. 64 at 66.

[67] Case 145/88 *Torfaen BC* v. *B&Q* [1989] ECR 3851.

[68] B&Q was able to show that about 24% of its turnover occurred on a Sunday; that 5% of its Sunday sales were of imported goods; and that people spend money on Sundays that they do not spend any other day of the week (known as the Sunday pound) therefore the sale of imports were reduced if shops could not open on Sunday. Thus, argued B&Q, the Shops Act was in breach of Article 30.

[69] Arnull points out that the European Court did not identify the objective of the Act, leaving it to the national courts see Arnull, 'What shall we do on Sunday?', 16 EL Rev. (1991), 112 at 118.

[70] This decision has generated critical commentaries see for example Arnull, ibid., Gormley, 'Some reflections on the internal market and free movement of goods', fn. 1 and his casenote on *Torfaen* 27 CML Rev. (1990), 141; Steiner, fn. 1.

[71] Gormley, Ibid.

policy considerations as to quality of life. In addition, Sunday trading regulation is to be found throughout the Community and there are significant differences between Member States.[72] If the Court applied its own test, it could then be called on to measure each national or regional Sunday trading rule against Article 30, a potentially lengthy and politically damaging prospect.[73]

The case failed to clarify the law and in a large number of cases proportionality was treated as a question of fact and led to lengthy argument in the Magistrates Courts which were ill-equipped to deal with such arguments and lacked the capacity to handle contentious cases.[74] Thus long delays developed in the courts without any clarification of the legal issues involved. After about six months, the question of Sunday trading arose in the High Court where Hoffman J. in *Stoke-on-Trent* v. *B&Q*[75] laid down some guide-lines for the lower courts, most notably, that judicial notice could be taken of the factors surrounding the Act and large amounts of evidence did not have to taken as to the nature of its operation and effects. This was to be welcomed but the second part of his judgment is unfortunate from a Community law perspective.[76] He examined the role of the judge in relation to the application of the test of proportionality from a British constitutional position: judges could not perform quasi-legislative functions, putting themselves in the position of the legislators. All the court could do was identify the objectives of the Act and see if no reasonable legislator would have passed the Act to advance those objectives. If on the basis of this test, the Act could have been passed, then it was proportionate. In others words, the English test of reasonableness as found in the Wednesbury principle was applied even though it is not the same as the Community principle of proportionality.[77] Steiner points out that this

---

[72] Weatherill and Beaumont argue that it is the pervasive nature of the rules in *Cinetheque* and the Sunday trading cases which led to the Court taking a different approach than in other marketing cases see Weatherill & Beaumont, *EC Law* (1993) at 471.

[73] Especially, as the Council of Ministers had been unable to agree to Sunday as the relevant rest day in the Directive on part time work. The Commissioner for Social Affairs favoured Sunday as the mandatory rest time but could only secure the compromise that in principle it should be Sunday see Article 5 Directive on Working Time OJ 1993 L 307/18. See Rawlings fn. 13 at 312 and Diamond, 'Sunday Service: Trading Restrictions', 135 SJ (1991), 564.

[74] Rawlings fn. 13 at 316.

[75] [1991] Ch. 48.

[76] See Arnull, fn. 72 at 119.

[77] *Associated Provincial Picture Houses Ltd.* v. *Wednesbury Corporation* [1948] 1 KB 223. The House of Lords was asked to consider how Hoffman J. applied proportionality in this case but refused to do so because the issue was no longer

approach was clearly contrary to EC law but that the judge was concerned about a national law being challenged regularly on highly dubious grounds.[78]

An approach more akin to that of the Community was taken in the *Peterborough* case where the High Court applied *Torfaen* and held that section 47 was a trading rule within Article 30.[79] It did state obiter that in seeing if the Act was proportional the courts were to see if it went further than the purposes demanded. This sets a different standard from that laid down by Hoffman J. but was only an obiter decision.[80]

The jurisprudence of the European Court had also developed further. In *Marchandise*[81] and *Conforama*[82] the European Court held that Sunday rules relating to employment, which affected Sunday opening, were proportionate i.e. it went a step further than it had in the *Torfaen* case and applied the proportionality test to the rules. This could have resolved the matter of the compatibility of the Shops Act but in the *Stoke-on-Trent* case, B&Q persuaded the House of Lords that there was sufficient difference between the rules in those two cases and the Shops Act to justify a reference, the House having no discretion but to refer where a decision on a point of EC law is necessary and is not clear, it being a court of last resort. Thus the regulatory gap continued with shops continuing to open on Sundays. In its decision, the European Court finally laid to rest the question of whether or not there was a breach of Article 30 by the Shops

---

relevant after the decision of the European Court in *Stoke-on-Trent* see *Stoke-on-Trent* v. *B&Q* [1993] 2 All ER 297 at 299. In *R. v. Secretary of State for the Home Department, ex p. Brind* [1991] AC 696 the House of Lords held that proportionality was not a separate ground for judicial review. Lord Bridge did indicate that proportionality might become a part of the law in the future at 749-750. See generally, Craig fn. 59 411-421.

[78] See Steiner fn. 1 at 52. Under Community law, a measure must not restrict trade between Member States any more than is absolutely necessary for the attainment of the legitimate purpose and if there are other ways, less restrictive of trade between Member States of attaining that purpose then the measures are not acceptable see case 261/81 *Walter Rau Lebensmittelwerke* v. *de Smedt PvbA* [1982] ECR 961.

[79] *WH Smith Do-It-All and Payless DIY* v. *Peterborough CC* [1991] 1 QB 304. The case stated had been sent to the High Court from the Crown Court before the European Court decision in *Torfaen*. Of course, it would have been more appropriate to make an Article 177 reference as the question was one concerning EC law see Arnull fn. 72 at 117.

[80] Hoffman J. leap-frogged the *Stoke-on-Trent* case to the House of Lords as it raised a question of exceptional public importance and the House of Lords sent a reference to the European Court see [1991] 4 All ER 221 at 239.

[81] Case 332/89 *Ministere Public* v. *Marchandise* [1991] ECR I-1027.

[82] Case C-312/89 *Union Departementale des Syndicats CGT de l'Asine* v. *Sidef Conforama* [1991] ECR I-997.

Act holding that the Sunday trading rules were compatible.[83] This ruling was unequivocally applied by the House of Lords, thereby ending the dispute as to the compatibility of the Shops Act with the free movement of goods rules.[84]

IV THE AFTERMATH: *KECK* AND *PUNTO CASA*

Thus the inapplicability of EC law to the Shops Act was at last resolved. While the question of the compatibility of Article 30 and the Shops Act was in doubt, large numbers of shops opened and large numbers of people shopped or worked on Sundays.[85] The discrepancy between the formal law and social practice was so great, the government was keen to reform the law as quickly as possible and the Sunday Trading Act was passed in 1994.[86] It completely deregulates Sunday trading for small shops while larger shops, subject to certain exceptions, can open for 6 hours a day.[87]

The role of EC law in the Sunday trading litigation has done nothing to enhance its status as a credible system of law as it seemed to engender a regime of lawlessness in relation to the Shops Act, styming enforcement by local authorities, and after *Factortame*, central government also. The amendment of the national law would probably have occurred in time irrespective of the invocation of EC law. However, it is unlikely that it would have occurred as quickly because the desired change in social attitudes might have taken longer to achieve. Thus EC law acted as a catalyst for social and legal change at the national level on a subject which it now holds to be beyond the purview of Article 30 entirely. This paradoxical position indicates the confusion that surrounded the issue when it was first raised in *Torfaen* and the uncertainty generated by the Court's approach, which it now seems to have abandoned.[88] It also highlights the vacuum in regulation that results from the temporary suspension of domestic law pending an Article 177 reference and the importance of the Court providing an interpretation which national courts are able to apply.

---

[83] Case C-169/91 [1993] 1 All ER 481.

[84] [1993] 2 All ER 297.

[85] See generally Freathy & Sparks, fn. 18.

[86] A white paper, *Reforming the Law on Sunday Trading: A Guide to the Options for Reform* cm 2300 (1993) was published in July 1993 and the Sunday Trading Act became law in November 1994.

[87] The Deregulating and Contracting Out Act 1994 deregulates trading hours for shops for other days of week see section 23.

[88] See below section 4 for a discussion of case C-267 & 268/91, *Keck & Mithouard* [1993] ECR I-6097.

The Sunday trading experience shows that the lower national courts in particular, cannot be expected to engage in sophisticated legal analysis unless they are provided with clear guide-lines. The chaos generated in the lower courts after *Torfaen* could be used to argue for a redrafting of Article 177 so that the lower national courts can no longer make a reference.[89] This would prevent the fiasco seen in this instance but would also cut off one of the most fruitful sources for the Court of cases where it can develop its vision of EC law and the Community itself. If the Court wants to continue to receive references from the lower courts, it needs to be more sensitive to the limitations of those courts in terms of their resources and their legal expertise.

With national courts unable to apply the proportionality test effectively and consistently in relation to the Shops Act, the Court had little alternative but to proceed and apply the test itself in the *Stoke-on-Trent* case.[90] Thus it resolved the immediate question of whether or not the Shops Act fell foul of Article 30 without offering much clarification of the test used. If anything, by looking to see if the effect on inter-state trade was direct, indirect or speculative in order to establish whether or not the measure was necessary, the Court seemed to be modifying the *Dassonville* formula thus creating further uncertainty and making more litigation on marketing rules inevitable.[91] Unless the Court devised a new test, it would be called on repeatedly to apply a test with few criteria which required it to identify the aim of a national measure and to balance the national interest in pursuing that aim, if legitimate under EC law, with the interest of the Community in establishing an internal market. In evaluating the socio-cultural characteristics of a national measure, the Court ran the risk of evaluating aspects of national life which had little or nothing to do with the completion

---

[89] See Weiler, fn. 6 at 444. At the same time, the Court has started to reject references from national courts where they fail to provide the full factual background to a case see cases C-320-322/90, *Telemarsicabruzzo SpA* v. *Circostel* [1994] ECR nyr noted by Arnull, 31 CML Rev. (1994), 377-386.

[90] Case C-169/91 *Stoke-on-Trent* at paragraph 14: 'The Court considered that it had all the information necessary for it to rule on the question of the proportionality of [Sunday trading] rules and that it had to do so in order to enable national courts to assess their compatibility with Community law in a uniform matter since such an assessment cannot be allowed to vary according to the findings of fact made by individual courts in particular cases.'

[91] Case 8/74 [1974] ECR 837 at 847. The *Dassonville* formula refers to direct or indirect, actual or potential effects on intra-Community trade. The question raised by the Stoke-on-Trent judgment was whether or not speculative effect was the same as potential effect or was the court moving towards some sort of de minimis rule.

of the internal market.[92] Such interference would be counter to the current concern with subsidiarity.[93]

The uncertainty surrounding the application of the test developed in the Sunday trading cases was exacerbated by the perception of Article 30 as a traders' charter ensuring unrestricted trade throughout the Community. If Article 30 did offer such guarantees, then any national measure which affected trade per se could be challenged under the free movement provisions even if it imposed an equal burden on domestic and imported goods. Hence, English traders, relying on Article 30, challenged Sunday trading rules which did not adversely affect imports any more than domestic goods but had the overall affect of reducing all trade.

In *Keck*, the Court departed from the test developed in the Sunday trading cases and also weakened the perception of Article 30 as a traders charter. The Court held that Article 30 did not apply to a measure prohibiting resale as a loss. It did not refer at all to the Sunday trading cases.[94] Instead, it stated that the purpose of the measure was not to regulate inter-state trade and even if it reduced the volume of trade, this in itself was not sufficient to make it a measure having equivalent effect to a quantitative restriction. It then specifically noted trader's increasing use of Article 30 to challenge any rule which affected their commercial freedom. After referring to *Cassis*[95] it indicated that contrary to what it had previously decided, measures which restrict or prohibit selling arrangements do not fall within Article 30 provided 'the measure applies to all affected traders operating within the national territory and provided that they affect in the same manner in law and in fact, the marketing of domestic products and of those from other Member States'.[96] Thus the Sunday trading cases and the test contained in them, seem to have been laid to rest,[97] while the role of Article 30 as a traders charter has been diminished with the Court in *Keck* expressly indicating that it is changing its previous position because of the frequency

---

[92] See Reich fn. 2 at 482 where he discusses the problem of legitimacy surrounding judicial activism.

[93] See Gormley fn. 64 at 67 where the desire of the Court not to decide on essentially local matters is seen as in keeping with current concerns about subsidiarity.

[94] There were two Advocate General opinions in this case. The first was handed down before the decision in *Stoke-on-Trent* and the second, reaching a different conclusion, was delivered after further questions had been put to the parties by the Court. See case C-267/91, *Keck* [1993] ECR I-6097. Noted by Gormley, fn. 64, 63-67; Rothe, 31 CML Rev. (1994), 845-855.

[95] Case 120/78 *Rewe-Zentral AG* v. *Bundesmonopolverwaltung für Branntwein (Cassis de Dijon)* [1979] ECR 649.

[96] Case C-267/91, *Keck* [1993] ECR I-6097 at paragraph 16.

[97] See Advocate General Van Gervan in case C-401 & 402/92, *Tankstation 't Heukske vof and Boermans* [1994] ECR I-2199 at paragraph 26.

with which traders had been invoking Article 30 to challenge any restriction on their commercial freedom. The Article is best seen as an instrumental rule primarily concerned with the completion of the internal market.[98]

The Court has since applied *Keck* in the most recent Sunday trading case to come before it. In *Punto Casa*,[99] the Court considered whether or not Article 30 applied to an Italian law prohibiting Sunday trading. The fact that the volume of trade was affected did not mean that the measure fell foul of Article 30. The rules did give regional authorities power to introduce rules so there were regional differences in opening hours. Advocate General van Gervan indicated that this did not prevent the application of *Keck* because the rules affected did not hinder access for traders outside Italy any more than those in the country. The Court did not refer specifically to regional differences but referring to *Keck* held that once the marketing rules do not prevent imports gaining access to the market any more than domestic goods then they fall outside Article 30.

Neither the Advocate General nor the Court referred to the previous Sunday trading cases although the Advocate General in his opinion in *Tankstation*[100] did discuss the previous case law and noted that, in light of *Keck*, that case law could not apply. Unlike *Keck*, where the Court referred to the fact the legislation was not for the purpose of regulating inter-state trade, no reference is made in *Punto Casa* to the motives of the legislation. This move away from seeking to establish the aims of the legislation is to be welcomed as considerations of intent are not relevant to the operation of a test based on access. Only if the measure fell within Article 30, would intention and objectives need to be considered to establish if a measure is subject to the rule of reason.[101]

In *Keck* and *Punto Casa*, the Court reduces the scope of Article 30 by developing a new test which allows for some national measures to fall outside it even where they affect the overall volume of trade.[102] The

---

[98] The Court could have reconciled the instrumental and liberalisation perspectives of the Article by developing an autonomous concept of a Community trader. Such a trader would be able to look to Article 30 to guarantee their commercial freedom but because such a concept would be free of national references, they would not be looking to challenge any national law which inhibited trade. However, as Reich has discussed, the Court seems to be moving away from the development of such autonomous concepts see Reich fn. 2 at 483 et seg.

[99] Case 69/93 & C-258/93, *Punto Casa SpA* v. *Sindaco del Commune di Capena* [1994] ECR I-2355.

[100] C-401 & 402/92, *Tankstation 't Heukske vof and Boermans* [1994] ECR I-2199.

[101] See Gormley fn. 64 at 66.

[102] See Reich fn. 2 at 461.

emphasis is on access to the market.[103]   This involves creating two categories of measures: those that are product-related and those that deal with marketing arrangements. As van Gervan points out, the Court in *Keck* does not explain why the two sorts of measures are to be treated differently but the distinction can be explained by the key question of access.[104] Where a national measure affects product requirements this imposes an extra burden on the imports such as the repackaging that would have been required in the *Clinique* case where German law would not allow the use of a medicinal name such as Clinique in relation to cosmetics.[105]   In other words, if the product has to be adapted to gain access to a market, then that is an additional burden which restricts its access to the market more than domestic products.[106]   Marketing arrangements are primarily concerned with regulating the domestic market and therefore are unlikely to affect the appearance or characteristics of an imported product.   As indistinct measures, domestic and imported goods will be similarly affected and both will have their access restricted to the same degree. In this situation, the Court has set up a presumption that if the measure is a marketing rule, it will be presumed to fall outside Article 30 as it does not adversely affect access.   The burden of proof then shifts to the party challenging the measure in light of Article 30 to show that one of the two conditions laid down by the Court have not been met[107] i.e. either access for traders from other Member States is impeded more than for domestic traders or that the effect of the measure either in law or fact is such as to differentiate between domestic goods and imports.[108]

If this analysis is adopted, then there remains the possibility that marketing rules may be scrutinized under *Cassis*.[109] This means that even if the Court has restricted the scope of Article 30, it has not done so to such a degree that all marketing rules will fall outside Article 30. Thus the Court will still be able to ensure the further integration of the market, while no

---

[103]   White discusses the question of market access see fn. 1 at 246.

[104]   C-401 & 402/92, *Tankstation 't Heukske vof and Boermans* [1994] ECR I-2199 at paragraph 20.

[105]   Case C-315/92 *Verband Soliazer Wettbewerb eV* v. *Clinique Laboratories SNC* [1994] ECR I-317. The measure was held to be contrary to Article 30.

[106]   See Weatherill and Beaumont fn. 75 at 473 et seg. for a discussion of the dual-burden test.

[107]   See Van Gervan in C-401 & 402/92, *Tankstation 't Heukske vof and Boermans* note 107 at footnote 53.

[108]   Van Gervan suggests that one way of invoking the second condition would be to show that the purpose of the measure was to regulate inter-state trade see paragraph 22 ibid.

[109]   See Reich fn. 2 at 486.

longer entertaining cases brought by traders asserting commercial freedom in the light of national socio-cultural measures reducing the volume of trade. One of the outstanding difficulties that remains is that the Court has not provided any criteria according to which marketing rules can be distinguished from product related rules. By not identifying those cases which it was departing from in *Keck* and by stating that only certain selling arrangements were affected, the Court will develop the law on a case-by-case basis.[110] This means that some uncertainty remains as to the scope of the *Keck* test e.g. Rothe and Reich both point to advertising measures and the difficulty of knowing whether or not they are marketing rules within *Keck*.[111] The reserve implicit in a case-by-case approach does not automatically imply indecision by the Court. It has given itself the discretion to take its jurisprudence forward cautiously. Caution per se is not a fault provided the Court gives sufficient direction and clarity of interpretation to allow national courts to apply its judgments without giving rise to the sort of chaos seen in the Sunday trading cases.

V CONCLUSION

One of the most important lessons to be learnt from the Sunday trading cases is that the effectiveness and implementation of EC law must take into account the effectiveness and implementation of national law within the framework of EC law.[112] The U-turn made by the European Court in *Keck* is perhaps best understood in terms of ensuring the effectiveness of EC law at the national level. A reduction in the scope of Article 30 where the access to the market is equally impaired for domestic and imported goods seems a small price to pay for restoring the status of EC law as a source of the rule of law within the domestic context.[113] In other words, sometimes less regulation by the Community will lead to more effective implementation of EC law by national courts and to greater respect for that

---

110 See Rothe fn. 97 at 852.
111 See Reich fn. 2 at 487 and Rothe ibid.
112 See Rawlings, fn. 13 at 334 where he concludes that in establishing the distribution of power between Community and national institutions, regard must be had to the implementation and effectiveness of national law within the Community framework as well as the implementation and effectiveness of Community law within the Member States.
113 Weiler discusses the inherent paradox in the Community where increased integration leads to calls for less regulation from the centre: reflected in the current debate on subsidiarity see 'The Transformation of Europe', 100 Yale LJ (1991), 2403 at 2410 et seg.

law among the citizens of the Europe. If the interplay of EC and national law is such that EC law is seen to be undermining the rule of law and creating a climate of lawlessness, then a broad interpretation of the EC rules may in fact be counter-productive as in the Sunday trading litigation.

The Court is unlikely to be faced with the sort of repeat litigation which arose in relation to the Sunday trading issue because of its implicit rejection of Article 30 as a traders charter. At the same time, because of the uncertainty surrounding the division between marketing rules and product related rules, the question of where competence lies between the Community and the Member States in the regulation of domestic markets remains. The Court can develop the law on a case-by-case basis but any broad ranging clarification of competence must occur at the political level. Until such developments, the tension between the scope of Article 30 and the powers of the Member States remains leading to continued uncertainty. Such uncertainty will not be as great a problem in the future if Article 30 is seen as instrumental in the creation of the internal market and not as a traders charter, thus preventing litigation on issues of marginal importance to the completion of the internal market.

* Lecturer in Law, University of London. Thanks to Colin Scott for comments. An earlier version of this paper was presented at staff seminars in University College London and Exeter University in March 1994.

8. The European Conventions on Criminal Matters[1]

Professor Theo Vogler – University of Giessen

I OVERVIEW

Criminal concerns have played an important role within the scope of operation of the Council of Europe[2] from the beginning. In 1957 the European Commission for Criminal Problems (ECCP) was already called into existence by the committee of ministers with the mission to 'prepare and administer a plan (of action) for the Council of Europe in the field of crime prevention and the treatment of offenders'. Within the European Commission for Criminal Problems there are subcommissions the members of which are entrusted with investigating specific criminal problems due to their special knowledge.[3] The works of the subcommissions deal both with fundamental research and with preliminary studies for international agreements. The studies done in the course of fundamental research are intended to give the member states information to assist in the development of their national law. The results of these efforts are reflected in the official publications of the Council of Europe which appear in French and English.[4]

---

1 The chapter is based on a previous publication in German: 'Die strafrechtlichen Konventionen des Europarats', Jura 1992, pp. 586 et seq.
2 The Council of Europe is a public international federation of sovereign states with its seat in Strasbourg. At the moment 38 member states belong to the Council of Europe: Belgium, Federal Republic of Germany, Denmark, Finland, France, Greece, United Kingdom, Ireland, Italy, Liechtenstein, Luxembourg, Malta, The Netherlands, Norway, Austria, Poland, Portugal, Romania, San Marino, Sweden, Switzerland, Spain, Czechia, Slowakia, Slowenia, Turkey, Hungary, Cyprus, Bulgaria, Latvia, Estonia, Lithuania, Moldova, Albania, Macedonia, Ukraine, Andorra and Iceland.
3 Cf. the description of the different areas of work in Vogler, Zur Tätigkeit des Europarats auf dem Gebiet des Strafrechts, ZStW 79 (1969), pp. 113 et seq.
4 E.g. The death penalty in European countries (1962); Suspended sentence, probation and other alternatives to prison sentences (1966); The effectiveness of punishment and other measures of treatment (1967); Aspects of the international validity of criminal judgements (1968); Legal aspects of extradition among European States (1970); New

Due to their practical significance the preliminary studies are a major focus of interest in the activity of the subcommissions. Over the years there have been over nineteen agreements on co-operation in the field of criminal law with corresponding Explanatory Reports.[5] At the beginning there were the classical instruments of extradition (1957, amended by two additional protocols) and legal assistance (1959, amended by an additional protocol), treaties about the supervision of conditionally sentenced or conditionally released offenders (1964), the international validity of criminal judgements (1970), the transfer of proceedings (1972) and the transfer of prisoners (1983) followed up to the present with the complex of problems concerning the confiscation of proceeds from crimes (1990); as well as nine agreements on special issues.[6]   Since 1984 an expert committee of the European Council has been discussing whether all the instruments on criminal law of the Council of Europe could be codified into a 'comprehensive agreement'[7] though it cannot be foreseen, whether this ambitious project will succeed.[8]

In addition, within the scope of the European Community, an attempt has been made to intensify co-operation in the field of criminal law by agreements.   In 1985 a team called 'Justizielle Zusammenarbeit' (co-operation in the field of justice) was set up and formulated – within the

---

trends in the treatment of young offenders (1974); Sentencing (1974); Alternative penal measures to imprisonment (1976); Compensation for victims of crime (1978); The contributions of criminal law to the protection of the environment (1978); Economic crime (1981); The role of criminal law in consumer protection (1983); Alcohol and crime (1984); Organisation of crime prevention (1988); Exterritorial criminal jurisdiction (1989); Computer-related crime (1990). The European Council issues a separate list of publications in the field of crime problems.

[5] Cf. the collection of Müller-Rappard, Bassiouni, European Inter-State Co-operation in Criminal Matters. The Council of Europe's Legal Instruments. Collection of Texts compiled and edited by Ekkehard Müller-Rappard and M. Cherif Bassiouni. Revised second edition (November 20, 1991). The collection also contains the 'Resolutions and Recommendations concerning the Application' of each convention.

[6] The Treaties are published in the official collection of Conventions of the Council of Europe (ETS) in English and French language printed under No. 24, 30, 51, 52, 70, 71, 73, 82, 86, 88, 90, 97, 98, 99, 101, 112, 116, 119, 141. Cf. the table in the 'Chart showing signatures and ratifications of conventions and agreements concluded within the Council of Europe' published by the Council of Europe.

[7] Cf. the suggestion of Jescheck, Möglichkeiten und Probleme eines Europäischen Strafrechts in: Festschrift für Jhong-Won Kim, 1991, pp. 947 ff, 958. The whole area has to be rethought to avoid the impression of a perfect European law which in reality only exists on paper. 'Was not tut, ist ein integrierter Text, eine Art Codex der europäischen Strafrechtspflege' (an integrated text is needed, some kind of a Code on European Criminal Law).

[8] Cf. Wilkitzki, Regionalisierung des internationalen Strafrechts, Deutscher Landesbericht zum Thema IV/1. Teil des XV. Internationalen Strafrechtskongresses, ZStW, Vol. 105 (1993), pp. 821, 828.

scope of the European Political Co-operation (EPC) – five EEC Agreements on criminal law. They deal with the transfer of sentenced persons (1987), the application of the principle 'ne bis in idem' (1987), the simplification of methods of the transmission of requests for extradition (Telefax, 1989), the transfer of criminal proceedings (1990) and the enforcement of foreign sentences (1991). Many of the agreements can be seen as a supplement to the relevant agreements of the Council of Europe and merely facilitate the application of the principles and mechanisms laid down in them.[9] They have not yet come into effect.

II LAW OF CONVENTIONS AND THE UNIFICATION OF LAW

Although the European Conventions express a hope for the assimilation of laws and the unification of law it cannot be said that the substantive criminal law has been harmonised within Europe. At the same time the unification of law appears as an element in and means of achieving the wider objective of political unity expressly mentioned in the statute of the Council of Europe[10] and it is frequently referred to in the conventions[11] and the resolutions of the Committee of Ministers.[12] Legal unity has always been lauded as an ideal.[13] [14] Although the prospects for the unification of law are quite propitious in Europe, even in the field of criminal law – the states linked together in the Council of Europe are connected by their history, tradition, custom and fundamental social and ethical beliefs and they also have corresponding attitudes towards criminality[15] – only limited attempts towards harmonising the substantive criminal law have been made

---

[9] Wilkitzki, op. cit., n. 7, p. 8.

[10] Constitution of the Council of Europe May 5, 1949. BGBl. 1950, 263.

[11] See e.g., the Convention on Terrorism January 27, 1977, ETS Nr. 90.

[12] Resolution by the Committee of Ministers concerning crime problems.

[13] Zitelmann, Die Möglichkeit eines Weltrechts, reprint of the 1888 edition, plus a forward of 1916.

[14] Cf. Vogler, Die europäischen Übereinkommen über die Auslieferung und die sonstige Rechtshilfe in Strafsachen, ZStW 780 (1968), pp. 480 et seq.; cf. also the documents produced within the framework of the UN on 'standard agreement' about the transfer of prisoners. UN-Document (1988) Nr. 40634, the transfer of prosecution, the transfer of supervision of conditionally sentenced and conditionally released persons, the extradition and legal assistance in criminal matters, UN-Document A/CONF. 144 Rev. 1, pp. 64-102.

[15] On the advantages of starting with a European Criminal Law due to its common cultural heritage in this area is hinted in Jescheck, op. cit., n. 6 p. 949.

in the European practice of the last decade. But the studies of the new subcommittee 'Europa im Wandel'[16] (Changing Europe) aim beyond merely harmonising the criminal policy of the member states. The subcommittee which is to consider the criminal dimension of the changes in Europe has the task of harmonising the definitions of offences by creating common definitions in particular fields of crime;[17] with the qualification that this is to be aimed at only insofar 'as it seems practicable and useful for the purposes of international co-operation and as far as definitions of offences of transnational character are affected'.[18] This 'realistic concept' has been applied in a number of areas. The Committee of Ministers of the Council of Europe has laid down detailed guidelines for the formulation of new definitions of offences in the Appendix to its Recommendation R (89) 9 concerning computer criminality, which will possibly be incorporated into binding international agreements in the future. The newly initiated activity of the Council of Europe in the field of environmental criminality[19] is an example. With the agreement of November 8, 1990 about money laundering, seizure and confiscation of profits from criminal offences, guidelines have been incorporated into a binding international instrument of the Council of Europe for the first time. Art. 6 imposes a duty on the contracting partners to embody the rather precisely formulated definition of the offence of money laundering into their national criminal law.[20]

The Treaties of Schengen[21] that extends the possibility of prosecution to compensate for the loss of security as a result of the opening of domestic borders do not provide for an assimilation of substantive criminal law. Given the intention to refrain from all types of personal checks at the internal border it is clear that the question has to be raised whether it will suffice to secure the interest in prosecution of criminals of the countries involved to give the police the right to make further observation of a suspected person beyond their own borders as well as the right to engage in 'hot pursuit' of a suspected person caught in the act.[22] Even timid attempts

---

[16] Project group 'Europe in a time of change: Criminal policy and Criminal law'.

[17] E.g. Computer Criminality, Dealing with Human Beings, Cultural Property, and Firearms, Money laundering and other types of Economic Criminality.

[18] Wilkitzki, op. cit., n. 7, p. 4.

[19] Project group on the Protection of the Environment through Criminal Law (PC-R-FN).

[20] Cf. Wilkitzki, op. cit., n. 7, p. 4.

[21] Convention of Schengen June 14, 1985 ('Schengen I'), GMB1. 1986, pp. 79 et seq., as well as the Convention for the application of the Convention of Schengen June 19, 1990 ('Schengen II'), BT-Drucks. 12/2453. Member states are France, Germany, The Netherlands, Belgium, Luxembourg, Italy, Spain, Portugal; cf. Kühne, Kriminalitätsbekämpfung durch innereuropäische Grenzkontrollen? 1991.

[22] Cf. Jescheck, op. cit., n. 6, p. 951.

which have been made in the Second Schengener Treaty to get national criminal law harmonised at least in the fields of the law dealing with drugs, weapons and explosives have not been without their political problems and are far from achieving the goal of an unified criminal law.[23]

What this short review shows is that one cannot yet speak of a European criminal law in any real substantive sense. Hence the use of the method of recommendations rather than some form of normative arrangement.[24] Even where an international law has been created by the signing of conventions the conventions are not self-executing though they do create duties on the part of the states to adapt their national law.[25] Nevertheless it is now accepted that the internationalisation of crimes demands an international criminal policy.[26] The activities of the European Committee on Criminal Problems (ECCP) reflects the development which this policy has achieved in the legal systems of individual states.

The following Conventions are examples of recent development

1. The Conventions on Extradition and Mutual Assistance

At the beginning stands the desire to give a criminal the sentence he deserves. In crime prevention it is of urgent priority that the prosecution of crime does not stop at the national borders. Because of this aim extradition has changed (since the 19th century) from a political instrument of the state to a means of criminal policy[27], that is why extradition and the other instruments of legal assistance in criminal matters were the first objects of a European unification of the law.[28] In the course of the preparatory work for these two agreements an important and not to be overestimated decision was made. It was resolved that a multilateral agreement was to be given priority over the standard form bilateral agreement between individual states. The European Convention on Extradition has since been completed

---

[23] Cf. Wilkitzki, op. cit., n. 7, p. 6.

[24] Cf. Recommendations, cited in Wilkitzki op. cit., n. 7, p. 6.

[24] 'Recommendations to member states'. Published annually by the Committee of Ministers of the Council of Europe.

[25] Cf. the Convention on the non-applicability of statutory limitation to crimes against Humanity and War Crimes, from January 25, 1974, ETS Nr. 82.

[26] Kielwein, Zum gegenwärtigen Stand einer internationalen Kriminalpolitik, Festschrift für Theodor Rittler, 1957, pp. 95 et seq.

[27] Grützner, Staatspolitik und Kriminalpolitik im Auslieferungsrecht, ZStW 68 (1956), pp. 501 et seq.

[28] European Convention on Extradition, December 13, 1957 (EuAlÜbk) BGBl. 1964 II, 1371 (German edition) and European Convention on Legal Assistance in Criminal Matters April 20, 1959 (EuRHÜbk) BGBl. 1964 II, 1386 (German edition).

through two additional protocols. The additional protocol of October 15, 1975)[29] deals with extradition in cases of political crimes. It restricts the exception to extradition of political crimes in the case of specific public international crimes. The second additional protocol of March 17, 1978)[30] provides for an extension of 'accessory extradition' for crimes which are only punishable with fines, and for extradition in cases of fiscal crimes as well as extradition for the execution of sentences imposed in absentia. The European Convention on Mutual Assistance in criminal matters has also been supplemented through the additional protocol of March 17, 1979).[31] It deals in general with the extension of legal assistance to fiscal crimes.

It is not possible here to give detailed descriptions of the Conventions and their individual provisions. But some essential aspects may be mentioned.

In connection with the European Convention on Extradition (EuAlÜbk) a certain relaxation of the rigid principle of reciprocity is noticeable. The Convention puts the application of the principle of reciprocity within the discretion of the requested state. The introduction of the so-called 'accessory extradition' makes a considerable concession to meet a practical need (Art. 2 sect. 2). The Convention does not include prohibition of the extradition of a state's own nationals; but the agreement gives each contractual party the right to exclude the extradition of its nationals (Art. 6 sect. 1 letter a), a regulation which seemed mandatory in the national law of some states, for example, the Federal Republic of Germany.[32] However provisions regarding the initiation of a prosecution in the requested state which have been added as a compensation for the non-extradition of nationals may be seen as an essential step in the direction of an effective fight against criminality. Even if no duty is imposed to undertake a prosecution, the requested state is nevertheless expected to inform its prosecuting authorities of the arguments in favour of initiating its own criminal proceedings (Art. 6 sect. 2).

The practical impact of the Convention lies in its priority over all other existing bilateral agreements between the contracting states, which it replaces. Bi- or multi-lateral conventions will in the future only be admissible between the contracting partners to complement or to simplify its application (Art. 28). A defect of this convention is that it makes it possible for the parties – as expressly mentioned in the treaty (Art. 26 sect. 1) – to make practically unlimited reservations.

---

[29] ETS Nr. 86.

[30] ETS Nr. 98, BGBl. 1990 II, 118, 119.

[31] ETS Nr. 99.

[32] Cf. Art. 16 Section 2 of the German Basic Law (Grundgesetz).

The European Convention on Legal Assistance also lays the foundations for an expansion and simplification of mutual assistance in criminal procedures. The attempt to give the most comprehensive legal assistance finds its most visible expression in renouncing a common element in relation to legal assistance in existing extradition requirements. It does so e.g. by basically dropping the principle of double criminality.

2. Convention on Supervision

After having made first steps towards an international regulation of criminal matters in Europe, the European Council felt encouraged to pursue more far-reaching plans. A properly understood international criminal policy could not limit itself to putting the penal function of criminal law into effect across the borders. In the last decades the stress on the preventive aspects of criminal law has led to a number of important reforms in national legal systems. The preventive possibilities of modern sentencing systems are characterised by the emphasis on giving the sentenced person a chance of rehabilitation. If these advances in national law are not to end at the national borders, they should not depend on the nationality of the criminal. National courts often abstain from ordering conditional measures because there is no way to observe the conduct of the sentenced person during the period of probation or to supervise the observance of conditions in cases where the sentenced person returns to a foreign state and escapes from surveillance. This is intended to be remedied by the European Convention on the Supervision of Conditionally Sentenced or Conditionally Released Offenders of 1964,[33] which provides for the observation of conditionally sentenced or conditionally released persons in the state of their residence. It also provides for the possibility of cancelling the postponement of a sentence and for its implementation.

3. The Convention on Road Traffic

The need for the enforcement of foreign sentences is shown also in traffic offences. Quite apart from the fact that the extradition of nationals may be prohibited – which often puts a bar to extradition – most cases are such minor offences that extradition is not considered. Therefore the European Convention on the Punishment of Road Traffic Offences of November 30, 1964[34] provides, among other things, for the possibility that the contracting

---

[33] ETS Nr. 51, Convention on Supervision.
[34] ETS Nr. 52, Convention on Road Traffic Offences.

partners may mutually request the enforcement of sentences, even sentences of imprisonment.

4. The International Validity of Criminal Judgements

The European Convention on the International Validity of Criminal Judgements of 1970[35] at last expands the possibility of enforcement to all sentences. With the recognition of the international effect of the principle 'ne bis in idem' this convention not only closes a gap within the national legal systems which often content themselves with the principle of deduction, it also closes a gap of the ECHR which does not in itself nor in an additional protocol guarantee the prohibition of double punishment.

5. The Transfer of Proceedings

An international criminal policy which is bound to modern principles cannot content itself with granting international validity to a criminal sentence at the end of a prosecution. The requirements of criminal policy have to be taken into account at the earlier stage of the regulation of competence. The European Convention on the Transfer of Proceedings in Criminal Matters[36] tries to balance the conflicting interests of an effective prosecution on the one hand and resocialization of the criminal on the other by the means of a new European competence, by limiting the reasons which justify a request for transfer of proceedings or its refusal. The convention thus modifies the legality principle of the national systems which impose a duty to prosecute by allowing every contracting state to fulfil its duty to prosecute by transferring criminal proceeding to the requesting state, in the cases covered by the Convention.

6. Convention on Terrorism

With the European Convention on the Suppression of Terrorism of January 27, 1977[37] a signal should have been set against the frequently practised means of blackmailing allegations in police states and military dictatorships. The Convention[38] is not a treaty on extradition. It does not

---

[35] ETS Nr. 70, Convention on the International Validity of Criminal Judgements.
[36] ETS Nr. 73.
[37] ETS Nr. 90, Convention on Terrorism.
[38] Cf. for a detailed discussion Bartsch, Das Europäische Übereinkommen zur Bekämpfung des Terrorismus, NJW 1977, pp. 1985 et seq.; Stein, Die Europäische Konvention zur Bekämpfung des Terrorismus, ZaöRV 1977, pp. 668 et seq.; Nowack,

create new duties to extradite; rather it modifies the respective treaty regulations about the non-extradition of political offenders. Art. 1 enumerates offences which are not to be considered as political crimes and are therefore not be excluded from extradition. Art. 2 defines violent actions of terrorists in a more comprehensive way than Art. 1. But the regulation is merely an optional clause.

7. Convention on Transfer of Prisoners

The European Convention on the International Validity of Criminal Judgements has basically been overtaken by the European Convention on the Transfer of Sentenced Persons from March 31, 1983.[39]/[40] The Convention on Transfer of 1983 differs from the Convention on the International Validity of Criminal Judgements in a number of respects. The request for transfer cannot only come from the sentencing state but also from the state of which the offender is a national (Art. 2 III). The consent of the sentenced person to be transferred is a prerequisition of admissibility (Art. 3 I letter d, Art. 7). It does not oblige the contractual states to transfer (and therefore it does not numerate reasons for a denial of a request) and it is open to accession by other states which are not members of the Council of Europe.

With the possibility of the offender's country requesting a transfer and the consent of the sentenced person being a prerequisition of any transfer the humanitarian aspect of the concern of a state for its nationals is taken into account as well as the question of mutual assistance in criminal

---

Die Europäische Konvention zur Verhütung der Folter. Regelmäßige Bersuche von Haftanstalten durch Europäisches Komitee zur Verhütung der Folter ab 1989, EuGRZ 1988, 537 et seq.; Puhl, Europäisches Anti-Folter-Abkommen, NJW 1990, pp. 3057 et seq.

[39] Convention on the Transfer of Prisoners, ETS Nr. 112, Gesetz zu dem Übereinkommen vom 1.3.1983 über die Überstellung verurteilter Personen, vom 26.9.1991, BGB1. 1991 II, 1006; with Überstellungsausführungsgesetz - ÜAG - vom 26.9.1991, BGB1 I, 1954; cf. Epp, Der Ausländer im Strafvollzug, ÖJZ 1982, pp. 119 et seq.; Bartsch, Strafvollstreckung im Heimatstaat, NJW 1984, pp. 513 et seq.; Schomburg, Lagodny, Richtlinien für den Strafverteidiger in Strafverfahren mit Auslandsbezug – neueste Entwicklung im internationalen Rechtshilfeverkehr, StV 1992, pp. 239, 240. Concerning the 'Legal Assistance in the Execution of Foreign Judgements', see sections 48-58 in Vogler, Wilkitzki, Kommentar zum Gesetz über die internationale Rechtshilfe in Strafsachen. Further Vogler, Das neue Gesetz über die internationale Rechtshilfe in Strafsachen, NJW 1983, 2114, 2121; also Vogler, Rechtshilfe durch Vollstreckung ausländischer Strafurteile, Festschrift für Jescheck, 1985, p. 1381.

[40] The scope of application of the Convention on Transfer is limited to sanctions limiting the freedom of a person and to cases in which the sentenced person still resides in the sentencing state.

matters. This makes it possible to execute a sentence in the home state particularly in cases in which the punishment is above the usual penalty and/or has to be executed under extremely difficult conditions in the foreign state.[41]

8. Money Laundering Convention

The Convention of the European Council Concerning Laundering, Search Seizure, and Confiscation of the Proceeds from Crime of November 8, 1990[42] extends – going beyond the Vienna Convention on Drugs of 1988[43] – the statutory definition of the offence of money laundering beyond the field of drug offences. The contracting states agree either to initiate proceedings for confiscation or to grant legal assistance.[44]

9. Protocol of Information

Although it is not strictly a Convention on criminal law an Additional Protocol to the European Convention on Information about Foreign Law of March 15, 1978[45] is nevertheless of considerable importance for the conventions on criminal law. The Additional Protocol includes the criminal law as part of the reciprocal system of information. It provides that the participating states may upon request give information about their substantive and procedural law as well as the organisation of courts in the field of criminal law and their procedures for enforcement of the law. This should facilitate co-operation between European states particularly in the area of double criminality[46] which is required in many cases.

---

[41] Cf. Vogler in: Vogler, Wilkitzki, Gesetz über die internationale Rechtshilfe in Strafsachen (IRG), before section 48, footnotes 10 et seq.

[42] ETS Nr. 141.

[43] Convention of the United Nations against illegal dealing with addictive drugs and psychotropic substances December 19, 1988, UN-Documentation E/CONF/82/15.

[44] Cf. Krauskopf, Geldwäscherei und organisiertes Verbrechen als europäische Herausforderung, ZStrR 108 (1991), pp. 385 et seq., 389.

[45] ETS Nr. 97.

[46] Jescheck, op. cit., n. 6, p. 958.

III THE IMPORTANCE OF THE EUROPEAN HUMAN RIGHTS CONVENTION ON CRIMINAL LAW

The European Convention on Human Rights of 1950 can be seen as a form of European basic law.[47] It too has had an impact upon the substantive and procedural criminal law and has been brought into force in all states of the European Council. Art.3 is for example significant for criminal law as it prohibits torture and inhuman or degrading punishment or treatment as well as Art. 7 which lays down the principle of legality.[48]

More important are the provisions of the ECHR in the field criminal procedure, Art. 3 guarantees – apart from the prohibition of torture – freedom of statement by the accused as well as witnesses. Art. 5, which regulates the preconditions of arrest, provides, in section 2 that every arrested person has to be informed about the reason for his arrest immediately and in a language which he or she is able to understand. It provides in section 3 that every arrested or imprisoned person has to be brought before a judge immediately. According to section 4 a 'habeas-corpus-proceeding' has to be provided which gives every person arrested or otherwise deprived of his liberty the right to appeal to a court which immediately has to decide about the legality of the arrest and which – in the case of illegality - is to arrange that the arrested will be set free. Of special importance is Art. 6 which sets out the European principles of a 'fair trial'. According to these principles everybody has the right that his case will be heard 'justly', publicly and within reasonable time and by an independent, impartial and legitimate court.

Section 2 contains the presumption of innocence. Section 3 sets out the minimum standard of rights which every accused has to be granted in criminal proceedings. The Convention does not grant the right to asylum or recognise the principle 'ne bis in idem'. This protection is included in the resolution of the European Parliament of March 16, 1984[49] but without becoming valid law automatically, because the European Parliament has no legislative power.[50]

---

[47] ECHR, BGB1. 1952 II, 686, 953; 1968 II, 1116, 1120; 1989 II, 547.

[48] The legality principle is in the form of the prohibition of retroaction contained in Art. 21 of the 'Declaration of Basic Rights and Basic Liberties' of the European Parliament April 12, 1989, EuGRZ 1989, p. 205.

[49] EuGRZ 1984, 355 et seq.; cf. also Karel de Gucht, EuGRZ 1984, pp. 349 et seq.

[50] Cf. Jescheck, op. cit., n. 6, p. 954.

IV CONCLUSIONS

The number of European Conventions – of which only a few could be mentioned here[51] – cannot hide the fact that the attempts to create a European law by means of Conventions on criminal law have achieved only limited success. Only the Conventions on Extradition, Legal Assistance and Transfer of Prisoners have had any real impact. The prospects of an extension of the system of Conventions are rather difficult to estimate. The limits on progress which have occurred even in the narrow circle of the member states of the Council of Europe can only be overcome, if the spirit that accompanied the European Council at its beginning can successfully be renewed and the mutual trust, without which effective co-operation will not be possible, can be strengthened. The work of the subcommittee 'Changing Europe' suggests that this may be happening.[52] A new incentive could also come from the creation of the European Union, the starting point of which was already made with the European Common Market according to Art. 13 of the Uniform European Act, which went into effect on December 31, 1992. Such a Union naturally needs the protection of a criminal law. Art. 18 of the Act takes this into account in providing measures for the unification of the laws of member states which include the criminal regulations for the protection of the Common Market.[53] But the limited role which the criminal law has in the process of unification can still be seen in the fact that the fight against criminality across the border will basically remain within the national domain. The Europeanisation of the administration of justice has been incorporated into the Community only to a very limited extent.[54]

---

[51] Cf. in detail under appendix VI.

[52] Cf. above II.

[53] Cf. Jescheck, op. cit., n. 6, p. 951; on the protection of the financial interests of the European Community see also the duty to co-ordinate which is expressly provided in Art. 209a of the EC-Treaty in the version of the Treaty of Maastricht of February 7, 1992 on the European Union. Concerning the Treaty of Maastricht see Graf Stauffenberg, Langenfeld, Maastricht – ein Fortschritt für Europa? ZRP 1992, pp. 252 et seq.

[54] Graf Stauffenberg, Langenfeld, op. cit., n. 53, p. 254.

V APPENDIX

List of the Conventions on criminal law of the Council of Europe in the order of the official collection of agreements of the European Council (ETS).

ETS Nr. 24   European Convention on Extradition December 13, 1957; became valid on April 18, 1960.

ETS Nr.30   European Convention on Mutual Assistance in Criminal Matters April 20, 1959; became valid on June 12, 1962.

ETS Nr. 51   European Convention on the Supervision of Conditionally Sentenced or Conditionally Released Offenders November 30, 1964; became valid on August 22, 1975.

ETS Nr. 52   European Convention on the Punishment of Road Traffic Offences November 30, 1964; became valid on July 18, 1972.

ETS Nr. 70   European Convention on the International Validity of Criminal Judgements May 28, 1970; became valid on July 26, 1974.

ETS Nr. 71   European Convention on the Repatriation of Minors May 28, 1970 which did not become effective.

EST Nr. 73   European Convention on the Transfer of Proceedings in Criminal Matter May 15, 1972; became valid on March 30, 1978.

EST Nr. 82   European Convention on the Non-Applicability of Statutory Limitation to Crimes against Humanity and War Crimes January 25, 1974 which did not become effective.

EST Nr. 86   Additional Protocol to the European Convention on Extradition October 15, 1975; became valid on August 20, 1975.

EST Nr. 88   European Convention on the International Effects of Deprivation of the Right to drive a Motor Vehicle June 3, 1976; became valid on April 28, 1983.

EST Nr. 90   European Convention on the Suppression of Terrorism January 27, 1977; became valid on August 4, 1978.

EST Nr. 97   Additional Protocol to the European Convention on Information on Foreign Law March 15, 1978; became valid on August 31, 1979.

EST Nr. 98   Second Additional Protocol to the European Convention on Extradition March 17, 1978; became valid on June 5, 1983.

ETS Nr. 99   Additional Protocol to the European Convention on Mutual Assistance in Criminal Matters March 17, 1978; became valid on April 12, 1982.

ETS Nr. 101   European Convention on the Control of the Acquisition and Possession of Firearms by Individuals June 28, 1978; became valid on July 1, 1982.

ETS Nr. 112   European Convention on the Transfer of Sentenced Persons March 21, 1983; became valid on July 4, 1985.

ETS Nr. 116   European Convention on the Compensation of Victims of Violent Crimes November 24, 1983; became valid on February 2, 1988.

ETS Nr. 119   European Convention on Offences Relating to Cultural Property June 23, 1985 which has not taken effect.

ETS Nr. 141   Convention on Laundering, Search Seizure and Confiscation of the Proceeds from Crime November 8, 1990 which has not taken effect.

9. Scholarship And Constitutionalism In The European Union: The Curious Absence of Critique

Gavin W. Anderson – University of Warwick

I INTRODUCTION

In his seminal 1986 article 'Eurocracy and Distrust,'[1] Professor Joseph Weiler noted that the already burgeoning literature on the European Court of Justice's fundamental human rights jurisprudence contained little or no critical scholarship.[2] In a co-authored work nine years later, and in spite of increased academic activity, he was able to remark that '[a] comprehensive truly critical analysis of the Court's human rights jurisprudence is yet to be written'.[3] This paper considers the issue of the lacuna of scholarship in this field suggested by Weiler in three ways. First, it considers the actual extent of the gap in the academic literature: This is approached by a detailed examination of the most controversial exchange of views in the area to date to demonstrate the narrowness of the ground presently being contested. Second, it is argued that there are undesirable consequences of conducting the discourse within such a limited framework of analysis: while the problem with the absence of critical scholarship is not necessarily that its conclusions are compelling and should be accepted, the most important question about the adoption of a fundamental rights jurisprudence goes unasked, namely, what is the political impact on the policy-making process. Third, some possible new directions for scholarship will be suggested, which, if followed, would articulate explicitly the political (as opposed to

---

[1] J.H.H. Weiler 'Eurocracy and Distrust: Some Questions concerning the role of the European Court of Justice in the Protection of Fundamental Human Rights within the Legal Order of the European Communities' (1986) 61 Washington L.R. 1103.

[2] *Ibid.* at 1105-6.

[3] J.H.H. Weiler & Nicholas J.S. Lockhart '"Taking Rights Seriously" Seriously: The European Court of Justice and Its Fundamental Rights Jurisprudence – Part I' (1995) 32 Common Market Law Review 51 at 57.

legal) issues of human rights, which it is submitted require to be addressed as a matter of urgency.

II THE DEVELOPMENT OF CONSTITUTIONALISM IN THE EUROPEAN UNION

The adoption of human rights discourse by the Court of Justice is familiar and well-documented. Although the EC Treaties (or any of their major amendments) do not contain a Charter (or Bill) of human rights, the ECJ has over the years developed a jurisprudence of fundamental human rights. Initially, the Court of Justice's human rights jurisprudence was developed to fight off a challenge to the supremacy of EC law from the German courts, which led the ECJ to declare that 'respect for fundamental rights forms an integral part of the general principles of EC law protected by the Court of Justice'.[4] The content for these rights was to be found in both the common constitutional traditions of the member states,[5] and the international treaties to which the member states were signatories, such as the European Convention on Human Rights.[6] For the 1970s and 1980s, these rights were held to apply only to acts of the Community, but in the late 1980s, the reach of fundamental rights began to expand into the field of member states' law.

The expansion of the ECJ's human rights jurisprudence came in two stages. First, the Court held that where member state legislation is implementing a Community measure, the member state measure must also respect human rights. Thus in *Wachauf* v. *FRG*[7], the ECJ examined a German law implementing an EC Regulation on the transference of milk quotas for its compatibility with human rights. The second stage of expansion was to hold that the Court of Justice's human rights jurisprudence would apply where member state measures would be illegal under EC law but for a derogation from one of the four freedoms of the Treaty of Rome e.g. on grounds of public policy or public health under Article 56 EEC. For example, in the *ERT* case[8] it was held that a otherwise justifiable derogation from the free movement of goods and services giving a broadcasting monopoly to the state channel must be appraised in light of

---

4   *Internationale Handelsgesellschaft* Case 11/70 [1970] ECR 1125 at 1134.
5   *Ibid.*
6   See *Nold* v. *Commission* Case 4/73 [1974] 491 at 507.
7   Case 5/88[1989] ECR 2639
8   *Elliniki Radiophonis Tileorassi* v. *Dimotiki Etairia Pliroforissis* Case 260/89 [1991] ECR I-2925.

its compatibility with human rights (and in particular, Article 10 of ECHR). Although there is disagreement as to how far these two developments extend into the laws of member states, at the most conservative estimate, the Court of Justice will assess member state legislation for its compatibility with human rights in at least two situations:

(1) where the member state legislation is implementing a Community measure, and ;

(2) where the member state measure would be illegal under EC law but for a derogation from one of the four freedoms of the Treaty of Rome e.g. on grounds of public policy or public health.[9]

III ACADEMIC LITERATURE

As a result of these developments, it is now possible to speak about constitutionalism in the sense of a supreme or constitutional court (the ECJ) having the ability to strike down laws because of their incompatibility with human rights, at least to some degree, in a European Union context. Not surprisingly, the appearance of the constitutionalist phenomenon has given rise to considerable academic activity, and this has taken at least three directions so far. Some commentators have concentrated on doctrinal analysis, and initially this involved the question of identifying the various sources of the Court's jurisprudence,[10] as well as trying to determine the precise extent of the reach of EC human rights guarantees *vis-à-vis* the actions of member states.[11] The dynamic nature of this enterprise (and therefore the difficulty in accurately characterising the state of the jurisprudence) is highlighted by various articles in response to recent developments which have either a potential impact on, or are themselves a development of the Court's jurisprudence.[12]

---

[9] Weiler & Lockhart, *supra* note 3 at 64.

[10] Most of this work has concentrated on the respective influences on each other of the European Convention of Human Rights and EC Law: see e.g. M.H. Mendelson 'The Impact of European Community Law on the Implementation of the European Convention on Human Rights' (1983) YBEL 99, and; N Foster 'The European Court of Justice and the European Convention for the Protection of Human Rights' (1987) Human Rights LJ 245.

[11] See e.g. M.H. Mendelson 'The European Court of Justice and Human Rights' (1981) 1 YBEL 125; M.A Dauses 'The Protection of Fundamental Rights in the Community Legal Order' (1985) European LR 398; H.G. Schermers' 'The European Communities bound by Fundamental Human Rights' (1990) Common Market LR 249.

[12] With regard to the former, see L.B. Kroosgaard 'Fundamental Rights in the European Community after Masstricht' (1993) Legal Issues of European Integration 99, for a

A second stream of writing embodies a more prescriptive element, and
has moved to perhaps the next stage, i.e. how the human rights basis in EU
law may be developed and strengthened.   This may be based on the
assumption that there may be omissions in the existing level of human
rights protection which need addressing,[13] or that there may be ways of
improving existing arrangements.   The latter idea arises in a number of
contexts: the possible EU accession to the ECHR,[14] the relationship
between the courts in Luxembourg and Strasbourg were that to happen,[15] or
the possibility of promulgating the EU's own Charter of Fundamental
Rights.[16] The majority of writing within this stream takes the value of the
enforcement of human rights by the European court of justice as a given,
and as a result there is an absence of reflection before proceeding to discuss
the various reforms suggested.[17] A third strand to the literature has taken a
more speculative form, questioning the motives for the Court of Justice
expanding its jurisprudence in this way, [18] and this will be examined in
greater depth *infra*.

There are perhaps two striking features which emerge from sampling this
literature.   The first is that virtually all of the contributions come from
people writing in the area of EC law; there have been little, if any,
contributions from people who have an interest in comparative
constitutionalism. It is certainly not surprising that those engaged in the
study of the EC would find much of interest in these important
developments;   however, it is noteworthy that the appearance of
constitutionalism on potentially its biggest stage should go unremarked by
constitutionalist scholars to this extent. The second and more important
feature (as Weiler has noted), and this is perhaps linked to the first, is the
complete absence of a debate well-rehearsed in the comparative literature
between advocates of constitutionalism – for convenience referred to as

---

detailed discussion of recent case-law extending the Court's jurisprudence, see G. de
Burca 'Fundamental Rights and the Reach of EC Law' (1993) 13 Oxford Journal of
Legal Studies 283.

[13] See D. O'Keefe & P.W. Twomey *Legal Issues of the Maastricht Treaty* (1994)
Chancery; London at Ch. 8 'The European Union: three Pillars without a Human
Rights Foundation', p. 121.

[14] *Ibid.* at p.125.

[15] See H.G. Schermers 'The European Court of Human Rights after the merger' (1993)
European Law Review 493.

[16] See K. Lenaerts 'Fundamental Rights to be included in a Community Catalogue'
(1991) European Law Review 367.

[17] For a welcome exception to this general rule see A. Clapham 'A Human Rights Policy
for the European Community' (1990) YBEL 309.

[18] See J. Coppel & A. O'Neill 'The European Court of Justice: Taking Rights
Seriously?' (1992) 29 CMLR 669.

those writing within the *liberal rights paradigm*[19] – and a tradition of *critical scholarship* which questions the desirability of judicially enforced constitutional rights as part of a system of governance. The absence seems doubly curious because although critical scholarship on constitutionalism has its origins in North America,[20] it has been quite forcibly advanced with regard to the constitutional courts of a number of member states,[21] and it is also well known in the Bill of Rights debate in the UK.[22]

IV THE CONSTITUTIONALISM DEBATE

It might be useful to outline some of the key elements of the above debate on constitutionalism before proceeding to consider the extent to which it is absent from the existing literature on the ECJ's human rights jurisprudence. To do so, it will be helpful to employ ideal-typical models of the liberal rights paradigm and its critique. The debate itself essentially turns on whether the protection of human rights by a constitutional court is a question of law or politics. For the critical tradition, constitutionalism represents an attempt to *depoliticise* political issues by *legalising* them. However, in the words of one long-standing critic of the constitutionalist enterprise, 'to require a supreme court to make certain kinds of political decisions does not make these decisions any less political'.[23] Both sides are then separated on how they approach the following issues:

i. Textual Authority of Constitutional Rights

One of the principal tenets of the liberal rights paradigm is the idea that judges are constrained by the text they interpret and apply. It is usually

---

[19] This is a more short-hand version of what Weiler and Lockhart refer to as 'the classical liberal rights theory paradigm,' *supra* note 3 at 54.

[20] See e.g. R.W. Galloway *Justice for All? The Rich and Poor in Supreme Court History 1790-1990* (1991) Carolina Academic Press; Durham, N.C.; M.V. Tushnet *Red, White and Blue: A Critical Analysis of Constitutional Law* (1988) Harvard University Press; Cambridge, Mass.; M. Mandel *The Charter of Rights and the Legalisation of Politics in Canada* (2nd ed, 1994) Thompson Educational Press, Toronto.

[21] See e.g. A. Stone *The Birth of Judicial Politics in France* (1992) OUP, Oxford; M.Mandel 'Legal Politics Italian Style' in *The Globalisation of Judicial Politics* (1994); & C. Landfried 'Judicial Policy-Making in Germany: the Federal Constitutional Court'(1992) 15 West European Politics 50.

[22] See J.A.G. Griffith 'The Political Constitution' (1979) Modern Law Review 1.

[23] *Ibid.* at 16.

accepted that there may be different approaches to interpretation open to the court,[24] but that there is a right, or at least more preferable, choice for the court to make. The most distinguished exponent of this approach is of course Ronald Dworkin, who argues that by the correct application of 'principled' reasoning, the court will be able to come to the 'right answer'.[25] The critical tradition points, *inter alia*, to inconsistency in legal doctrine to dispute the notion of constraint. According to Mark Tushnet, there is nothing inherent in the U.S. constitution which would prevent that document being interpreted according to a form of socialism or alternatively racist or sexist values.[26] Thus, terms such as 'freedom of expression' are too vague in themselves to provide an answer to any constitutional dispute before the court.

ii. The Role of the Judges

The answer to the question of constraint in turn determines the importance placed by either side on the role of the judiciary. Advocates of constitutionalism within the liberal rights paradigm who would not rely wholly on the constraint position might instead argue that by virtue of their training and insulation from the political process, judges are to be trusted, in preference to politicians, to decide issues of human rights. In either case, their personal input is negligible. For the critic, because the issues raised in constitutional litigation are inherently political and as judges are not constrained by the text, *their* politics must have a key role in deciding cases. Accordingly, given the background of most members of the judiciary, the key question is 'why we should trust, and privilege over any other, the value judgements of an elite group of predominantly white, upper middle class, male lawyers'.[27]

---

[24] For a survey of differing techniques employed by the US Supreme Court see P. Bobbitt *Constitutional Fate* (1982) OUP, Oxford; and for a critical account of the impossibility of distinguishing between them, see P. Brest 'The Fundamental Rights Controversy: The Essential Contradictions of Judicial Review' (1982) 90 Yale Law Journal 1082.

[25] See R. Dworkin 'Political Judges and the Rule of Law' in *Comparative Constitutional Law (Festschrift in honour of Professor P.K. Tripathi)* (1989) M.P. Singh (ed) Eastern Book Co., Lucknow at p.3.

[26] Tushnet, *supra* note 20 at p. 140; Tushnet's comments are specifically made in response to Dworkin's thesis that the judicial role is to interpret the constitution by implementing principles which are to be found in the existing institutional morality of society. However, they should also be read in the wider context of the impossibility of compelling judges towards a particular decision by mere words alone.

[27] J.C. Bakan 'Constitutional Arguments: Interpretation and Legitimacy in Canadian Constitutional Thought' (1989) 27 Osgoode Hall Law Journal 123 at 175.

iii. Democracy and the Rule of Law

The foregoing also informs whether constitutionalism can be reconciled with democracy and the rule of law. Within the liberal rights paradigm, democracy embodies more than the simple one-person one-vote notion of majoritarianism, and the protection of individual rights is a substantive element necessary in any true democratic society. That this protection is administered by unelected judges is justified by contrasting the principled resolution of disputes by judges within the rule of law with their resolution on policy grounds by politicians, where the ability of the majority to oppress the minority is all too evident. For the critic, handing political decisions over to unelected and generally unremoveable judges, who are not constrained by the texts they interpret, seems a strange way of correcting the faults of majoritarianism. The rule of law which is upheld by these means is the authoritarian version whereby the judges' rules prevail, rather than the democratic version, where judges too are restrained.[28]

Criteria of assessment
Accordingly, the criteria by which a constitutional court's human rights jurisprudence is assessed differs sharply between the two models. For the advocates within the paradigm, what is important is the extent to which individual rights are being protected by the court in question, an important element of which is the doctrinal coherence of the courts in effecting this protection.[29] The critique does not necessarily accept that protection of individual rights is the *raison d'être* of constitutionalism[30]; instead it evaluates constitutionalist jurisprudence by reference to *political* criteria, that is in terms of its likely impact on political outcomes. In Tushnet's words, the key question is: '[are constitutional rights] likely to have a relatively *progressive* effect, or a relatively *conservative* one?'[31] The

---

[28] See Mandel, *supra* note 20 at pp.42/3.

[29] Weiler and Lockhart refer to this methodology as 'doctrinal': 'examining the jurisprudence of the Court on the basis of textual reading, explication and exegesis and evaluating the cases by reference to formal criteria such as consistency, clarity, consistency of 'legal reasoning' and broader teleological considerations.' *supra*, note 3 at 54.

[30] E.g. in the US context, Galloway suggests that the constitution had more to do with the preservation of pre-war debts than preserving human rights (*supra*, note 20 at pp.11-15); Mandel places the Canadian Charter of Rights and Freedoms in the context of defeating the Quebec independentiste movement (*supra*, note 20 at pp. 19-27); and Stone links the creation of the *Conseil Constitutionnel* with establishing de Gaulle's authority over the National Assembly (*supra*, note 20 at pp 46-50).

[31] M.V. Tushnet 'Living with a Bill of Rights' in Understanding Human Rights (1996) C.A. Gearty & A. Tomkins (eds.) Mansell, London (emphasis in original).

answer to this takes two forms in the critical tradition: the weaker version stresses the formal nature of the process of judicialisation, and questions whether the form of legal discourse, with its emphasis on a dispute *inter partes* and using the language of individual rights, is appropriate for decisions of a political nature, where the wider impact of the decision should be considered. The stronger version looks to the substantive impact of constitutionalism, and claims that the resolution of political issues by this means is more likely to lead to a relatively conservative or deregulatory effect on political outcomes i.e. the preservation of the legal *status quo* which means constitutionalism is particularly advantageous for the economically powerful.

V THE 'TAKING RIGHTS SERIOUSLY?' CONTROVERSY

By far the most contentious exchange of views to date on the subject is that conducted in the pages of the Common Market Law Review between Joseph Weiler and Nicholas Lockhart, and Jason Coppel and Aidan O'Neill. This arose from Coppel and O'Neill's controversial 1992 article *'The European Court of Justice: Taking Rights Seriously?'*[32] in which they launch a sustained attack on the ECJ's motivation for expanding its human rights jurisprudence. Their conclusion that the Court had used fundamental rights instrumentally and so brought its standing into disrepute[33] might at first glance suggest that they were attempting to fill the critical gap Weiler had identified in 1986. In his co-authored response, Weiler employs some forceful language to dispute Coppel and O'Neill's conclusion, claiming at one point that there is 'a huge gap between their scathing condemnation of the Court [of Justice] and the intellectual apparatuses on which their condemnation is based'.[34] Given the strength of the views expressed one might have thought that this was a disagreement of some import: however, it will be argued that in fact there is more on which the two camps agree than disagree on fundamental jurisprudential matters (and that the gap in scholarship Weiler identifies still exists). Before proceeding, it would be useful to outline the terms of the debate.

The Coppel and O'Neill article makes the claim that 'in the cases in which the Court has adopted fundamental rights discourse, it has been the

---

[32] *Supra*, note 18.
[33] *Ibid.* at 690.
[34] Weiler and Lockhart, *supra* note 3 at 57.

general Community rule or the Community objective which has prevailed against claims as to the violation of fundamental human rights'.[35] This result is not considered merely accidental: it is the result of manipulation of the case-law on the Court's part. They develop their argument by an analysis of some of the important cases. Taking first the case of *Wachauf* v. *FRG* (referred to above) which concerned a dairy farmer who was not entitled under German law to compensation on the transference of his milk quota on the expiry of the farm lease. The German law being questioned was in implementation of an EC Regulation on the transference of milk quotas, and it was argued that the absence of compensation was an 'unconstitutional expropriation' and that his rights to property were protected under the fundamental rights jurisprudence of the ECJ. Although the Court ruled that national implementing legislation must be in accord with its fundamental rights requirements, it held that the Regulation in question allowed compensation to be paid, and so the fault lay with the implementing legislation. What troubles Coppel and O'Neill about this case is that the Court also commented on the fact that the fundamental rights it protects are not absolute and that national implementing legislation is only bound to respect them 'as far as possible', which leads them to the conclusion that as far as Community legislation is concerned, the Court if necessary will elevate the Community objective over the fundamental right at issue.[36]

They contrast the Court's treatment of Community measures in *Wachauf* with its treatment of national law in the *ERT* case. This case involved a challenge by a private TV station to the monopoly of broadcasting in Greece enjoyed by the nationalised television station ERT on the grounds, *inter alia*, that this constituted an infringement of the freedom of goods and services guaranteed by the EC Treaty. The Court held that this infringement was justified under the public policy derogation of Article 56 of the EC Treaty, but also stated that where a member state sought to rely on this derogation, it could only do so insofar as this was compatible with the Court's fundamental rights case-law. In this case, this resulted in the national court being told that the derogation allowing the broadcasting monopoly must be appraised in light of the guarantee of freedom of expression in Article 10 of the ECHR. For Coppel and O'Neill, this shows the Court erecting a further obstacle to the validity of the national law in question, in contrast with the more lax treatment of the Community measure in *Wachauf*. This contrast between the constitutionality of the

---

[35] Coppel and O'Neill *supra* note 18 at 682.
[36] *Ibid.* at 684.

Regulation in_*Wachauf* with the extension of Community law into what would otherwise have been an exempted area of Greek law in *ERT* is used by them to support their analysis that the Court is in fact using the language of human rights while its resolution of cases in fact depends on extending the competences of the Community.[37]

In their response Weiler and Lockhart disagree with Coppel and O'Neill in fairly forthright terms. Their argument is basically two-fold. First, dealing with the ECJ's motive, they agree that Coppel and O'Neill may well be right that the Court's jurisprudence has had the effect of furthering EU-integration, but state that this is not necessarily incompatible with protecting human rights. In an earlier work, Weiler had commented on the use of the fourteenth amendment by the US Supreme Court in the process of American integration.[38]   As far as the implicit manipulation of fundamental rights doctrine is concerned, they find the charge not proven: instead, they explain apparent inconsistencies in the doctrine like *Cinetheque*[39] (where the ECJ rejected the argument that a French law which relied on Art 56 exemption was thereby subject to its human rights jurisdiction) as evidence of an aversion on the part of the Court to the integrationist consequences of expanding its human rights jurisprudence. Instead, their conclusion is of 'an almost reluctant Court, pushed *perhaps in the interests of taking rights seriously*, to gradually expand the exercise of its [human rights] jurisdiction so as not to allow potential violations under the canopy of Community law to escape European Community judicial protection'.[40]

Their second point is to refute the empirical basis of Coppel and O'Neill's claim that the Court of Justice has always subordinated human rights interests to the Community will at issue, and lists a number of cases in which the Court of Justice has actually struck down a Community measure for its alleged violation of human rights standards. These include cases asserting procedural rights, such as *Al-Jubail Fertilizer* v. *Council*[41] where an anti-dumping duty was declared void because it infringed the right to a fair hearing; or cases upholding the right to equal treatment, e.g. *Weiser* v. *Caisse nationale des barreuax francais*[42] where a staff regulation was struck down as it treated officials differently depending on their previous occupation; or cases following the principle of *non bis in idem* like

---

[37] *Ibid.* at 684/5.

[38] Weiler, *supra* note 1 at 1136/7.

[39] Cases 60-1/84 [1985] ECR 2605.

[40] Weiler and Lockhart, *supra* note 3 at 71 (emphasis added).

[41] Case C-49/88 [1991] ECR 3187.

[42] Case C-37/89 [1990] ECR 2395.

Vandemoortele NV v. *Commission*.[43] Their conclusion on this point is that the Court's human rights record is far more complex than Coppel and O'Neill would suggest.[44]

Extent of disagreement?

In terms of the broad spectrum of academic viewpoints which are located within the literature on constitutionalism in other jurisdictions, what is striking from the exchange, especially given language often used, is how little Coppel and O'Neill, and Weiler and Lockhart actually do disagree. As stated above, one might have expected a controversy of significance, possibly in terms of the debate between the liberal rights paradigm and the critical tradition, but from reading the various articles, it becomes clear that there is much more on fundamental jurisprudential matters on which they agree than disagree.

First, both sides' framework of reference is the gap between what should be the level of human rights protection in the EU constitutional regime, and what prevails, i.e. while they disagree on the extent of that gap, they do agree that the primary function of human rights is the protection of the individual. This is apparent from the empirical claims which each side makes, the proving or disproving of which is crucial to the claims they make about the Court's motivation. Implicit in this methodology is that constitutionalist scholarship is to a large extent about the mechanical measuring of the distance between what ought to be and what is, where what ought to be is the better protection of the individual's rights. Thus Coppel and O'Neill attack the Court's conclusion with regard to both *Wachauf* and *ERT* on the grounds that it ignored the task of normative reconciliation (in order to promote integration), while Weiler and Lockhart reading of the situation is a gradual narrowing of the gap as the Court (perhaps reluctantly) embraces more the concept of individual protection. The tests both apply are the same: it is in their application of the tests that discord emerges.

Second, implicit in their disagreement is the assumption that an optimal, although not necessarily a complete, level of human rights protection is possible and attainable by means of constitutional adjudication, i.e. that there is a right way for a constitutional court to interpret human rights in order to maximise individuals' protection, and that individuals' rights are protected to the extent this is done properly. The cause of Coppel and O'Neill's opprobrium with regard to the same two cases is their contrasting

---

[43] Case C-172/89 [1990] ECR 4677.
[44] Weiler & Lockhart, *supra* note 3 at 94.

of a court deciding these cases against the benchmark of integration as opposed to fundamental rights, and again implicit in their analysis is that a court deciding these cases (properly) on human rights grounds would have reached a different conclusion. For Weiler and Lockhart, this approach is explicit, as they frequently deploy Dworkinian language on behalf of their argument that the Court is engaging in legitimate human rights reasoning.[45] Again they agree on what is the proper role of a court adjudicating human rights issues: their disagreement is whether this role is being fulfilled by the ECJ.[46]

In essence, the disagreement just outlined is about how to measure the ECJ's jurisprudence with reference to the assessment criteria of the liberal rights paradigm. Weiler and Lockhart acknowledge this by stating at the outset that their response is entirely within (in legal scholarship terms) a 'rather traditional'[47] perspective which is not really engaging with critical theories of constitutionalism. That is not to say their debate is not worth having: the range of debate within the liberal rights paradigm itself is considerable, and as the protagonists in this debate demonstrate, not without passion. However, if one were reading Coppel and O'Neill's arguments in the hope of discovering the application of critical theory to constitutionalism in the ECJ, then one would come away disappointed.

Omissions

As a result of conducting their debate within this relatively narrow framework, there are some striking omissions from the discussion of the ECJ's human rights jurisprudence which are particularly striking to anyone familiar with the critical literature. The tendency (on both sides) is to try to explain and analyse the Court's decision form within the liberal rights paradigm, with any difficulty which this poses dismissed as a blip (e.g.

---

[45] See e.g. their explanation of Cinetheque's apparent inconsistency with fore-going and preceding doctrine on the basis that 'in Dworkinian terms, *Wachauf* is the predictable chapter in the chain-novel, *Cinetheque* the chapter that does not fit.' *supra*, note 3 at 73.

[46] To digress for a moment: it is not necessarily to be assumed from Coppel and O'Neill's position that they advocate the practice of constitutionalism on the part of the Court (as Weiler and Lockhart clearly do). It is possible to read their article so that their main target is the unjustified integrationist practices of the Court, and that if the Court were not following this agenda then the need for it to pursue (proper) human rights adjudication would be diminished. However, it is reasonable to characterise their article as saying that if human rights issues do arise in the (however regrettable) context of European integration, then a constitutional court in the position of the ECJ which 'took rights seriously' would have come to a different conclusion in the cases they highlight.

[47] *Supra*, note 3 at 54.

Weiler and Lockhart's accounting for *Cinetheque* as the maverick contribution to the otherwise coherent chain novel). The only other possible source of explanation either side acknowledge is from the wider context of EC law. The possibility that the ECJ's jurisprudence could be informed by ideas coming from the critical tradition is not addressed.

To give a couple of examples. In *Eurocracy and Distrust*, Weiler himself takes a relatively critical stance with regard to the Court's record, and in the example of the *Van Duyn* case notes how faced with a conflict between preserving the integrity of EC law (which for him was the original motive for the Court developing its human rights jurisprudence) and upholding individual rights, the latter can be sacrificed to the former.[48] Among the factors which he identifies as explaining this decision was the impending referendum in the UK on the question of remaining within the EEC, and the Court's sensitivity to the impact on that vote of its allowing the Dutch scientologist entry to Britain. Turning to the critical tradition, Weiler's acknowledgement of the importance of the Court as a political actor would certainly be welcomed, but what would be striking would not be the specific factor of the referendum, but that Van Duyn could be added to a long list of socially undesirable plaintiffs, including e.g. Japanese Americans imprisoned during the Second World War,[49] or Communist party members during the Macarthy period,[50] who have been unable to rely on constitutional rights to defeat the majority's prejudice against them. The question which the critical tradition would want answered from the Van Duyn case is why judges and the politicians who appointed should be expected to disagree (the possibility of which, after all, is the essence of formal constitutionalism) on matter of this nature, and would point to studies which show a very low 'disagreement rate' between courts and politicians.

By far the most remarkable omission from the debate is the question which neither side asks, but which in the critical tradition is crucial, viz.: what is the political impact of the Court's human rights decision on the EU decision making process? This is the crux of the issue under review, and it is when the issue is seen in these terms that the undesirable nature of conducting the debate to date within the confines outlined becomes clear. Weiler and Lockhart state that Coppel and O'Neill's 'traditional' perspective is valid and that they are not to be criticised for adopting this.[51] This is without dispute. However, the question as to the political impact of

[48] Weiler, *supra* note 1 at 1120, fn.48.
[49] *Korematsu* v. *US* (1944) 323 US 214.
[50] *Dennis* v. *US* (1951) 341 US 494.
[51] Weiler & Lockhart, *supra* note 3 at 54.

the jurisprudence lies at the heart of the issue of constitutionalism, and raises the subject's (already considerable) significance in terms of forensic exegesis to the realm of high politics. Casting constitutionalism as the legalisation of the political process means that it has to answer questions about the nature of society and our system of government, the distribution of social and economic entitlements, and our ability to exercise change them. Therefore, although there is no fault in those who so believe pursuing their scholarship within a more 'traditional' perspective, the absence of discussion of the politics of human rights is most certainly worthy of censure.

That the absence of this question has a limiting affect on how scholars have treated the Court's jurisprudence is evident from where the debate ends for those participating in the 'Taking Rights Seriously?' controversy. For both sides the debate ends after it is established whether the ECJ has upheld the protection of human rights or not. For the critical tradition, this is where the really interesting questions begin. The question of whether a court adjudicating human rights issues is to be praised or condemned is much more subtle and multi-faceted than appears in the existing literature, and requires asking questions about the very question about the political content of the decision which, as we have seen, is curiously absent. For Coppel and O'Neill, and Weiler and Lockhart the protection of human rights by the Court of Justice is self-evidently a welcome development: to take the example of *Wachauf* again, Coppel and O'Neill's criticism is that protection of property may have been subordinated to the promotion of the EC Regulation at hand. There is an implicit higher value attached to the protection of property as a human right, and if this had been asserted over the Community law measure in question, then one presumes Coppel and O'Neill's complaint would have been dealt with. However, at no stage does anyone query why the right to property should be valued in this manner. The question of whether the Court's decision should be welcomed or not is linked to its decision on the plaintiff's assertion of his right to compensation: once that is made, the decision is praised or condemned accordingly.

In the critical tradition, courts' human rights decision should be assessed according to a number of criteria, not just whether they uphold a human rights provision in question, because that in itself is not necessarily a benevolent development. If the criterion of assessment changes from the protection of the individual to the likely political impact of the decision, i.e. whether it is more likely to have a progressive or a conservative effect, the range of options for assessment change. Seeing the decision in terms of their political impact on the relations of social power, the Court is assessed in terms of whether its decision affects the prevailing *status quo*: here the options are (a) the court striking down a regulatory measure seeking to change the *status quo* (b) the court leaving intact the law in question or (c) the court using human rights to impose regulatory measures itself. From here the perspective changes: again to return to *Wachauf*, rather than asking whether the Court upheld the human right at issue, the question becomes what is the political impact of a Court upholding a right to property in this way (it is only when we reach the stage of (c) that Tushnet's earlier question can be answered in terms of a tendency towards progressive results). A critical account might highlight the possibility of the Court being able to use this right as a deregulatory device, that is, to impede attempts at economic redistribution. The development of Weiler's 'truly comprehensive critique' will have to wait till another day, and it is only when this is undertaken will we see if the tentative critical conclusion advanced above is appropriate. However, there are perhaps a few impressionistic remarks that can be made which seem to indicate the viability of pursuing scholarship down this (as far as the ECJ is concerned) uncharted road.

VI PROSPECTS FOR CRITICAL SCHOLARSHIP

If one were to embark on the project of a more critical appraisal of the ECJ's human rights jurisprudence, what seams of scholarship could be mined, and how rich would the pickings be? There are at least three aspects of the ECJ's human rights jurisprudence where the debate would be enhanced by investigating the implications of a more critical approach. In each instance, this would require a thorough reappraisal of the doctrine, and whether this would lead to the conclusions suggested by the critical tradition would remain to be seen. However, it is hoped that the brief remarks that follow will at least indicate the potential enrichment of the academic debate which could occur by following a more expansive approach..

i. Source of EU Fundamental Rights

The dearth of critical scholarship does seem particularly remarkable in light of the absence in the EC Treaties of a clear, single textual basis for the Court's development of its fundamental rights jurisprudence. Remembering that one of the key features of the constitutionalism debate outlined above is the question of to what extent courts are constrained by the texts they interpret, the flexibility inherent in the court's formulation of where it may draw its inspiration from is all too evident. The idea that the Court will draw inspiration from the constitutional law of the member states begs many more questions than it answers. Is the test the lowest or highest common denominator? How many jurisdictions need to be canvassed: all or a majority or merely a number sufficient to sample a range of viewpoints? Turning to the other source, international human rights agreements and treaties, although the European Convention has clearly been a significant influence in the evolution of the jurisprudence, the Court does reserve the right to draw inspiration from other treaties as well. Although these potential contradictions have been acknowledged in the mainstream scholarship, this is generally pointed out to assist the Court in setting intelligible standards and so avoid these pitfalls. To the critical scholar, what is significant is that the malleability inherent in these tests militates forcefully against any notion of judicial constraint. A case-study which sought to establish the actual discretion employed by the ECJ in terms of the provenance of rights would be a welcome addition to the literature.

ii. Hierarchy of Rights

The second point is that within national constitutions, there is often a choice to be made between deregulatory rights removing the state's influence from individual's affairs – such as the right to property – and those that may need more intervention to secure their operation - e.g. social and economic rights, or the right to national ownership. These rights often exist side by side without any explicit textual guidance for their normative resolution, and constitutional courts are frequently called on to choose between them.[52] In the EU context, the hierarchy of rights is not so ambiguous: the ECJ has elevated the four freedoms of the Treaty of Rome (goods, services, people and capital) to the status of fundamental rights.[53] On the other hand, the clearest statement in favour of social and economic rights is found in the 1989 Charter of the Fundamental Rights of Workers, which has no binding legal status, instead relegated to the level of 'soft law'. In other words, the deregulatory bias of rights adjudication in the EU may be even more blatant than in national constitutions. Whether this apparent bias towards deregulation results in the tension between these two

---

[52] E.g. the French nationalisation cases of the 1980s discussed in Stone, *supra* note 21 at Ch.6.

[53] *UNECTEF* v. *Heylens* Case 222/86 [1987] ECR 4098.

forms of rights being resolved in this manner would again require more detailed consideration.

iii. Deregulatory Nature of Jurisprudence

Finally, it could be argued that some of the key cases can be read in a deregulatory manner. We have already seen how *Wachauf* is potentially protective of property rights against state intervention. The *ERT* judgement affords another example: from a critical point of view, it at best is an example of a blinkered approach to making political decisions, with the importance of control of the media in the modern technological age never featuring once in the Court's judgement. At worst, it can be seen as favouring the economically powerful: by dealing with the issue at the abstracted level of the principle of freedom of expression, the ECJ ignores the relative economic strength of the private corporation plaintiffs, and gives them an advantage in legal proceedings which they had hitherto been unable to secure through the Greek political process.

VII CONCLUSION

It seems likely that questions of constitutionalism and human rights are going to be increasingly relevant and important in the development of the European Union. The potential for a more expansive reading of existing case-law by the Court of Justice has already been canvassed, but it is important to place this in the context of growing political support for the idea of entrenched rights. This is evident in a number of ways, such as the approving reference to the Court's human rights jurisprudence in the Common Provision of the Treaty on European Union. In the Inter-Governmental Conference of 1996, this may have the support of a British Labour Prime Minister keen to entrench a Bill of Rights in the UK. The charge made by the critique makes important claims about the impact of constitutionalism on political decision-making, and yet these important questions affecting the future of the European Union are at present being considered in a very one-sided manner. It may well be that the conclusion of a detailed examination of the operation of constitutionalism in the EU is that it would not have the negative effects found in other jurisdictions, but at the very least it is not a debate which ought to be lost by default.

10. Understanding Legal Systems – The case of German Law

Professor Geoffrey Wilson – University of Warwick

In any division of legal systems into categories, it is usual to find the German legal system grouped with the French under the general heading of civil law systems. Two features are said in particular to characterise such systems, they have been influenced by Roman law, and they are codified. The Roman law influence is traced back to the Digest compiled on the orders of Justinian in the 6th century in Byzantium. It consists of snippets taken mainly from the classical Roman jurists of the first and second centuries AD, arranged under separate headings, with some attempts to reconcile and modernise them. It was the rediscovery of this collection of texts which sparked off a revival of legal learning at Bologna in the twelfth century, attracting scholars from all over Europe which then spread to Universities elsewhere. Groups of scholars, the Glossators and Postglossators took it upon themselves to write commentaries or glosses on the original texts to make them more readily usable in the administration of law and justice throughout Europe in the thirteenth and fourteenth centuries.

The various ways in which Roman law came to influence German law are complex and varied. But the common explanation presents the impact of Roman law as occurring at several stages. In the earliest stages jurists trained in Roman law in the Universities became advisers to princes, administrators and judges and both supplemented and rationalised the customary law with principles, concepts and classifications taken from Roman law. This is a time when Germany was fragmented into different political units and different jurisdictions. There did exist for a time a Reichskammergericht which in principle had jurisdiction throughout the Holy Roman Empire of the German Nation but its direct influence on the content of German law was minimal. More influential in generalising a common Roman/German law was the development of the usus modernus Pandectarum, a common law based on Roman law. The Universities also played an influential part in the development of a common law in their responses to requests for guidance from the courts, which were regarded as authoritative, a tradition of attaching authority to the opinions of German scholars which continues to the present day.

Three further opportunities arose for Roman law to have an influence in the development of German law. The first was in the eighteenth century when books of natural law were written which used Roman law concepts to create a systematic body of law. The second was at the beginning of the nineteenth century as a result of Savigny's plea for a more intensive study of Roman law as a means of understanding the true nature of the development of German law, which in turn led to the Pandectist studies which preceded the enactment of the BGB, the German Civil Code, at the end of the century. It is these Pandectist studies that not only left the mark of Roman law on the BGB but also gave it the scholastic character which distinguishes it so sharply from its neighbour in the civil law family, France. Every commentator points to the eloquent simplicity of the language of the Code Civile, in contrast to the conceptual, abstract, even professorial, character of the German civil code. In it the influence of Roman law through the Pandectists was combined with rigorous organisation to provide a conceptual basis and style for German law as a whole, reinforced over the years by the use of the BGB as the basic training ground for students of German law, and this in spite of the fact that much of it is no longer in force, that many of its provisions have been developed in a way that would have come as a surprise to the original draftsmen, and that its provisions have been supplemented by legislation and by judicial decisions.

The BGB however no longer stands alone as the basis of the German legal system. Since 1949 there has also been the Grundgesetz which, as befits a constitutional document, is not drafted in such a systematic way and owes nothing at all to Roman law. It is in fact a reminder that the traditional contrasts made between legal systems and their grouping into families have their roots mainly in private law. When it comes to public law, and particularly constitutional law, a different set of criteria applies for distinguishing one from another, which will put legal systems in quite different families, federal and unitary, parliamentary and presidential, and in particular, when it comes to comparing the German constitution with the British, written and unwritten constitutions, the guarantee or absence of guarantee of basic rights, and the existence or absence of a constitutional court.

Adding the Grundgesetz and public law generally to private law is an important corrective to seeing the characteristics of German private law as determining the character of German law as a whole. But, of course, even if one adds public law to private law and includes other branches of substantive law as well that does not exhaust the special features of a legal system. Besides the law of procedure, there are the other elements which go to make up clearly visible features of the system as a whole, the appointment, status and role of the judges, for example, and their responsibility for supervising the day to day working of the system in individual cases and for developing and applying the law; the lawyers and public prosecutors who service the courts; the structure and division of jurisdiction and functions of the courts themselves; the administrative responsibility for the system's reliability and efficiency; the procedures for making new law; the techniques for using the raw materials of the law as a basis for the decisions in individual cases and for developing principles to meet new challenges or changes in circumstances, values and expectations; and the whole system of legal education and training. And it is not just a question formal matters such as questions of responsibility and technique, it is also a question of what the system has achieved in terms of effectiveness, as a means of regulating society, as a means of settling disputes, as a means of providing remedies, including problems of comprehensibility, the availability of advice, and accessibility and the question of cost, and quality in terms of representation and judgment.

All of these are important features of any legal system and they are all elements which can give a special character to a particular legal system as one can easily see as soon as one contrasts the German version and experience of these elements and the British. In spite of the enormous growth in the importance of legislation the judge remains at the heart of the English legal system. Appointed late in life, individual judges, of which there are a much smaller number in England than in Germany, have a higher status and a more important role than their German equivalents, at least so far as the application and development of the law is concerned. The system too is much more highly centralised, not only at the level of first instance, where judges still travel out from London to hear the most important civil and criminal cases throughout the country, but at the appellate level as well which peaks in a single one chamber court and where a single decision of a higher court can set a precedent not only for all the courts below it, but to a great extent and with only an occasional exception for itself as well.

In public law the contrast is even greater with Britain being almost the last home of the unwritten constitution, having no guarantee of legal rights other than that in the European convention, which, unlike Community law, is not a part of English law recognised by or enforceable in the British courts, and having no constitutional court.

Of course when one puts both systems in the larger European context there are major similarities between the two systems. They are both non-socialist and secular and so stand in marked contrast to the old DDR, East German system, and religious systems throughout the world. And apart from being signatories of conventions designed to iron out problems arising from differences in the field of international trade, and harmonise rules of private international law, and providing for the mutual recognition and enforcement of awards and judgment, they are both now subject to the harmonising and other enactments of the European Community, which have come to make up an important element of the domestic law of member states. And in other respects too old differences have softened. In Germany more attention is paid to judge made law than in the past, a trend which is particularly noticeable in the field of public law, and legislation has frequently broken the symmetry of the BGB which for many years appeared to lie at the heart of the legal system and as well as setting its character and tone.

It would be possible of course to characterise all the differences and special features of the German and English legal systems as being no more than different instruments or ways of reaching the same goals and the German legal system as meaning no more than the legal system in Germany just as the English legal system would simply be the legal system in England. But it is not clear that this is the whole truth or that the systems are in fact interchangeable, so that the choice of one or the other is like the choice of one or other brand of motor car, with British people finding it no more difficult to drive a German car than a German to drive a British one, with after sale services and familiarity being the only plausible advantages for preferring the one to the other. Or is there more to it than that? The question is important as the pressure to move towards a more European private and public law increases, the one to provide a context which will facilitate transactions across European borders, the other as a means of developing new constitutional arrangements for the Community. Are disputes or differences about future community law simply disputes about the policy to be embodied in it, or a preference for one technique rather than another, or do they go deeper? Do they reflect perhaps views, and assumptions about law itself and its functions in the wider community?

If one looks at public law the answer is bound to be yes. The very fact that the British constitution is unwritten is more than a matter of fact. It is a matter of value. It involves a view about the role of law and judges in the establishment and maintenance of constitutionalism. The British constitution rests not on law but on a political tradition. This can be seen not only in the role that conventions have played in the past in shaping the constitution but also in the role they play today in its day to day working. In spite of the increasing assertion by the courts of their role in relation to the government's use of the legal powers it has been given, the grant of those powers in the first place lies outside of their control. They have neither the power nor the responsibility for securing that the constitutional proprieties are observed. This is the responsibility of the main political actors, the Government and its ministers, the Opposition, the back benchers of both parties, the Speaker of the House of Commons, the media, and, ultimately, public opinion, enforceable through the ballot box. The line between what is constitutional and what is not is not a legal one. It is a conventional one and one which is often the subject of debate, negotiation and even disagreement between the major political parties.

The absence of a guarantee of basic rights points in the same direction. There is no code of basic legal rights which can be used as the basis of an argument that this or that action is unconstitutional. In spite of the impact, actual and potential, of the European convention, its provisions have not been incorporated into the legal thinking of the United Kingdom. Successful applications to the European Court of Justice are still regarded as relatively rare and as individual exceptions rather than something which requires to be taken on account in any fundamental way. So far as public law is concerned English law remains largely remedy based rather than rights based.

Even as regards private law there is at least a question mark. One of the features of a code is that it claims to be comprehensive. It is expected that an answer to all legal problems will be found within it and justifications for decisions will be based on its provisions. In practice this does not mean the code, it means the framework of concepts and principles developed from, and around the code. But the comprehensivness remains a value as does the coherence of the developments made from the code and around it. They are intended to be systematic and provide a comprehensive framework. It is seen as one of the functions of legal scholarship to see that this is the case. The quality of being systematic and comprehensive is easily carried over to the law as a whole. Is there a further step that is also easy to take, not only that the law that there is should be comprehensive but law itself should be capable of providing solutions for every kind of problem? Does it lead to a built in preference for legal solutions?

It is clear that in public law there is such a preference. The Grundgesetz was seen as the only way in which a new start could be made after the collapse of the Nazi regime. It was around this legal document, and its provisions, in particular the guarantee of basic rights and the constitutional court for which it provided, that a new political tradition was to be built. This was not merely a question of technique. It was something to which importance and value was attached. If the German state was to be a Rechtsstaat, in deliberate contrast to the arbitrary rule which had preceded to it, it was not simply the basic rights of individuals that needed to be guaranteed by law, but constitutionalism itself. As in private law so in public law the pressure was in the same direction, a reliance on law as the major regulator of relations, in private law between individuals, in public law between public bodies and between public bodies and individuals citizens.

It is interesting to notice that just as in the field of public law the same pressure towards reliance on law does not exist in the United Kingdom, so in private law the approach to law is far more pragmatic. No one pretends, or even regards it as a value, that English law is or should be gapless. It is in fact the essence of the common law system that it is full of gaps which are only resolved in the course of litigation. No one pretends that English law is systematic or that it should be in any general over-arching way. Such principles as it has developed are always provisional and always rooted in the facts of particular cases, real or hypothetical. Just as there are no attempts to make the law comprehensive so there is no temptation to see law as a comprehensive solution to society's problems. Even where law is used the discretion given to the judges is often paralleled by a discretion given to administrators. Like the politicians in the constitution at large who have developed a political tradition without recourse to law, administrators have developed their own bureaucratic traditions which are not based on law. Administrators are rarely lawyers and lawyers rarely play a central role in administration.

Reference to administrators, particularly in the form of the German word Beamten, however, opens up much wider questions than a comparison of the different balance of rule and discretion in the two systems. For the Beamte along with the soldier is always seen from outside of Germany as a typical part of the Prussian heritage. This conception does not have its roots in the BGB or the Grundgesetz. Its roots and its implications lie outside and go beyond the legal system, particularly the current legal system. And the reason it gives a pause for thought is that it raises the question whether the path we have chosen, to move out from what we know of distrinctive features of the German legal system, gradually adding aspects of the system to get a more rounded picture is the most fruitful path to take, even when we contrast them with those of the English legal system. In trying to understand the German legal system in this way will there not be parts of the explanation of its character that we will never reach? In concentrating on the special features of the German legal system will we ever be able to discover what is particularly German about it? Would we reach a different conclusion and understanding if we approached it not from the German legal system looking out but from German society looking in, till we reached that particular aspect of it which we recognised as the legal system? Is it enough to list the features that we have so far, all features of the legal system itself, law, procedure, courts, judges, lawyers, prosecutors, codes, contributors, administrators, legislation, judicial decision. What of the relevance of education, education at large, that is, and not just legal education, of traditions of scholarship, of historical experience? The Grundgesetz already contains implicit references to the Weimar Constitution and its fate and the period of the Nazi regime and the post-war occupation of Germany. Does the role of the judge still carry with it traces of the judge as official? Is the Rule of Law simply an updated version of an older tradition of autocratic government? What of the conventions governing the relations between individuals, between individuals in employment, between individuals in business relationships, between individuals in families, between individuals and government? What of the role of unions, employer associations, pressure groups, voluntary organisations? What of the media, press, television and cable? How significant is religion and church membership, regionalism, the distinction between town and country, industry and agriculture? What are the implications of the shift from being a western European country to being once again a central European power, the shift from Bonn to Berlin? Are there echoes of German scholarship in German legal scholarship or German reasoning in German legal reasoning? Does the notion of comprehensiveness implicit in the notion of a code or a constitution really carry over into a notion of comprehensiveness of law at large and then into a notion of law as the basic determinant of the social structure and relations within it? What is the role of political parties and the balance of responsibility between them and the courts for achieving constitutionalism? None of these can easily be reached by the patient step by step approach from the original characterisation of the German legal system by reference to its system of private law through its public law to the wider structural components and personnel that make up the obvious features of the formal system.

It is at first no more than a question, but it may turn out to be a lesson. If we were anthropologists like Malinowski and we went to the Trobriand Islands, where there were none of the features which we associate with a legal system, we would be forced to move cautiously, taking the whole society as our frame of reference and beginning with an open mind which saw everything as potentially relevant. Most of us, because of our ignorance of Japan, would probably do the same if we intended to study the Japanese legal system. The study of German law and the German legal system raises a quite simple question. Is there anything different about a country with which we think we are more familiar?

11. Modernising the Law: Theories of Legislation in 18th and 19th Century Germany

Professor Diethelm Klippel – University of Bayreuth

I INTRODUCTION

The general subject of this colloquium – 'Challenges to European Legal Scholarship' – can be understood as referring to legal problems of today. But it can be looked at from a historical perspective as well. One of the greatest challenges to German legal scholarship was to come to terms with new ideas about the law put forward in the Age of Enlightenment and with the political, economic and social changes during the Napoleonic era and in the years between 1815 and 1848. In Germany, this was considered to be a task which had to be accomplished by legislation as well as by legal scholarship. Therefore, I shall look at both the history of legal scholarship and the history of legislation and ask whether and how the theory of legislation in Germany in the second half of the 18th and the first half of the 18th century tackled these problems. I shall try to show that, around 1800, German lawyers and philosophers, mostly professors at universities, developed new theories of legislation which they called 'the science of legislation' ('Gesetzgebungswissenschaft'). It was part of the wider academic discipline of natural law which, contrary to what legal historians have assumed until now, continued to exist during the 19th century and played an important role in modernising the law and legal scholarship in Germany.

II LEGISLATION AND THE LAW IN GERMANY IN THE 18TH AND 19TH CENTURY

First of all, I would like to briefly outline the history of legislation and of the theory of legislation in Germany in the 18th and 19th century, as one would find them in textbooks on legal history. Two developments are usually considered to be important. The first one comprises the four decades around 1800 and is commonly, yet misleadingly referred to as the era of natural law codifications ('Naturrechtskodifikationen'). It is seen as a European phenomenon, the most important and influential results of which are supposed to be the Prussian Code of 1794, the Austrian Civil Code of 1811/1812 and the French codifications. In terms of Germany, one might describe the projects and results of this movement towards codifying the law as the legislative efforts of enlightened absolutism and of the age of reforms. Both the history of the codes themselves and the political and legal theory upon which they were based are covered relatively comprehensively by scholarly literature. In Germany these legislative efforts aimed at replacing Roman law which clearly dominated legal theory and practice since its so-called Reception. However, there is considerable controversy about the political aims which enlightened rulers in Germany pursued with planning or, in Prussia, actually putting into force, new codifications.

The second crucial development is usually seen to be the vast legislation by the second German Empire after its foundation in 1871. In fact, the many codes enacted during that period have moulded even the German legal system of today; quite a number of them are still in force, though they have been altered to a greater or lesser degree since then. Legislative efforts before 1871, for instance by the German Union ('Deutscher Bund'), were seen as mere predecessors of the legislation of the German Empire.

This view of the history of legislation in Germany seems to be illustrated by the result of one of the most famous controversies in German legal history.[1] In 1814, Anton Friedrich Justus Thibaut, professor of law at the University of Heidelberg, had argued in favour of a civil code for Germany.[2] His Berlin colleague, Friedrich Carl von Savigny, opposed this view and pleaded that Roman law should retain its central position in

---

[1] For a thorough and scholarly analysis of the Thibaut-Savigny controversy, see Joachim Rückert, Jurisprudenz und Politik bei Friedrich Carl von Savigny, Ebelsbach 1984, pp. 160-193; cf. Hans Wrobel, Die Kontroverse Thibaut-Savigny im Jahre 1814 und ihre Deutung in der Gegenwart, jur. Diss. Bremen 1975.

[2] Anton Friedrich Justus Thibaut, Ueber die Nothwendigkeit eines allgemeinen bürgerlichen Rechts für Deutschland, Heidelberg 1814.

Germany.[3] As a German civil code did not come into force before 1900, it seemed that Savigny and the historical school of law had effectively prevented legislative efforts for codification for more than half a century.

Yet this view, which neglects the considerable legislative activities of the German states after 1815, is distorted, and it has to be revised. Recent research indicates that it is in fact this legislation, mostly in the field of criminal law, public law and several areas of private law, which adapted German law to the social, economic and political needs of that time.[4]

But what were the theoretical concepts which were put forward to legitimise these legislative activities? As the 19th century in German legal history is usually regarded as the age of the historical school of law it might even seem absurd to ask this question. Yet a vast number of books and articles about the theory of legislation were published, about which we know nearly nothing. The reason for this neglect is that this sort of literature is part of the literature on natural law and legal philosophy which, in their turn, have hitherto not been considered important legal disciplines in 19th century Germany.

But, if a 19th century lawyer wanted to read about the theory of legislation, he would have referred to the literature of legal philosophy, either to a comprehensive textbook or to a special treatise about legislation. To what extent then did legal philosophy and natural law influence German law and lawyers in the 19th century?

III NATURAL LAW IN GERMANY IN THE 18TH AND 19TH CENTURY

It is well known that the non-theological natural law did play an important role in legal history and in the history of political theory in the 17th and 18th centuries. However, especially with regard to Germany, scholars

---

[3] Friedrich Carl von Savigny, Vom Beruf unserer Zeit für Gesetzgebung und Rechtswissenschaft, Heidelberg 1814.

[4] Cf. Rolf Grawert, Gesetzgebung im Wirkungszusammenhang konstitutioneller Regierung, in: Gesetzgebung als Faktor der Staatsentwicklung, Berlin 1984, pp. 113-160; Barbara Dölemeyer, in: Helmut Coing (ed.), Handbuch der Quellen und Literatur der neueren europäischen Privatrechtsgeschichte, Vol. 3/II, München 1982, pp. 1403-1561; Stephan Buchholz, ibid., pp. 1626-1773; see also the introductory essays by Helmut Coing (Allgemeine Züge der privatrechtlichen Gesetzgebung im 19. Jahrhundert) and Dieter Grimm (Die verfassungsrechtlichen Grundlagen der Privatrechtsgesetzgebung), ibid., Vol. 3/I, pp. 3-16 and 17-173; as to the criminal law of that time see the reprinting project 'Kodifikationsgeschichte Strafrecht', Goldbach 1988 et seq. (ed. and with introductory remarks by Werner Schubert et al.).

disagree on the political impact of natural law. In my view, up to the end of the 18th century, it mainly provided the theoretical basis for absolutism and enlightened absolutism. But in the last two decades of the 18th century German natural law underwent a radical political change.[5] As regards its method the change was based on the philosophy of Immanuel Kant or at least influenced by it. In the political domain, it took up ideas expressed by English and French authors like John Locke, Montesquieu and Rousseau, and it was, in a complex way, deeply affected by the French revolution. Consequently, the numerous proponents of this type of natural law opposed enlightened absolutism and put forward liberal and sometimes even democratic points of view. For instance, most authors drafted sometimes very extensive catalogues of human rights and civil liberties in their textbooks or systems of legal philosophy. Others demanded the introduction of a written constitution or discussed the separation of powers or a representative government as constitutional principles.

For my present purpose it is important to note that, contrary to the common beliefs of legal historians, natural law and especially its liberal version continued to flourish in Germany in the 19th century.[6] Indeed, it may be considered one of the major academic disciplines which influenced German politics and law. This view which might seem a bit exaggerated is supported by a number of facts. I would like to mention just two of them.

First of all, an astonishingly large number of books and treatises on natural law and legal philosophy were published in the 19th century. To some extent, this can be established by consulting 19th century bibliographies. The sheer number of publications on the various aspects of natural law came as a surprise when, in the last years, I worked on a new bibliography which I hope to publish next year. Counting only comprehensive textbooks on natural law, around 130 titles were published between 1800 and 1850 alone, not including the 30 new editions.

Secondly, university courses on natural law and later on the philosophy of law did not cease to exist during the 19th century but remained an

---

[5]   Cf. Diethelm Klippel, Politische Freiheit und Freiheitsrechte im deutschen Naturrecht des 18. Jahrhunderts, Paderborn 1976.

[6]   Cf. Diethelm Klippel, Naturrecht und Politik im Deutschland des 19. Jahrhunderts, in: Karl Graf Ballestrem (ed.), Naturrecht und Politik, Berlin 1993, pp. 27-48; Diethelm Klippel, Naturrecht und Rechtspilosophie in der ersten Hälfte des 19. Jahrhunderts, in: Otto Dann and Diethelm Klippel (eds.), Naturrecht - Spätaufklärung – Revolution. Das europäische Naturrecht im ausgehenden 18. Jahrhundert, Hamburg 1994, pp. 270-292.

important part of teaching of the law faculties of the German universities up to the last decades of the century.[7]

Of course, the mere facts that natural law was taught at the universities and that it was a subject of many publications does not reveal its exact significance and role for politics and for the law. Unfortunately, a lot of research has yet to be done to answer this question definitely. Provisionally, a list of topics that were dealt with in natural law publications and which were regarded as problems specifically of natural law can give us a first indication of the range and the interests of natural law: human and civil rights, the social contract, the purpose of the state, the separation of powers, voting rights and representation, the death penalty, intellectual property, pauperism and, last but not least, legislation.[8]

Looking at these and other topics, it becomes obvious that natural law and legal philosophy provided both a forum for the discussion of the problems which faced legal scholarship in the 19th century and suggestions for solutions to these problems. Thus, natural law and legal philosophy complemented the science of positive law, as the latter, for various reasons, sometimes showed a remarkable inability to solve certain problems. A striking example of this in private law is its reluctance to acknowledge the notion of intellectual property. From the political point of view natural law and legal philosophy provided the theoretical foundations of German liberalism. Thus one author, Leopold August Warnkönig, wrote in 1839: 'German liberalism is based on France on the one hand and on the principles of the eternal law of nature on the other hand.'[9]

However, as natural law had a complementary role, this could also be seen as a problem, the problem of the discrepancy between natural law theory and the practice of the actual law. One needs to inquire, therefore, how natural law, positive law and legislation related to each other.

---

[7] Cf. Jan Schröder and Ines Pielemeier, Naturrecht als Lehrfach an den deutschen Universitäten des 18. und 19. Jahrhunderts, in: Dann and Klippel, op.cit., n. 6, pp. 255-269.

[8] Cf. Karl David August Röder, Grundzüge des Naturrechts oder der Rechtsfilosofie, Heidelberg 1846; Felix Eberty, Versuche auf dem Gebiete des Naturrechts, Leipzig 1852; both Röder and Eberty give more examples, as does Karl Ignaz Wedekind, Von dem besonderen Interesse des Natur- und allgemeinen Staats-Rechtes durch die Vorfälle der neueren Zeiten. Eine Einladungsschrift zu den Vorlesungen über diese Wissenschaften, Heidelberg 1793.

[9] Leopold August Warnkönig, Rechtsphilosophie als Naturlehre des Rechts, Freiburg i.Br. 1839, p. 148; similar views: Röder, op. cit., n. 8, 2nd ed., Vol. 1, Leipzig and Heidelberg 1860, p. XI; Joseph Gambihler, Philosophie und Politik des Liberalismus, Nürnberg 1831.

IV NATURAL LAW AND POSITIVE LAW

The natural law of enlightened absolutism in the 18th century was not seen as having a binding force on the prince and his statutes. Thus Ludwig Julius Friedrich Höpfner, a law professor at the University of Gießen, stated in 1785: 'The controversy, whether the legislator can decree anything contrary to natural law is only a verbal one. Everybody agrees that the legislator can command, permit or forbid something which, by natural law, is indifferent, forbidden or permitted, if he acts in the interest of the common weal and attempts to avoid a greater evil.'[10] Höpfner's position is consistent with the role of natural law of enlightened absolutism in legitimising the absolutist powers of the monarch. These included the legislative power which, however, natural law was supposed only to legitimise not restrict.

This began to change in the last decade of the 18th century. Now natural law began to require that its rules should also be observed by the state. Natural law authors did not cease to point out and criticise the deplorable discrepancies between natural and positive law and to stress the superior validity of natural law. Natural law was seen as an unchangeable norm for all positive law.[11]

If, as a result, natural law positions were to be realized in positive law, legislation could not but become the vital link between natural law theory and legal practice. Therefore, legislation and the theory of legislation formed a major part of natural law. New codes were regarded as a means of implementing natural law ideas. This was one of the crucial aims of natural law at the end of the 18th and in the first half of the 19th century: to base legislation firmly on natural law ideas, i.e. to put into practice the political ideas of liberalism. To quote just one author, Carl Friedrich Wilhelm Gerstäcker (in 1837), thought that the 'science of natural law' is 'the one and only source by which positive legislation can be criticized, the one and only source of good statutes ...'[12]

---

[10] Ludwig Julius Friedrich Höpfner, Naturrecht des einzelnen Menschen, der Gesellschaften und der Völker, 3rd ed., Gießen 1785, p. 168.

[11] Cf. Jan Schröder, 'Naturrecht bricht positives Recht' in der Rechtstheorie des 18. Jahrhunderts, in: Staat, Kirche, Wissenschaft in einer pluralistischen Gesellschaft. Festschrift für Paul Mikat, Berlin 1989, pp. 419-433 (432).

[12] Carl Friedrich Wilhelm Gerstäcker, Systematische Darstellung der Gesetzgebungskunst sowohl nach ihren allgemeinen Prinzipien, als nach den, jedem ihrer Haupttheile, der Civil-, Criminal-, Polizei-, Prozeß-, Finanz-, Militair-, Kirchen-und Constitutions-Gesetzgebung eigenthümlichen Grundsätzen, Vol. 1, Frankfurt a.M 1837, p. 154; a similar view is expressed by Carl Dresler, Ueber das Verhältniß des Rechts zum

If legislation was deemed to be the most important connecting link between natural and positive law, then it became necessary to look more closely at the contents and the form of the state's legislative activities. This was the particular task of the science of legislation as part of natural law. Thus, in 1806, Karl Salomo Zachariä made it quite clear that, in his opinion, the science of legislation was to be 'the science of those principles which guide the drafting and enacting of laws'.[13]

It follows that virtually every question concerning legislation, i.e. its content, forms and procedures, was the subject of discussion in the science of legislation.[14] I would like to concentrate on two aspects which are especially illuminating from a political point of view: firstly, the purpose of the state and civil liberties as guidelines for legislation, and secondly the problem of continuity and change of codes.

V THE PURPOSE OF THE STATE AND CIVIL LIBERTIES AS GUIDELINES FOR LEGISLATION

Both the theory of the purpose of the state and the theory of human rights and civil liberties concerned the limits of legislation. According to natural law, civil society, i.e. the state, was founded by the social contract for a certain purpose. Only this purpose justified the existence and the concerns of the state and, consequently, the contents and the scope of its legislation. But the ideas about the chief end of the state fundamentally changed at the end of the 18th century.

In the natural law of enlightened absolutism, the concept of happiness ('Glückseligkeit') was seen as the major purpose of the state.[15] Happiness both of the state as a whole and of its subjects was regarded as the chief end of all the activities of the state. This led to a vast extension of the concerns of the state, as it was regarded as the task of the state to achieve the happiness of the individual. Accordingly, the state had to legislate very comprehensively. I quote from a book on legislation, published anonymously in 1777: '... if they (i.e. the laws) do not regulate everything

---

Gesetze, Berlin 1803, pp. 162 et seq., 191 et seq., 202 et seq; Karl Salomo Zachariä, Die Wissenschaft der Gesetzgebung, Leipzig 1806, pp. 222 et seq.

[13] Zachariä, op. cit., n.12, p. 18.

[14] Cf. Zachariä, op. cit., n. 12, pp. 26 et seq.; Gerstäcker, op. cit., n. 12, Vol. 1, pp. 194, 210.

[15] Cf. Ulrich Engelhardt, Zum Begriff der Glückseligkeit in der kameralistischen Staatslehre des 18. Jahrhunderts (J.H.G. v. Justi), in: Zeitschrift für Historische Forschung, Vol. 8, 1981, pp. 37 et seq.

which can be regulated; if they do not put the whole of society into such an order that all its parts and their changes correspond with the common weal, then disorder will more or less prevail in them.'[16]

At the end of the 18th century, natural law assumptions about the aims of the state changed radically. Many authors now write polemically against the view that happiness was the purpose of the state. For instance, in 1795, the philosopher Johann Christian Gottlieb Schaumann summed up these objections to the theory of happiness.[17] Though no state may make a person unhappy, 'it is wrong that happiness should be the immediate, legal purpose of the state and the centre of all princely power'. No man, he continues, can make another man reach true happiness, because nobody knows what another man's happiness requires. Schaumann concluded that everybody is responsible for his own happiness. He also points out the undesirable consequences of regarding happiness as the purpose of the state: 'If one allows happiness to be the legal purpose of government, one must also sanction what others call an abuse of the powers of government. Because then the rulers of states are entitled to meddle with all their subjects' affairs, they can attend to everybody's most secret thoughts and wishes. How else could they fulfill their duty to make everybody happy?' Schaumann also argues that the states are insufficiently organized to guarantee the people's happiness, because ideally there should be government-authorities dealing with happiness, whose special function it would be to get the necessary information about everybody's wishes.

Accordingly, new liberal concepts of the purpose of the state were developed. Christian Daniel Voss, for instance, followed John Locke and wrote: 'Man only entered into the social contract to reach his personal objective, the preservation of his life and his property.'[18] This new liberal natural law put forward the theory that the purpose of the state lies in the security of the private good, in the guarantee of human rights, or liberty generally.[19]

But if the purpose of the state consisted in the guarantee of human rights and civil liberties and if natural law set obligatory rules for positive law, then legislation was bound to respect human and civil rights. This, in turn,

---

[16] Entwurf der allgemeinen Grundsätze der Gesetzgebung, Frankfurt and Leipzig 1777, pp. 117 et seq.

[17] Johann Christian Gottlieb Schaumann, Kritische Abhandlungen zur philosophischen Rechtslehre, Halle 1795, pp. 222 et seq.

[18] Christian Daniel Voss, Handbuch der allgemeinen Staatswissenschaft, Vol. 1, Leipzig 1796, p. 301.

[19] Cf. Klippel op. cit., n. 5, pp. 133 et seq.

was the starting point for numerous political demands. I would like to briefly mention only three of them.

Firstly, the demand for equality had several consequences for legislation. For instance, the power of the prince to grant special privileges was not consistent with the idea that every human being should have equal rights. Accordingly, the state could not grant privileges even by way of legislation.[20]

Secondly, as the purpose of the state and of legislation was derived from the rights of the individual, the individual should have the chance to get to know what the law of the land was. Consequently, codes and statutes had to be published.[21]

Thirdly, statutes had to be intelligible and, therefore, could not be in a foreign language. Though this was already a demand in the eighteenth century, the natural law of enlightened absolutism did not contest the right of the prince to draft legislation in a foreign language or to adopt such codes.[22] But this was no longer the case in the science of legislation in the 19th century. Politically, both liberals and conservatives demanded that codes must be written in German.[23] The liberal demand was critical of the role of Roman law in Germany, whereas conservatives were critical of the French codes which were in force in parts of Germany throughout the 19th century.

---

[20] Cf. Prosper Bracht, Die Ansprüche unserer Zeit an die bürgerliche Gesetzgebung, Düsseldorf 1834, pp. 161 et seq.; Gerstäcker, op. cit., n. 12, Vol. 3, Frankfurt a.M. 1838, p. 145. For a broader picture, see Heinz Mohnhaupt, Untersuchungen zum Verhältnis Privileg und Kodifikation im 18. und 19. Jahrhundert, in: Ius commune, Vol. 5, 1975, pp. 71 et seq.

[21] This demand can be found in nearly every textbook on natural law, see e.g. Leopold Friedrich Fredersdorff, System des Rechts der Natur, auf bürgerliche Gesellschaften, Gesetzgebung und das Völkerrecht angewandt, Braunschweig 1790, p. 178; Karl Heinrich Gros, Lehrbuch der philosophischen Rechtswissenschaft oder des Naturrechts, Tübingen 1802, pp. 182 et seq.; Zachariä, op. cit., n. 12, p. 275; Gottlob Wilhelm Gerlach, Grundriß der philosophischen Rechtslehre, Halle 1824, p. 273.

[22] That is still the position of some 19th century authors, cf. Fredersdoret seq, op. cit., n. 21, pp. 170 et seq.; Gros, op. cit., n. 21, p. 181; Zachariä, op. cit., n. 12, pp. 309 et seq.; Ernst Wilhelm von Reibnitz, Aphorismen über die Formation der Gesetzbücher, Breslau 1818, pp. 31 et seq.

[23] Burkhard Wilhelm Pfeiffer, Ideen zu einer neuen Civil-Gesetzgebung für Teutsche Staaten, Göttingen 1815, pp. 16, 75 et seq.; Aphorismen über bürgerliche Gesetzgebung und Rechtspflege, Stuttgart 1826, p. 32; August Ludwig Reyscher, Ueber die Bedürfnisse unserer Zeit in der Gesetzgebung, Stuttgart and Tübingen 1828, pp. 36 et seq.; Gerstäcker, op. cit., n. 12, Vol. 2, Frankfurt a.M. 1837, p. 124; Marum Sam Mayer, Ueber Römisches Recht und Neue Gesetzgebung, Tübingen 1839, p. 26. Against French law in Germany: Johann Paul Harl, Rationelle Beiträge zur Reform der Gesetzgebung, Vol. 1, Erlangen 1822, pp. 22 et seq., 28.

VI CONTINUITY AND CHANGE OF CODES

If positive law has been properly enacted and as a result corresponds with natural law, then the difficulty arises whether changes in the law can still be necessary, and if that is so, how these changes can be legitimised.

In the 18th century, there was no theoretical problem in this respect, as natural law as we have seen, did not lay down obligatory rules, and thus the prince could ensure that any changes in the law were made. Astonishingly perhaps, 19th century authors also took the view that legislation, even if it complied with natural law, could be changed. It was true that natural law and legal philosophy provided some rigid principles; but the state was to put these principles into practice and to adapt them to the variant conditions of reality. Therefore, the science of legislation postulated that the law had to be adapted by legislation to the economic, social and political changes of the 19th century - thus proving, once again, that natural law provided the field in which lawyers could take note of these changes and their possible legal effects.

All this becomes very obvious in a booklet published in 1847 with the title 'The Relation between Natural and Positive Law, from an Ethical Point of View' by Heinrich Michael Och.[24] First of all, Och explained why legislation was so important a subject. 'Entirely new aspects of life arise, the number of inventions radically changing life increase day by day, commercial relations seem to undergo a change, and thus there are many questions ..., which science has to answer and which legislation, taking into account these entirely new aspects of life, has to order and to realize ...'[25] As examples, Och mentions pauperism, usury and the jail system, which were topics much discussed in his time.[26] The science referred to is natural law, which was seen as the place to discuss the legal aspects of current political, economic and social problems. In the words of Och: '[If natural law presents its answers, the legislator] is not allowed to swim against the tide and to reject the demands of natural law, but he has to act as a mediator and has to reconcile science and theory with life and practice and create harmony between them, and thus has to promote the demands of natural law into positive law.'[27]

Thus, the problem of continuity and change of both codes and statutes was not only a question of the relation between natural and positive law,

---

[24] Heinrich Michael Och, Das Verhältniß des natürlichen Rechts zum positiven, vom ethischen Standpunkte aus, Würzburg 1847.

[25] Op. cit., n. 24, p. 96.

[26] Ibid.

[27] Op. cit., n. 24 pp. 96 et seq.; cf. Aphorismen, op. cit., n. 23, p. 140.

but was regarded as a fundamental problem of any legislator. It is, Wilhelm Arnold wrote in 1865, 'the inevitable fate of legislation that it falls back behind life'.[28] Consequently, the science of legislation had to provide the answer to the question how it could be discovered whether codes and statutes had to be changed and how, eventually, appropriate changes could be implemented.

In the 18th century, the theory of legislation of enlightened absolutism had thought of two ways of adapting codes and statutes to the demands of the time. Firstly, the legislative power of the prince included the power to give an authoritative interpretation of codes and statutes.[29] However, the 19th century science of legislation voiced grave doubts about the legality of this power of the prince. It was argued that it was not compatible with the principle of the division of powers, that it was a form of retroactive legislation, and that it undermined the certainty and security of the law.[30]

The second means was to have a permanent Commission of Legislation ('Gesetzgebungskommission'), as was the case in Prussia, whose function was to to deal with suggestions by the enlightened public and with questions from the courts and to ensure that the code and legislation generally were constantly improved. Though the Prussian Commission was abolished at the beginning of the 19th century, the idea behind it was taken up and developed further by Gerstäcker and other authors. Though statutes, according to Gerstäcker, are laid down for the future, they are not unchangeable. On the contrary, their practicability, their influence on real life, has to be ensured by their form and contents and by organizational measures. Therefore, he suggested that every five years - other authors suggest ten years – it should be decided whether the codes and statutes ought to be changed or abolished or whether new legislation should be introduced.[31] In 1855, Leopold von Morgenstern outlined in detail the reasons why changes in legislation could be justified: if existing statutes had serious deficiencies, if there had been substantial changes affecting the nation's life, if new inventions or new intellectual and economic developments created new demands, if the organism of the state

---

[28] Wilhelm Arnold, Cultur und Rechtsleben, Berlin 1865, p. 379.

[29] As a late example, cf. Ludwig Heinrich Jakob, Philosophische Rechtslehre oder Naturrecht, Halle 1795, p. 406.

[30] Reibnitz, op. cit., n. 22, pp. 42 et seq.

[31] Gerstäcker, op. cit., n. 12, Vol. 2, Frankfurt a.M. 1837, pp. 156 et seq.; cf. Johann Friedrich Reitemeier, Ueber Gesetzgebung insbesondere in den Deutschen Reichsstaaten, Frankfurt a.d.O. 1806, pp. 119 et seq.; von Reibnitz, op. cit., n. 22, pp. 37; Joseph Kitka, Ueber das Verfahren bei Abfassung der Gesetzbücher überhaupt und der Strafgesetzbücher insbesondere, Brünn 1838, pp. 1 et seq., 154 et seq.

('Staatsorganismus') underwent changes and if changes in the codes and statutes of other nations affected the nation's law.[32]

VII THE DECLINE AND FALL OF THE SCIENCE OF LEGISLATION

It remains to be asked why this science of legislation gradually ceased to exist in the second half of the nineteenth century, so that Ernst Zitelmann, in 1904, could no longer refer to a 'science of legislation' ('Gesetzgebungswissenschaft'), but wrote of the 'art of legislation' ('Gesetzgebungskunst'). At most, the old science of legislation influenced the codifications of the German empire from 1871 in only a marginal way. The political theory of the German "Vormärz", the era before the revolution of 1848, did not provide the political ideas which were prevalent in the German empire. Accordingly, the science of legislation lost its influence, as did natural law and legal philosophy. As the science of legislation was a part of natural law and legal philosophy, their fate was linked together.

A first reason for the loss of influence can be found in a changed relationship between natural law and political science in the 19th century. Political science, for a long time, was regarded as a discipline which considered the means of fulfilling the purposes given by natural law.[33] That changed in the second half of the 19th century. Political science itself now provided the aims, and the reality of the state dominated political theory. In 1853, Ludwig August von Rochau wrote, that power prevailed over law, and that the opposite principle - the ideal of natural law - had broken down.[34]

But the loss of influence of natural law and legal philosophy went still further, as it concerned the whole academic discipline of law. By the end of the 19th century, they were not regarded as having any binding force with respect to positive law, and they were increasingly regarded as part of ethics rather than of the science of law. Legal philosophy no longer played an important role within the science of positive law. Paradoxically, in this respect it was joined by the history of law, which had contributed to a considerable extent to the undermining of the status of both natural law and

---

[32] Leopold von Morgenstern, Mensch, Volksleben und Staat, im natürlichen Zusammenhange, Vol. 1, Leipzig 1855, pp. 277 et seq.

[33] See Klippel, Naturrecht und Politik, op. cit., n. 6.

[34] Ludwig August von Rochau, Grundsätze der Realpolitik, angewendet auf die staatlichen Zustände Deutschlands (1853), ed. by Hans-Ulrich Wehler, Frankfurt a.M. 1972, pp. 3 et seq.

legal philosophy. In 1889, Josef Schein thought that neither philosophy of law nor the history of law were of any use for the science of law.[35] Both of them became a sort of ornamental accessory. It was the science of positive law that now started to play the dominant role.

---

[35] Josef Schein, Unsere Rechtsphilosophie und Jurisprudenz. Eine kritische Studie, Berlin 1889, p. 120.

12. Challenges to Democracy – and Constitutional Law Barriers Against Meeting Them

Professor Brun-Otto Bryde – University of Giessen

Democratic politics in the last two hundred years in Europe, as far as there have been any, have taken place almost exclusively within the framework of nation states. Constitutional law and theory are therefore little prepared for the major challenges to democracy posed by the diminishing importance of the nation state.

In the first part of my paper I will sketch three such challenges:
1. transnationalisation in a world society;
2. increasing loss of social homogeneity in 'multicultural' societies;
3. loss of regulatory power of states;

and in the second part I will address some basic deficiencies of German (though probably not only German) constitutional law theory in meeting these challenges.

I will conclude with some comparative remarks.

I CHALLENGES

1. Democracy in the World Society

In a world society women and men everywhere are dependent on economic and social processes anywhere. This is, of course, no new phenomenenon. To cite an author from the early 18th century: 'We must think of the states of which Europe is composed as being joined together by all kinds of necessary commerce, in such a way that they may be regarded as members of one Republic, and that no considerable change can take place in any one of them without affecting the condition, or disturbing the peace, of all the others.'[1]   And one of the founding fathers of sociology, Durkheim, explained the increasing effectiveness of international law by reference to the interdependence of European nations: 'This is because in certain respects they are all part of the same society, still incohesive, it is true, but one becoming increasingly conscious of itself.'[2]

The ascendancy of nationalism in Europe in the last two centuries – which in a longer historical perspective was merely a nationalist interlude between two eras of a transnational organisation of Europe – tended to obscure this simple fact of interdependence.   But references to prescient authors can hardly make us overlook that this interdependence today has reached a new dimension.   Chernobyl should have made clear to those who didn't know before (and Scandinavian victims of acid rain certainly did know before) that air knows no borders; our economic well-being is much more dependent on the US-deficit, crises in the Gulf or an earthquake in Japan than on good or bad economic policies of our own governments; we are threatened by international organized crime which national police-forces are ill-equipped to control; and our schools fight a losing battle with MTV for the education of our children.

One can define the problem more systematically: the boundaries of social systems like economy, culture, science do not coincide with state boundaries, but it is only within state boundaries that national lawmakers can exert control (Luhmann, 1971; Kennedy, 1994, pp. 122 et seq.)

Obviously, therefore, many of the major challenges that have to be met in the future cannot be handled within the framework of the nation state.   If democracy remains wedded to the nation state this bodes ill for the future of democracy.[3]

However, up to now neither ideologies nor institutions are ready to accomodate this loss of meaning of the nation state.

We have become members of a world society in practice but not in our minds.   This is not just due to ignorance: a world view that retains the nation states as the main actors provides a useful orientation.   In a democracy, e.g., it makes it possible to put blame and praise on the elected government and to sanction it through elections (even though it might be neither responsible for the good nor the bad conditions we are in).

And up to now there have not been many models for transnational democratic institutions, either, so that the theoretical recognition that democracy has to transcend the boundaries of the nation state to survive has

---

[1]   Callières, 1716, cit. by Held, 1991, p. 144.

[2]   E. Durkheim , The Division of Labor in Society, as cited in W. Streeck (1992), p. 514.

[3]   For a critique of democratic theory's inability to deal with this problem cf. Streeck, 1992; Held, 1991.

little practice to rely on. In an important paper on our subject, in which one of the leading authorities in democratic theory, David Held (Held, 1991), develops an ambitious world-wide 'federal model of democratic autonomy', he names the European Parliament as an important example. One need not be as cynical about this much maligned institution as many eurosceptic writers are (given its modest powers it does an outstanding job), to be sceptical when this is acclaimed as the most progressive form of transnational democratic institution developed thus far. So there is obviously much room for imaginative thinking if we hope to democratize the transnational processes governing our lives.

But there is a danger that the identification of democracy and nation state may defeat this effort from the start.

2. Democracy Without Homogeneity

Historically, the idea of democracy in Europe (it has always been different in America) is closely linked to the idea of the nation.

In political and constitutional theory, at least in Germany, this historical coincidence has been transformed into an ontological one. For many authors, democracy requires an ethnically and/or linguistically homogeneous group as demos in order to function (Böckenförde 1987; Kirchhof 1991; Grimm, 1994). The reality of modern politics is very different. The homogeneous nation state has always been the exception. It existed only in Western Europe and in East Asia, and only in a sort of fashion, usually with a lot of open or suppressed minority problems. International migration has transformed all European societies into multicultural ones. But the heated discussion, for instance in Germany, whether one should accept the definition of our societies as multicultural is not only somewhat unreal when it ignores the fact of immigration (Bryde, 1992). Much more fundamentally the concurring processes of individualization and globalization have irrevocably destroyed the homogeneous societies for which there is so much nostalgic longing in many parts of Europe. Modern societies do not need immigrants to become multicultural: the gay scene, feminists, traditionalist groups or fundamentalists (Islamic as well as Christian) don't share the same culture. So democracies can no longer rely (if they ever could) on a pre-political community of values, culture, ethnicity, religion or language but have to function under conditions of increased diversity (Wolin, 1993).

Obviously, this is not easy. It is the tragedy of the present condition that increasing multicultural differentiation asks for the development of political forms that would allow for unity in diversity, while in practice the fear of the loss of identity threatens in many European societies to lead to the suppression of minorities, a regression towards nationalism and tribalism. But these dangers only make the challenge for democratic theory to develop answers for democratic practice in multi-cultural societies more urgent.

Quite obviously, the solution for the problems of democracy in a non-homogeneous society cannot be to reserve political rights to a homogeneous core electorate and to subject the other members of society to the rule of such a narrowly defined 'demos'[4]: a society in which minorities are not only culturally different but in addition lack political rights is even less homogeneous than one in which they are at least able to take part in the political process.

The insistence on a quasi-identity of historical nations and democracy is astonishing not only in the light of the fact that, historically, nation building, including the development of a vernacular, usually followed political organisation rather than the other way round (Hobsbawm, 1990; Anderson, 1991; Schulze, 1994, pp. 172 et seq.) Very sucessful examples of democratic government managed without an ethnically or culturally defined 'demos' to build on. In Europe, Switzerland is the most prominent example.[5] Perhaps more important, however, is the experience of the USA. Here, the coexistence of people of different origins, race, religion, and language has led to conflicts, discrimination, violence – so that this example may prevent us from being too optimistic about the future of multicultural democracies. There has always been the temptation of regression towards an ethnically defined concept of the American nation (white, Anglo-Saxon, Protestant or, more modestly, at least European and Christian).[6] On the other hand, oppressed minorities were tempted to define themselves as separate nations, as in the 'two-nations' concept of DuBois and its radicalization in black American thought.[7] Against both temptations the pluralist foundations of American democracy, unity in diversity, has been maintained. For Hannah Arendt this is the essence of the American republic: '(The people) never became a singular to the founders. The word 'people' retained for them the meaning of manyness, of the endless variety

---

4   This, however, is the definition of democracy by Carl Schmitt, still subconsciously influential in Germany: democracy as the rule of a homogeneous group over those who do not belong: C. Schmitt, 1985, p. 14.

5   While for many authors linking democracy to an ethnically and/or linguistic 'Volk' or nation, Switzerland is treated as the aberrant exception proving the rule, for Renan 'La Suisse est peut-être la nation de l'Europe la plus légitiment composé' (Renan, 1934, p. X).

6   For a recent example cf. Fleming, 1993, p. 114: 'The reassertion of our old cultural identities as European and ... Christian nation.'

7   Cf. for a critical discussion Early, 1993, p. 86.

of a multitude whose majesty resided in its very plurality.' (Arendt, 1990). In contrast, the substitution of a quasi-monarchical collective head of state 'people' or 'nation' ('the cheapest and most dangerous disguise the absolute ever assumed in the political realm') for the deposed king seriously impaired democracy in Europe at the outset.[8]

3. Democracy From Below

The insistence on the challenge of globalization does not mean that state regulatory competences should only move upwards, towards the supranational and international level. The regulatory powers of states are also affected from within by the differentiation that exists in modern complex societies.

Both systems theory (Willke, 1983) and economic analysis[9] have adduced much evidence about the inability of the political system on the state level to control economic and social processes.

So, as with the question of globalization, democracy faces the simple challenge of either to follow social decisions to where they are made or to become irrelevant.

More important than this technocratic argument is a positive reconstruction of democracy from below: in all western societies we find increasing alienation of citizens from the governmental process (in Germany this is called 'Politikverdrossenheit'). But in critiques of this phenomenon it is often overlooked that such withdrawal is restricted to the formal political process (elections, party-membership etc). If we define the political process more broadly and include all forms of public activities, citizens action groups, environmental groups etc. we would find an increase rather than a decrease of public participation, less 'vote' but more 'voice' in the language of modern political science (Baumann, 1991, pp. 276 et seq.; Brunkhorst, 1994, pp. 82 et seq.).

In order to rebuild meaningful democracies one has to bring decision-making closer to the people, to empower them to organize their own lives.

Here there is no lack of models: attempts to address environmental problems by a re-drawing of jurisdictions according to ecological rather than historical boundaries ('river basin communities') (Berry, 1993), communitarian proposals for economic democracy (Walzer 1983, p. 318), bargaining and community-centred concepts etc. This is not the place to

---

[8] H. Arendt, 1990, p. 24: '... it is as though the nation-state, so much older than any revolutions, had defeated the revolution in Europe even before it made its appearance.'

[9] For a critical discussion, especially a critique of the dangers of anti-democratic thought in economic theory cf. Pildes/Anderson, 1990, p. 2120.

discuss their merits but it should be possible to discuss them at all. An understanding of democracy that restricts the meaning of democracy to the nation is conceptually unable to take part in this discussion.

II CONSTITUTIONAL BARRIERS TO DEMOCRACY

1. Democracy as the Rule of the German 'Volk'

Let me now turn to the task of the constitutional lawyer. Before we can even think of employing our creative fantasy towards inventing institutions and procedures for meeting these challenges (e.g. more effective transnational parliaments, new institutions of grass-root democracy, arrangements for integrating immigrants into the political system) we have to try to abolish the barriers in constitutional legal thinking. Of these there are many, especially, but I fear not only, in Germany.

I have already mentioned the most important one, namely the close relationship of the concepts of the nation state and democracy. In German constitutional law doctrine this relationship has been transformed from a historical coincidence into a legal dogma by the 2nd senate of the Bundesverfassungsgericht and many writers.

The starting point is the formulation of the democratic principle in the Grundgesetz: 'Alle Staatsgewalt geht vom Volke aus', or, for some authors, an artificially narrow understanding of the original Greek meaning of 'democracy', kratos of the demos; rule of the people. While in English 'people' is both a singular and a plural so that when we speak of 'government by the people' we never lose sight of the manyness of the people, of human beings, the semantics (or socio-linguistics) of the term 'Volk' in German constitutional theory tend to be different: the 'Deutsches Volk' has historically been reified since the 19th century into a super-human being, a krypto-monarchical head of state above human beings (Koselleck, 1992; Sontheimer, 1978, pp. 244 et seq.; Brubaker, 1992). So when one defines the meaning of democracy in Germany by reference to the concept of 'Volk'[10] one imports a lot of pre-democratic thinking into German democracy.

This has been obvious in all three dimensions discussed:

In the Maastricht-debate there were many authors (Kirchhof, 1991; Huber, 1992; Murswiek, 1993; di Fabio, 1993) who held that the principle of democracy thus conceived forbade further integration, because European

---

[10] I call this approach 'volksdemokratisch'; for a critique cf. Bryde, 1994, p. 305

lawmaking was not legitimated by the German people. Contrary to a widely accepted consensus in Europe up to this point, the democratic deficiencies in Europe could, on this view, not be redressed by strengthening the European Parliament as this did not represent 'a people', a nationally defined group in the sense of the German 'Volk'.

In the Maastricht-decision[11] the Constitutional Court was obviously influenced by this position without following it to its radical conclusions. The Court stresses the primacy of democratic legitimacy brought to the European political process through the member states' parliaments. In an obiter dictum it also links democracy to 'social homogeniety', a very dangerous (and contra-factual) statement that the court tries to defend by drawing on the authority of Herrmann Heller – erroneously, as Heller attempts to show in the article cited (Heller, 1971) that democracy is endangered by class conflicts and therefore democracy requires socialism. The Court could have cited Carl Schmitt who appears to be the main influence behind positions linking homogeniety and democracy (Schmitt, 1983, pp. 231 et seq.; 1985, pp. 14 et seq.).

But the court accepts in principle that supranational power is compatible with democracy, pointing out that the opposite assumption would hinder democracies from taking part in integration processes. While this is correct, the Euro-sceptic plaintiffs had a right to be disappointed because in their pleadings they had relied on the ratio of the courts fusion of national principle and democracy in the alien suffrage cases.[12]

In these cases it was held that giving votes in local government elections to foreigners, i.e. people born and educated in Germany but not in possession of a German passport, would be undemocratic, because an election in which foreigners take part cannot provide democratic legitimacy to government. As this reasoning (at least in the Hamburg case) was based on the reading of the Basic Law's Art. 20 (All state power derives from the people) as 'All state power derives from the German people' the opponents of supranational power can be forgiven for thinking the Court was on their side.

Finally, if we take the understanding of democracy as the rule of the collective 'Deutsches Volk' to its logical conclusion, any devolution of power to self-governing bodies or participatory mechanisms is in principle in conflict with democracy, as decisions taken in such forums might

[11] BVerfGE 89, 155, for an English translation cf. Winkelmann, 1994, p. 751.

[12] BVerfGE 83, 37 (Schleswig-Holstein); 83, 60 (Hamburg); I was counsel for the state parliament of Schleswig-Holstein; my written and oral pleadings are documenented in Isensee/Schmidt-Jortzig, 1993; for an excellent critique of the German constitutional debate in English cf. G. Neumann, 1992.

conflict with the will of the German people as a whole (Böckenförde 1987; H. H. Klein, 1972).

So, taken together, conclusions from the concept of 'Volks-Demokratie', which are supported by a relatively broad tendency in German constitutional writing, could effectively bar progress in exactly those fields where democratic theory is in most urgent need of new thinking: transnational democracy, multicultural democracy and grass-root democracy.

2. The Openness of the Grundgesetz

This tendency of a large part of German doctrine, supported by the Bundesverfassungsgericht, to restrict democracy to the nation state, is to be regretted, because it forces me to criticize the German constitutional law doctrine in front of a foreign audience while a correct reading of the Grundgesetz would allow me to boast of the openness of the German constitution for new challenges.

The German Constitution was prescient in 1949 in opening the national constitutional space to transnational power processes. In the preamble it looks towards a future European union and in Art. 24 it allows the transfer of sovereign power to international agencies, thus leading the way to the eventual development of a supra-national law of European integration.

Similarly, the Grundgesetz in principle should be more and not less open to pluralist conceptions of democracy than comparable constitutional systems because it is federalist, guarantees local self-government constitutionally (Art. 28) and is open to the exercise of public authority by non-state agencies (e.g. in the social security system). Obviously, neither the state power exercised within the Länder nor within local communities derives from the 'German people' as a whole. Interestingly enough, when an early draft of the Weimar constitution located sovereignty in the 'German People' this was rejected as being incompatible with a federal system of government (Anschütz, 1933, p. 38).

Perhaps most important, the restriction of democracy to the national level is also astonishing in view of the fact that the Grundgesetz quite definitely does not put national sovereignty or the nation or the state at its beginning, but the principle of human dignity (Häberle, 1987; Maihofer, 1983). The older jurisprudence of the Bundesverfassungsgericht took this central feature of the constitution also as the starting point for its definition of democracy which it understood as a process of self-determination by which all those affected by decisions took part in decision-making.[13]   In conformity with this approach, the court held self-government (not only local government specifically regulated in the Grundgesetz, but also forms of professional self-government so important in the German tradition) to be an integral part of democracy, not an opposing idea.[14] It was mainly the discussion about alien suffrage that contributed to the substitution of a man-centred concept for a nation-centred.

III COMPARATIVE REMARKS

Let me end by some comparative remarks. I started by outlining some challenges to democratic theory and showed how developments in German constitutional theory tend to pose obstacles to meeting those challenges. I wonder, whether this is only a German problem. In a more general analysis, one might see that the heritage of the nation state hinders all European national legal systems in meeting new challenges, and this for very basic reasons: with the secularization of power in the development of the modern state, constitutional theory was looking for new sources of earthly power. Most legal systems developed a Grundnorm which allocated ultimate earthly power somewhere within the legal system: the Crown, Parliament, la nation francaise, Deutsches Volk. This creates basic difficulties in transcending the national legal system.

The solution should be to transfer power from those artificial krypto-monarchical sovereigns to the people seen in their manyness. Only then could the world-wide system of federal autonomy David Held is advocating be constructed without the logic of our different national legal systems frustrating even the first steps.

---

[13] BVerfGE 5, 85 (147); 44, 125 (142).
[14] BVerfGE 33, 125 (158 f.)

REFERENCES

Anderson, B. (1991) *Imagined Communities*, Rev. ed. London.

Anschütz, G. (1933) *Die Verfassung des Deutschen Reiches*, 14th ed. Berlin.

Arendt, H. (1990) *On Revolution*, London.

Baumann, Z. (1991) *Modernity and Ambivalence*, Cambridge.

Berry, Th. (1993) The context for reinhabiting the earth, in Walker S. (ed.) *Changing Communities*, Saint Paul, pp. 185 et seq.

Böckenförde, E. W. (1987) Demokratie als Verfassungsprinzip, in Isensee, J., Kirchhof, P. (eds.) *Handbuch des Staatsrechts*, Vol. I, pp. 906 et seq. Heidelberg.

Brubacker, R. (1992) *Citizenship and Nationhood in France and Germany*, Havard.

Brunkhorst, H. (1994) *Demokratie und Differenz*, Frankfurt am Main 1994.

Bryde, B.-O. (1993) Immigration and Asylum in Germany, in Weick, G. (ed.), *National und European Law on the Threshold to the Single Market*, pp. 159 et seq., Frankfurt Main et al.

Bryde, B.-O. (1994) Die bundesrepublikanische Volksdemokratie als Irrweg der Demokratietheorie, Vol. *5 Staatswissenschaften und Staatspraxis*, pp. 305 et seq.

di Fabio U. (1993) *Der neue Art. 23 des GG, Staat 1993*, pp. 191 et seq.

Early, G. (1993) Their Malcolm, my problem, in Epstein, J. (ed.) *Best American Essays*, pp. 86, et seq. New York.

Fleming, Th. (1993) A League of our own, in Walker, S. (ed.) *Changing Communities*, pp. 101 et seq..

Grimm, D. (1995) *Braucht Europa eine Verfassung?* Münich.

Häberle, P. (1987) Die Menschenwürde als Grundlage der staatlichen Gemeinschaft, in Isensee, J., Kirchhof, P. (eds.) *Handbuch des Staatsrechts*, Vol. I, pp. 845 et seq. Heidelberg.

Held, D. (1991) Democracy, the Nation-State and the Gobal System, *Economy and Society*, Vol. 20, pp. 139 et seq.

Heller, H. (1971) Politische Demokratie und soziale Homogenität, in *Ges. Schriften II*, pp. 421 et seq., Tübingen.

Hobsbawn, E. J. (1990) *Nations and Nationalism since 1780*, Cambridge.

Isensee, J., Schmidt-Jortzig, E. (eds.) (1993) *Das Ausländerwahlrecht vor dem Bundesverfassungsgericht*, Heidelberg.

Kennedy, P. (1994) *Preparing for the Twenty-First century*, London.

Klein, H. H. (1972) Demokratie und Selbstverwaltung, *Festschrift für Forsthoff*, pp. 165 et seq.

Koselleck, R. (1992) Stichwort Volk, Nation XIII - XV, in Brunner, J., Conze, W., Koselleck, R. (eds.) *Geschichtliche Grundbegriffe*, Vol. 7, p. 407

Luhmann, N. (1971) Die Weltgesellschaft, *Archiv f. Rechts- und Sozialphilosophie*, Vol. 57, pp. 1 et seq.

Maihofer, W. (1983) Prinzipien freiheitlicher Demokratie, in Benda, E., Maihofer, W., Vogel, J. (eds.) *Handbuch des Verfassungsrechts*, pp. 173 et seq., Berlin.

Murswiek W. (1993) Maastricht und der pouvoir constituant, *Staat 1993*, pp. 161 et seq.

Neumann, G. (1992) "We are the people": alien suffrage in German and American perspective, *Mich. J. Int'l L.*, Vol. 13, pp. 259 et seq.

Pildes, (1990) Slinging Arrows at Democracy: Social Choice Theory, Value Pluralism, and Democratic Politics, *Columbia Law Review*, Vol. 90, pp. 2120 et seq.

Renan, E. (1934) *Qu'est-ce qu'une Nation* (1882)

Schmitt, C. (1983) *Verfassungslehre*, Berlin.

Schmitt, C. (1985) *Die geistesgeschichtliche Lage des heutigen Parlamentarismus*, Berlin.

Schulze, H. (1994) *Staat und Nation in der Europäischen Geschichte*, Munich.

Sontheimer, K. (1978) *Antidemokratisches Denken in der Weimarer Republik*, Munich.

Streeck, W. (1992) Inclusion and Secession: Questions on the Boundaries of Associative Democracy, *Politics and Society*, Vol. 20, pp. 513 et seq.

Walzer, M. (1983) *Spheres of Justice*, New York.

Willke, H. (1983) *Entzauberung des Staates*, Königstein/Ts.

Winkelmann, I. (ed.) (1994) *Das Maastricht-Urteil des Bundesverfassungsgerichts*, Berlin.

Wolin, S. (1993) Democracy, Difference, and Re-Cognition, *Political Theory*, Vol. 21, pp. 464 et seq.

13. Studying a Foreign Legal System: The Case of Japan

Dr. John McEldowney – University of Warwick

I SUMMARY

Japanese law cannot be studied in isolation from Japan, its people and culture. In this essay some of the difficulties in understanding Japanese culture and law are examined[1] Uniquely Japan draws on the two major legal systems of the world. Both civil law and common law systems are combined in a culture that has embraced modern Western values while preserving Japanese tradition. A new modern Western style Constitution (1947) provides individual rights and creates new legal duties. The potential for radical constitutional change is tempered with a profound cultural inertia. Individual rights modelled on Western influences are in contrast to a group culture and the influence of family, neighbours and employers which act as strong constraints on individual behaviour. Conflict co-exists with the desire for compromise. Eclectic decision making accommodates decisions based on principle. Sharp tensions exist between formal law and customary law. Understanding Japanese law must take account of strong influences in Japanese society such as history, religion, politics, economics, employment, art, literature and geography. The value of law and the relevance of legal rules, including the use of the courts, must be studied as part of the rich cultural traditions that make Japan such a curiosity for the foreign scholar.

---

[1] See: Friedman, 'Some thoughts on Comparative Legal Culture' in Clark (ed.), *Comparative and Private International Law: Essays in Honor of John Henry Merryman on his Seventieth Birthday* (Berlin, Duncker and Humblot, 1990).

II STUDYING JAPANESE LAW[2]

Japan' modern legal system offers some stimulating curiosities[3] to the interested Western jurist. The fundamental parts of the legal system were developed in the nineteenth century and modelled on the Prussian Constitution[4] and the French and German Codes[5]. Japan's full scale adoption of a civil law system as a source of law, came after considering but rejecting, the introduction of the English common law[6].

It is significant that Japan's adaptation of the civil law system was assisted by academics. In 1873 the influential jurist Gustave Emile Boissonade[7] taught at the Law Institute attached to the Ministry of Justice and gave lectures in the preparatory training of future lawyers and judges in Japan. Foreign law professors visited and taught at Tokyo's Imperial University[8] Law Faculty and were influential in training future judges. But the reasoning and principles of the common law were also studied, including the use of precedent in deciding similar cases. Since 1877 Anglo –American law has been taught at the University[9] with an emphasis on legal precedent and the development of judge-made law.

After the second world war a new Japanese Constitution[10] (1947) drafted on an American constitutional model was adopted. The new Constitution

---

[2] I am very grateful to Professors Fuke, Kaino, and Ishida from the University of Nagoya for their help and assistance in developing my thinking about Japan. Also to Judge Fuiji, of the Tokyo District Court for his helpful advice and to Professor Geoffrey Wilson for his encouragement of Japanese studies at the School of Law at the University of Warwick.

[3] See: T. Gorai, 'Influence du Code Civil Francais sur le Japon' dans *Le Code Civil: Livre du Centenaine* (Paris, 1904).

[4] See: The Japanese Constitution (1889) or otherwise known as the Meiji Constitution. An analysis is provided in L. Beer, Constitutional Revolution in Japanese Law, Society and Politics *16 Modern Asian Studies* 39 (1982).

[5] See: The Japanese Constitution (1889), the Civil Code 1896 and 1898, the Commercial Code (1890), the Code of Civil Procedure (1890), Penal Code and Code of Criminal Procedure (1880). See: Professor Oda, *Japanese Law* (Butterworths, 1992) also J. McEldowney, *Public Law* (Sweet and Maxwell,1994), Yosiyuki Noda, *Introduction au droit Japonais* (1966).

[6] Translations were undertaken of A.V. Dicey's, *An Introduction to the Law of the Constitution* (Macmillan, 1885).

[7] (1825-1910).

[8] This was the first University Law School in Japan. See for a description of the value of foreign law studies in Japan: T.Kawasima, 'The Concept of Judicial Precedent in Japanese Law' in *Festschrift fur Max Rheinstein Ius Privatum* pp. 85-101.

[9] The subjects taught included precedent, civil and criminal procedure and rules of evidence. H. Terry, *The First Principles of Law* (1878) was influential.

[10] Nihon koku kempo.

brought an end to the monopoly of civil law and encouraged the adaptation of civil and common law values in the one legal system. It Constitution contains Western values[11] strikingly expressed in terms of individual rights and freedoms and provides for an independent Supreme Court and judiciary. Sovereignty is vested in the people exercised through a Parliamentary democracy centred around a strong executive Cabinet with constitutional protection. There is limited autonomy granted to local government. The Constitution reflects a radical break with the past militarist state and dominant feudal culture. It is uniquely pacifist in nature and abandons the notion of the Emperor as a deity, but maintains the Emperor in the form of an hereditary monarchy. Some, at least of Japan's feudal past is assimilated into a modern working democratic state.

The new Constitution has become a fundamental part of Japanese legal and social culture. As a result Japan offers an interesting example of the way in which the two major systems of the world may be combined; the civil law tradition in terms of its Codes and procedures and the common law tradition in the form of a modern written liberal Constitution based on precedent. This combination of traditions offers an intriguing glimpse of compromise and contradiction in the fusion of two distinct systems of law.

It is undeniable that the Japanese Constitution has a powerful influence on the life of the nation. It has legitimated public values and institutions and although the Constitution is almost fifty years old it has not been amended. Political stability has been gained, though the period of virtual one party rule has worried analysts about the state of the political well being of the nation.

The life of the Japanese Constitution has been accompanied by a period of unprecedented economic prosperity and peace in the 1980's. Although Japan's economic recession since the late 1980's has been more severe than many comparable nations, Japan's place in the world as a major economic power is unquestioned. Recognition of its economic status in international affairs has steadily increased: The first Nobel prize for literature was awarded to a Japanese in 1992; Japan is likely to gain full member status and voting rights in the Security Council of the United Nations; and Japan has become a major donor nation to the developing countries of the world.

There are, however, formidable difficulties facing a foreign scholar interested in studying the law and culture of Japan. This paper begins with an analysis of the difficulties facing a scholar interested in Japanese law because of the distinctive nature of the Japanese legal system. This is

---

[11] See: R.C. van Caenegem, *An Historical Introduction to Western Constitutional Law* (Cambridge, 1995).

followed by consideration of Japanese culture and society. Finally, there is an analysis of the role of law in Japan and the value of studying Japanese law to the foreign scholar.

The Distinctiveness of the Japanese Legal System

Unlike many other foreign legal systems, Japanese law and culture have not developed in a unilinear manner within one tradition of legal institutions and public values[12]. The formidable difficulties that face the foreign scholar include understanding the language and culture of Japan. Overcoming such difficulties may prove impossible for many and in many instances reliance has to be made on English translations of Japanese materials. Interpreting materials, largely written by American lawyers and scholars, requires careful judgement when assessing issues and perspectives.

The bulk of Japanese legal writing is not readily available in many libraries in the West. Japanese legal scholars do not warrant much attention in any history of Western legal theory[13] or in the development of Western substantive law. Japanese scholarly interest in Western systems of law has also been narrow and specific to particular issues[14]. Viewing law mainly in terms of a national or even a European legal system has largely confined the study of comparative law to Western systems and this may also have contributed to the lack of interest in the study of Japanese law and its values. Only if law is considered from a global or international perspective does the study of Japanese or Chinese law assume significance.

More difficult than the practical obstacles to the study of Japan and its laws is the need to overcome prejudices and preconceptions. The ferocity of the second world war and its aftermath has left an enduring legacy. Overcoming prejudice and misunderstandings has been slow and this has inhibited understanding Japan, Japanese culture and Japanese law.

A foreign student of Japan and its legal system must also overcome difficulties in understanding a complex history of tradition and culture that may appear to be in conflict with modern day Japan but which retains a fundamental relevance to our understanding of modern Japanese society.

---

[12] An insight into this analysis is provided in L. Beer, *Freedom of Expression in Japan: A Study in Comparative Law, Society and Politics* (1980). See also: D. Henderson, *Conciliation and Japanese Law: Tokugawa and Modern* 2 Vols. (1965).

[13] For example in J.M. Kelly, *A Short History of Western Legal Theory* (Oxford,1992). A relatively small reference to Japan is contained in the **Encyclopaedia Brittanica**.

[14] There appears greater interest in German, French, American and Chinese law than in English law or in the English legal system.

Within Japan itself there are problems arising from the diversity of interpretations of its legal culture. Scholars, judges, attorneys, prosecutors, civil servants and politicians offer different attitudes and interpretations reflecting their respective roles in the legal system. The part that culture plays in the legal system is the starting point of understanding Japanese law.

Japanese Culture and Society

Japan's geographical position and typography has an important significance for Japanese society. Japan consists of four major islands[15] off the east coast of the Asian continent. Its land mass is only slightly larger than that of Finland or Italy.Its population is the seventh largest in the world[16] and the population density per unit area under cultivation is the highest in the world. A high percentage of the population is based in three major urban areas, Tokyo, Osaka and Nagoya.

Japan's typography and situation has shaped the character of its people and its economic development. Japan lies on the Pacific rim and as a result earthquakes and active volcanoes form part of the Pacific earthquake zone and are relatively common. Volcanic eruptions have shaped the typography of the country and together with earthquakes have caused the deaths of many Japanese people from earliest history. The high peaked and steeply sided mountains on the Northern side of the islands make human habitation impossible. The low mountain districts and plateaus on the Pacific South side provide the main areas of population density. Japan is situated in the monsoon zone of the Eastern coast of Asia, it has a wide range of temperatures and a high rainfall.

Japan's agriculture is based primarily on large fishing industry and arable farming of crops such as rice, grain and vegetables. Japan's feudal past and agricultural economy has been transformed in modern times into the foremost industrial economy in the world.

(i) The Japanese economy and history
Tracing the origins of contemporary Japan requires some explanation of the economic, political and social culture of Japan. The origins of Japan's modern economy[17] may be traced back to developments during the Edo period of Japanese history (1600-1868). At the beginning of the

---

[15] Hokkaido, Honshu, Shikoku and Kyushu.

[16] In 1990 population was estimated to be 123,612,000.

[17] The most illuminating account is provided in T. Ito, *The Japanese Economy* (Cambridge, 1992).

seventeenth century Japan was an agrarian society, but by the end of the nineteenth century Japan had become highly commercialised.

Japan's society was centrally organised and unified in Edo (now Tokyo) during the Tokugawa shogunate (1543 – 1616)[18]. While political and military power rested with the Tokugawa family in Edo, the Emperor and the imperial family resided in Kyoto. The pretence that the Emperor had appointed the shogunate concealed the fact of political and economic power rested with the Tokugawa shoguns. Japanese society was ordered into a highly structured hierarchy[19] – warriors, farmers, artisans and merchants representing the major divisions of society. By the mid 18th century Edo's population had reached 1 million, Osaka had become a major port and Japan's economic development was rapidly changing. Currency was introduced in Japan earlier than in Britain. The value of gold and copper coins was standardised, while that of silver coins depended on their weight. Exchange rates for the coinage were determined daily. Bills of exchange and certificates of deposit were in common circulation and treated as equivalent to money. Government was organised around Edo with the allegiance of provincial war-lords (shugo daimyo) ensured through the requirements to spend alternate years in Edo (sankin kotai) to attend on the Shogun.

The characteristics of this period have been noted by Ito[20]:

> The social structure of the Tokugawa era was marked by Sakoku (isolation from foreign countries), Shino-kosho (a kind of caste system), and Sankin-kotai (the alternative attendance of local lords).

The Edo period provided a unity of purpose through central control and feudal organisation. It also prohibited foreign travel by Japanese and foreign trade was mainly confined to trade with Holland through Nagasaki. Japan appeared isolated from the world, though there was some trade with Korea through Tsuhima as well as trade from Nagasaki. There was some trade with China. Isolation gave rise to stability but also internal change. The birth of a Japanese enterprise culture is noticeable through the activities of small family merchants and larger merchant houses mostly in Tokyo and Osaka. The shift from the agricultural past to the development of retail trade and craft production was accompanied by changes in the social order. The development of guilds, crafts and trades is one aspect of this

---

[18] This account is drawn from *Japan, Profile of a Nation* (Kodansha International,1994) and *Japan: An Illustrated Encyclopaedia* (Kodansha International). I am very grateful for the assistance of the Japanese Embassy in London, for helpful advice and assistance in preparing this paper.

[19] Ito, *op. cit.*, p.8 .

[20] *Ibid.*

development. More significant were the changes in the allocation of wealth and property. Urban life proved costly and the revenue from agricultural taxes inadequate to meet the requirements of the Daimyo. Borrowing was necessary and credit instituted to subsidise the life styles of the samurai and the Daimyo. Merchants who managed the rice warehouses became major creditors. The consequences of change were not always clearly foreseen but the need for change was apparent. The economic indebtedness of the daimyo and shogunate was noticeable in contrast to the new found wealth of the merchants. The demand of foreigners for foreign trade eventually forced Japan to confront the world economy.

At the end of the Edo period Japan emerged remarkably unified and stable compared to many Western societies. Throughout the Edo period, Japan had been free from external war, although isolated in its perceptions about the world. Its agricultural and feudal society had gradually been transformed. There was a large educated population led by a wealthy merchant class experienced in commercial transactions and able to rely on a large surplus of agrarian labour. In addition Japan developed well trained and highly motivated craftsmen. More importantly administratively Japan could draw on the experience of the samurai to provide leadership and direction. Militarism was thereby linked to civilian society in a distinctive way. Japanese culture was identified with distinct social groups and internal cohesion provided the antidote to radical change.

In 1859 Japan's ports were forced to open to foreign trade after a series of negotiations with the United States[21]. Inevitably this led to a number of treaties signed between Japan and Britain, Russia, France, and the Netherlands[22] between 1854 to 1858. Foreign trade pressure and disputes between the Daimyos over the fairness of the treaty arrangements considerably weakened the Tokugawa Shogun. The end of the Tokugawa period came through an effort to unify Japan. Following criticism by many Daimyos the imperial court was unified through marriage between the young Tokugawa shogun and Princess Kazu. In 1867 the Emperor Meiji aged 16, came to power and the Imperial court moved from Kyoto to Tokyo.

The Meiji restoration which followed marked the beginning of the early modern Japanese economy and endured until the second world war. Modernisation of industries was accompanied by the creation of special banks[23] after 1897 which provided financial support for Japanese

---

[21] See: K. E.Calder, *Crisis and Compensation* (Princeton,1988).

[22] Ito, *op. cit.*, p.11.

[23] Leading banks included Dai-Ichi Bank, Mitsui Bank, the Mitsubishi Bank, the Sumitomo Bank and the Yasuda Bank (now Fuji Bank).

investments. Parallels are often made between industrialisation experienced in Western countries and the Japanese experience during the Meiji period. At this time the challenge Japan faced was how to adapt and change as an economic trading partner in the world economy while maintaining and preserving its own integrity and independence.   Two principles were adopted to confront this challenge: industrialisation and a strong military. Japan's economic and military power was demonstrated in two wars against its neighbours – with China (1894 -95) and Russia (1904-5). Japan was at the time of the first world war the major colonial power in Asia[24]. Ito[25] notes how Japan developed after the first world war:

> Japan entered the First World War and came out a big victor in the Treaty of Versailles, becoming the major colonial power in Asia. In 1910 Japan annexed Korea.

Early military success and later failure after the second world war has left an enduring legacy on Japan. Re-building Japan after defeat into one of the great economic powers of the world has come about through a curious combination of circumstances. At first glance it is easy to see the role of the state as the guiding strategist in building economic development and making Japan into the first of the East Asian developmental states[26]. The development of Japan's modern economy is analogous to a military operation of attacking key sectors of the world economy and building on success in areas such as textiles, car manufacturing, steel production, optics, ship building and electronics. However, trial and error as much as forward planning appears equally plausible as an explanation. The key to Japan's success up to the outbreak of the second world war depended on the adoption and mastery of imported techniques. Japan was the first country to achieve a high level of economic development from a rice-growing agricultural economy. Japan was the first Asian economy to industrialise while preserving a large and dynamic small-scale business sector. Cheap sources of labour and flexibility combined to provide a responsive labour force for each sector of the Japanese economy. As Francks has noted[27] Japan's domestic market was important to its economic success as well as Western economic strategies towards Japan:

> The domestic consumer market remained dominated by traditional, highly differentiated, food products and other consumption goods, for which only relatively labour intensive production methods (perhaps with the addition of an electric motor) were known and in which large-scale advanced-country producers had no interest.   Labour-intensive

---

[24] Japan had control over Korea, the Southern half of Sakhalin Island, the southern tip of Manchuria and the Manchurian railway.
[25] T. Ito, *The Japanese Economy* (Cambridge, 1992)pp. 13-14.
[26] See:P. Francks, *Japanese Economic Development* (Routledge, 1992).
[27] Francks, *op. cit.*, p.250.

Japanese producers, aided by general trading companies, by developments in Japanese shipping and by the fortunate withdrawal of Western competition at crucial times, found a ready export market in Asia for their lower-quality but cheaper consumer goods. Meanwhile, large-scale Japanese firms, with their easier access to investment funds and their ability to meet the demand for heavy industrial products for which more capital-intensive production techniques had come to be developed in the advanced economies.

It is clear that assessing Japan's modern day economic success depends on evaluating many of the historical forces and political circumstances that make up Japan. Many of these were eclectic. Also significant is the role of religion in Japanese society. Many Japanese beliefs and traditions owe their origins to Japan's prehistoric customs. Shinto, ('the Way of the gods'), is the only major religion indigenous to Japan. Different foreign contributions such as Indian Buddhism and various Chinese religions have all undergone transformation in the combination of native tradition and outside influence. It is estimated that by the 8th century myths and traditions were unified in Japanese teaching[28] setting out a single account of the creation and descent of the emperor from the gods. Shintoism took root in opposition to the strict regularity of Buddhist teaching. Buddhism was officially introduced into Japan from Korea around 552, though some scholars put this date to be earlier in 538. Studies of Buddhist teachings in Japan began in earnest at a much later date probably in the 7th and 8th centuries mainly influenced by six schools from China. In the Nara period (710-794) Buddhism became the state religion. Different sects developed placing their own emphasis on aspects of Buddhism. Zen Buddhism was introduced from China and found support in the military. The Tokugawa shogunate (1603-1867) experienced the entrenchment of Buddhism as an alternative to Christianity. Attempts were made in the eighteenth century to return to the origins of Buddhism through the interpretation of the original Sanskrit texts. After the Meiji restoration the government attempted to make Shinto the national religion and this became influential in maintaining the power of the Emperor and in education. A number of characteristics may be found: An emphasis on the importance of human institutions; an observance and respect for symbolic significance; a respect for ancient practices and Shinto; and the development of a lay leadership. Traditional Japanese religion pays great respect to the sacred relationship between God and man, the importance of the family, ritual purification, festivals as a means of religious celebration and the close relationship between religion and state.

---

[28] See: Kojiki 712, Record of Ancient Matters and Nihon shoki 720, Chronicle of Japan. See: *Japan Profile of a Nation* (Kodansha International, 1995).

In recent years there has been a growth in interest among Western states and companies about Japan. Often the inquiry is motivated by the desire to learn from Japan's success and to understand Japan as a model of how Western society might improve. Thus Japanese studies have been dominated by the analysis of the Japanese company, the structures of management, employer and employee relations and the organisation of the workforce and of Japanese society. Such studies are of useful value but this approach fails to appreciate the way the Japanese look at the world. What is required is an evaluation of how international precedent has a part in determining how Japan developed its economy and the intellectual debates that accompanied that development[29] in Japan itself. One of the important ways Japan is distinctive is its interest in borrowing ideas from the world. Innovation and ideas outside Japan are carefully monitored on a systematic and ongoing basis. For example, particularly in the 1960's the powerful Japanese Ministries kept a watchful eye on developments in public health in the United States and in agriculture in Germany and in Europe. In the development of the Japanese legal system an important dimension to the intellectual debate in Japan was the Europeanisation of Japanese law begun in the Meiji period.

(ii) The europeanisation of Japanese law

Japanese curiosity about Western philosophy and legal thought encouraged[30] the study of Mill, Bentham, Montesquieu, de Tocqueville and Rousseau[31]. The legal systems and laws of France, Germany and England were carefully studied by Japanese scholars. Their motives were mixed. Some regarded Western society as a model for Japan's future development economically and materially. Others saw Western economic influence and control as a threat to Japan's independence that required the development of strategies for Japan's survival.

Europeanisation of Japanese law was limited to the role of the state and the legal system. It did not affect the lives of ordinary Japanese people. Social rules, culture and conventions that were formed during the centuries of Japanese isolation from the world remained intact and often contradictory to the reception of foreign law and ideas. The Janus quality of Japanese attitudes dominated. The Japanese looking to the external world at large took on a different face than when looking to the internal world of Japanese society and culture. Any contradictions were accepted as

---

[29] H. Heclo, *Modern Social Politics in Britain and Sweden* (Yale University ,1974).

[30] See: O.F. Robinson,T.D. Fergus and M.W. Gordon, *European Legal History* (second edition, Butterworths,1994).

[31] See: R. Storry, *A History of Modern Japan* (Penguin, 1960), p. 107.

the inevitable consequences of attempting to reconcile the material success of European civilisation with Japanese morality. This demonstrates the paradox that often characterises Japan and the Japanese attitudes to change particularly the way change is accommodated in Japanese society[32].

In 1880 an influential liberal movement in favour of human rights grew in popular support and challenged government policy[33]. The liberal credentials of this movement were heavily questioned – some saw it as comprising disillusioned pro-government supporters with a radical agenda seeking power, others saw it as a mask to hide discontent over economic links with western governments and a reactionary movement seeking to make Japan isolationist. The movement was suppressed by the government. Arguably the link between liberal sounding human rights and reactionary forces left the Japanese government fearful of rights orientated Constitutions and its previous attraction to the French legal system and codes was rejected. Professor Noda explains[34]:

> From 1881 on the absolutest character of government policy became more accentuated, and this political tendency was reflected at the legal level too. The decline in the influence of French law was only one of its aspects. Another aspect was the increasingly important role that German law was playing in the Japanese legal world.

In 1882 Ito Hirobumi a senior official in the Imperial Government began work in Europe studying European Constitutions. In 1886 after returning to Japan he began work on a new Japanese Constitution. Inoue Kowashi, another government official, was given prime responsibility for drafting the text. A new Japanese Constitution was adopted in 1889 modelled in part on a British parliamentary system[35] but also heavily influenced by the Prussian Constitution of 1850. The legislative power was exercised by the Imperial Diet and the executive power was entrusted to the Prime Minister and Cabinet. The courts had limited jurisdiction but lacked constitutional authority to review the acts of the Diet. The Emperor bestowed the Constitution on the Japanese people.

The essential characteristics of the Constitution were its preservation of the past and its aspirations to bring democratic elements into Japan such as elections to the Diet. This Meiji Constitution combined many Western values with Japanese culture. Past traditions were preserved by the

---

[32] J. Woronoff, *Japan: The Coming Social Crisis* (Yohan Publications, 1988).
[33] *Jiyu Minken Undo.*
[34] Y. Noda, *Introduction to Japanese Law* (Tokyo University, 1976).
[35] The upper house comprised former court nobles, feudal lords, the samurai and the new merchants. The lower house was composed of representatives limited to males who paid more than 15 yen in taxes (no more than 1% of the electorate). The franchise was broadened in 1925 ehan all adult males received the vote.

acceptance of the independence of the military and considerable legal powers vested in the Emperor: he was Head of State; all laws were made with his consent; legislative powers could be exercised by the Emperor; a variety of regulatory functions could be exercised by the Emperor; and budget making could be decided by the Emperor who could influence the time-table of the debate in the Japanese Diet and thereby control the acceptance of budget measures.

In the case of the military, the Constitution failed to regulate the jurisdiction of the Diet over military affairs. This permitted past practices to be continued.Military autonomy thus preserved allowed militarist objectives to set the agenda of civil government.

The constitution began a path to democratic government that was both liberal and reformist. For the first time the Meiji Constitution introduced the concept of the separation of powers, providing for an independent legislature, executive and judiciary. The Constitution did not provide for judicial review of government decisions and the three elements of the Constitution gave way to executive influence. At the time of the first world war, Japan was a centralised state, bureaucratic in organisation and militarist in outlook.

A significant part of the reform of the Japanese legal system came through the adoption of European codes[36]. In 1893 a council for codification was commissioned to draft a Civil Code[37]. After considering many foreign legal systems,including the French[38] , the draft German Civil Code was chosen as a main model for the Japanese Civil Code and a draft contained in two books was completed and came into force on 16 July 1898. It was, however, more than a simple re-enactment of the German Civil Code.Many parts of the Japanese code contained substantial parts retained from the French Civil Code. And the influence of other European codes such as the Swiss, Austrian and Dutch may be found in some of the articles relating to damages for non-performance of obligations (see Articles 415-22 of the Japanese Civil Code). Such choices often reflected the differences in the education of the three draftsman[39]. In fact the model of

---

[36] See: O.F. Robinson, T.D. Fergus and W.M. Gordon, *European Legal History* (Butterworths,1994).

[37] The commission involved in drafting the Civil Code consisted of three Tokyo University Law Professors: Hozumi Nobushige,Tomii Masakira and Ume Kenjiro.

[38] Boissonade's code had been the first choice but this was rejected as the basis of a re-enactment.

[39] Ume and Tomii had been educated in French law Hozumi had been educated in English law and at the University of Berlin.

the French Code was seen to be as important as that of the German Code. Professor Ume explained[40]:

> The new code is based on the French Code and other codes of French origin at least as much as it is on the German Code.

Other Codes were also modelled on the German and French Codes. In the case of the Penal Code and the Criminal Procedure Code these were drawn up by Boissonade and modelled on the French Codes. In the case of judicial organisation and civil procedure French law was the most influential but here there were also some English influences. Prior to the introduction of the Japanese codes judges had decided most cases according to principles of French or English law. Judicial precedent was an important legacy from the English common law.Japanese jurists found the English doctrine of precedent important despite the reception and influence of German Codes[41]. This is a legacy which forms an important debate amongst Japanese lawyers today. In Japan some scholars prefer to see precedent as a flexible source of judge made-law and judicial creativity but others see judicial decisions as nothing more than interpretations of codes or statutes[42].

The development of an independent Supreme Court separate from the Ministry of Justice began in 1875. Training in French legal procedures was a core activity in the training of Japanese judges. French law formed a discrete part of the teaching at Tokyo University in 1885 and it was estimated in 1904 that sixteen out of the twenty nine judges of the Supreme Court were educated in French law.

In 1887 Otto Rudolph, a German scholar, was given the task of drawing up the law on the organisation of the courts and influenced by the French code on civil procedure. In 1884 Techow, a German jurist, was asked to draw up a draft civil Procedure Code based on the German law of 1877. As a result in 1890 a Code of Civil Procedure was drafted and a year later came into effect. In 1881 H. Roesler, a German jurist began work on a study of the commercial laws of the civilised world. He drew up a Japanese Commercial code based on the French Code. In 1890 the Japanese Commercial code was accepted and a year later came into effect. At the end of the nineteenth century Japan's codification was complete and this formed the basis of a modern legal system. This transformation was not in response to the demands of Japanese society, but more the formation of a

---

[40] Professor Ume, Centenary Celebrations on the French Civil Code in 1904 at the Faculty of Law at the Imperial University of Tokyo.

[41] See: T. Kawshima, 'The Concept of Judicial Precedent in Japanese law' in *Festchrift fur Max Rheinstein Ius Privatum pp.*85-101.

[42] M. Kaino, *Hanrei Kenkyu no Mokuteki* (1962).

legal order that might address the world. Newly imported western values and European ideas contained in the Meiji Constitution and the various codes co-existed with a Japanese society deeply rooted in Confucian thinking, culture and social habits. The basis of Japanese social order and morality was preserved and the Europeanisation of Japanese law appeared not to interfere with the life of the ordinary Japanese[43].

The role of law in Japanese society

Japan's unconditional surrender in 1945, after the second world war, resulted in the imposition of peace conditions on Japan by the Allies[44]. This resulted in the most radical break with past Japanese practice and tradition. The Emperor was replaced as law giver and the Meiji constitution was replaced with a new Constitution in 1947 which, as has been mentioned already, was strongly influenced by the United States. For the first time sovereignty lay with the people rather than the Emperor who was retained as[45] 'the symbol of the state'. State Shintoism was disestablished. The Japanese Supreme Court received a new constitutional authority to review legislation and government action. This has presented a new challenge of developing case law and interpreting constitutional doctrines in an American style of jurisprudence with an emphasis on the rule of law and civil liberties. The Japanese legal system comes under the influence of both common law and civil law traditions in the one legal system. This has led to an even sharper consideration in Japanese thinking of both civil law and common law systems and how to combine them.

The 1947 Japanese Constitution lists extensive individual rights, provides a level of local government autonomy, limits the use of military force to self defence[46], and provides for a separation of powers between the legislature, executive and judiciary[47]. In 1952 Japan regained its sovereignty and more than forty years have now passed since the enactment of the 1947 Constitution. Significantly for the development of the Japanese legal system the courts were separated from the Ministry of Justice and under the 1947 Constitution the courts were given freedom to determine their own

---

[43] A fascinating account is given in: K. Rokumoto, Problems and Methodology of Study of Civil Disputes Part 1 5 *Law in Japan* 97 *(1972)*.

[44] See: J. C. Grew, *Ten years in Japan* (London, 1943). Grew was United States Ambassador to Japan 1932-1942.

[45] Article 1 of the 1947 Japanese Constitution.

[46] See Article 9 of the 1947 Constitution on the role of the Japanese self defence forces.

[47] P. R. Luney, *The Constituion of Japan – the Fifth Decade Law and Contemporary Problems* Winter 1990.Duke University,1990.

jurisprudence. To date only four occasions have arisen when the Supreme Court has rejected as unconstitutional a legislative Act of the Diet[48].

How has Japan adapted to the rights formulation of its 1947 Constitution, and the civil law tradition of its Codes? The answer is partly to be found in Japanese attitudes to law.

It is apparent that Japanese attitudes to law and litigation share the essential characteristics of Japanese culture and history. Respect for the law is both symbolic and ritualistic. One writer described the Japanese as[49] 'ritualistic, restrained, aesthetic and authoritarian', a description that fits Japanese past tradition and modern pragmatism. The communal solidarity that flows from strong religious and cultural pressures is present in the organisation of Japanese schools, universities and companies. The Japanese reliance on others within society fits a pattern of life which in Japan is crime free and well ordered. Individual rights are therefore not the main determining factor in relationships. Generally the traditional Japanese tend to be submissive to public authority and the State. However, there are signs that such traditional approaches to law are changing. In recent times law and legal rights have become critical to the success of campaigns by environmental groups and by women seeking employment rights. Economic recession has cast doubts on the stability of the bed-rock of Japanese employment relationships such as the system of life-time employment.

Japanese perceptions about legal rules are also distinctive. Although Western lawyers may well recognise some similarity in approach, there are marked contrasts. For example in the law of contract the codified rules of contract provide only a conceptual framework that permits bargains to be worked out beyond the application of legal rules. The creation and maintenance of long term relationships is against the background of a closely knit community and this has paramount influence on the terms and conditions of the contract.By analogy the contract is seen as a communal relationship. Many of the elements of contractual relationships in Japan has been summarised by Kawashima[50] to include: the powerful party attempts to win favours from the weaker side; requirements of trust are high on the agenda of the relationship; and the elimination of future conflicts is seen as important. Significantly the stronger party may not see it as illogical to

---

[48] See: H. Oda, *Japanese Law* (Butterworths, 1993) pp. 43-44. The cases are as follows: Supreme Court 28 November 1962, Supreme Court 4 April 1973, Supreme Court 30 April 1975, Supreme Court 14 April 1976.

[49] See: J.T. Swada, 'A social legal study of current Japanese business practice in its total cultural context' in *Laws, Contract and Dispute Resolution* (Tokyo,1968) pp. 173-93.

[50] Kawashima, *The Notion of Law, Right and Social order in Japan* (1964).

attempt to assist the weaker party as part of a contribution to the conduct of future relationships and the general interests of the community.

One area of considerable controversy and debate is the question of Japanese attitudes to litigation.   Scholars have noted that in general litigation was less likely in Japan than in comparable situations in Western societies.   The argument that the Japanese are reluctant litigants was supported by a number of observations; the small number of lawyers in Japan[51] compared to the United States and England; the absence of legal aid for civil cases; the long time delay in obtaining decisions by the higher appellate courts; the absence of large law firms and outside Tokyo the relatively small number of legal practices; and the wide use of para-legal or quasi-lawyers.

More fundamentally it is asserted that the Japanese prefer a conciliation approach to dispute resolution. Sawada concludes[52]:

> the Japanese generally abhor impersonal,logical and clear solutions. The parties to a dispute prefer (1) quietly working out solutions themselves (2) without resort to the objective rule (3) in vague, quantitative indeterminate ways.

In contrast other scholars, most notably Haley in 1978, assert that the evidence suggesting that the Japanese are reluctant litigants is based on a myth. Haley points to the obvious difficulties of litigation in Japan. This may be explained in the way the profession has been regulated.The few law graduates that qualify as lawyers and the small number of legal practices in Japan is commensurate with the small number of judges in Japan and the relatively high work-load of the Japanese courts. Haley concludes[53]:

> Few misconceptions about Japan have been more widespread or as pernicious as the myth of the special reluctance of the Japanese to litigate. In emphasising this peculiar Japanese response, most commentators ignore the distaste for litigation and preference for informal dispute resolution common to most societies.

> The myth also directs attention away from factors that may help us to understand better some of the dynamics of Japanese life and hides from view relationships that we might otherwise profitably explore. Does the failure of the courts to provide adequate relief explain, at least in part, such apparent social abnormalities such as gangsterism and recurrent bouts of violence in Japan's otherwise remarkably crime-free society? On the other hand, does limited access to the courts also have the effect of promoting beneficial forms of mediation and other mechanisms for dispute resolution?   What is the relationship between the number of lawyers and litigation in other societies?

---

[51] Population per Attorney: Japan 9,199, U.S.A. 358, U.K. 879, Germany 1,291 and France 3,468. Source: H.Oda, *Japanese Law* (Butterworths, 1993) Appendix 2.

[52] Swada *op. cit.*, p.179.

[53] J. Haley, 'The myth of the Reluctant Litigant' (1978) *Journal of Japanese Studies* 359-390.

The Japanese use of mediation and other forms of conciliation provides an important agenda for future research on the role of law in Japan. The Japanese appear reluctant to wreck personal relations and the social pressure typified in a communal society compels both parties to a dispute to preserve 'harmony' and not to open controversy. What of the future? Will the Japanese continue to make personal relations perform such an important part in the process of dispute resolution? How will the intellectual difference between civil and common law systems exert pressures on the Japanese legal system? Will Japanese become more litigation conscious and Japanese law develop on the basis of individual rights?

III CONCLUSIONS: THE VALUE OF STUDYING JAPANESE LAW

Comparative legal studies is one of the most challenging areas of the curriculum. In this essay the perspective for the study of Japanese law is firmly rooted in the belief that legal institutions, ideas and influences may only be understood in the context of the culture and society in which they are found. The task ahead is a formidable one. Finding the intellectual connections between different legal systems and cultures demands skills and techniques that go beyond the conventional legal ones. Thus understanding history,economics and politics as part of legal culture is a pre-requisite to understanding particular laws and legal disciplines. This is not simply an intellectual debate. As Europe undergoes the considerable changes and transitions inherent in the development of the European Union, different religions, cultures and perspectives may collide in seeming disunity. This has an important relevance for the English common law. How might common law and civil law systems be combined successfully? Japanese law addresses this question and may provide a future perspective for the development of civil and common law systems within the European Union.

In conclusion it is possible to summarise many reasons why the study of Japanese law is important. Professor Oda[54] has noted a number of perspectives. Japan has been influenced by many legal systems of the world which underlines the value of the study of Japanese law as a study in comparative law. The Europeanisation of Japanese law in the nineteenth century was accompanied by a deep intellectual curiosity about the role of law in society. Japan provides a useful case study of the role of law in

---

[54] *Ibid.*

modernising society. Japanese experience may provide a model for foreign legal systems in specific fields of dispute resolution such as consumer credit, pollution control and in traffic accident disputes. Japan's financial institutions provide an important international centre linked to foreign securities and markets. Foreign companies are increasingly reliant on trade with Japanese companies and in areas such as intellectual property, competition and company law knowledge of the Japanese legal system is desirable.   Litigation arising out of trade arrangements with Japanese companies requires an understanding of the Japanese system of courts and approaches to litigation. Finally there is the significance of law as part of the culture of a country. Japanese law holds its own distinctiveness and it has been shown how this uniqueness makes the study of Japanese law an intellectual curiosity.   At a time when pressure through law, at both European and international levels, is to rationalise and harmonise, Japan's uniqueness provides lessons of how culture and law may be combined.

14. The Art Of Mirroring
Comparative Law and Social Theory

Dr. Ralf Rogowski LL.M – University of Warwick

I INTRODUCTION

Comparative law has struggled since its beginnings to acquire the status of a separate discipline in law. Ernst Rabel, for many scholars the founder of academic comparative law, assumed that it could become a fully-established 'branch of law'. He believed that comparative law could transcend from being just a 'method', added to existing branches of law, into a separate legal field.[1] The way to achieve this status was clear for Rabel: by becoming 'scientific' in its approach and methods.[2]

Rabel, who became the first director of the Berlin-based Kaiser-Wilhelm-Institute for Foreign and International Private Law in 1926,[3] presumed that legal scholars in general adhered to a common concept of legal science. It was the world view of a civil lawyer educated on the European Continent who believed in the value of pure knowledge-increasing comparative law. However, Rabel's assumption was not universally shared; it was swiftly rejected by comparative lawyers trained in common law systems. The former professor of comparative law at Cambridge University, H.C. Gutteridge, criticized Rabel's scholarly attempt as an unrealistic, abstract and speculative approach. He suggested instead a paradigm for comparative law which is derived from its practice. For Gutteridge the discipline only encompassed the two forms of 'descriptive' and 'applied'

---

[1] E. Rabel (1944) 'On Comparative Research in Legal History and Modern Law', reprinted in E. Rabel (1967) *Gesammelte Aufsätze III: Arbeiten zur Rechtsvergleichung und zur Rechtsvereinheitlichung 1919-1954*. Ed. by H.G. Leser. Tübingen: J.C.B. Mohr, pp. 247-260.

[2] E. Rabel (1925) 'Aufgabe und Notwendigkeit der Rechtsvergleichung' and (1937) 'Die Fachgebiete des Kaiser-Wilhelm-Instituts für ausländisches und internationales Privatrecht', both reprinted in Rabel, *op.cit* (Fn. 1), pp. 1-21 and 180-234.

[3] After World War II the Kaiser-Wilhelm-Institute became the Max-Planck-Institute for Foreign and International Private Law. It now resides in Hamburg.

comparative law, both reflecting the practical nature of comparative legal work of legal practitioners and legal scholars.[4]

The scientific character of comparative law has been debated ever since.[5] Recent discussions emphasise that comparative law is still characterised by the divide into theoretical ambitions and practical constraints which constitutes its major weakness.[6] Academic discussions, on the one side, tend to focus on theoretical and contextual issues in order to improve the methods used in comparisons of legal systems. On the other side, the practice of comparative law is still largely dominated by single-country studies of particular foreign jurisdictions which rarely reflect on their methods in analysing a legal system for comparative purposes.

A step forward could be to rethink the relationship of theory and practice of comparative law. A socio-legal approach, which utilizes general assumptions of a sociology of knowledge, could be of assistance. Such an approach evaluates the field of comparative law by focussing on the reality of comparative legal practice. It is likely that in this view comparative law can at best claim to be an 'art' or 'craft' which, despite the many scholarly efforts, is still characterised by unrelated activities and unsophisticated methods.[7]

The following chapter analyses both the methods of comparative law and the use of theory in comparative legal practice. In the first part, four approaches are reconstructed which in my view characterise the practice as well as the discourse of methods in comparative law. In the second part, an example of a theoretically guided comparison of legal systems is presented which resumes system theoretical efforts to define new dimensions for a comparison of judicial systems, and in the third part, the concept of mirroring is suggested to characterise the process of advanced comparison. Mirroring is contrasted with observation and systemic reflexion which offer alternative views on the function of comparison.

---

4 H.C. Gutteridge (1949) *Comparative Law.* An Introduction to the Comparative Method of Legal Study and Research. Second edition. Cambridge: Cambridge University Press, pp. 7-10.

5 See, for example, M. Ancel (1961) 'Valeur actuelle des études de droit comparé', in K.H. Nadelmann, A.T. von Mehren, J.N. Hazard (eds.) *XXth Century Comparative and Conflicts of Law.* Legal Essays in Honor of Hessel E. Yntema. Leyden: Sythoff, pp. 15-28.

6 B. Grossfeld (1990) *The Strength and Weakness of Comparative Law* Oxford: Clarendon. See also B. Markesinis (1990) 'Comparative Law: A Subject in Search of an Audience' 53 *Modern Law Review* 1-21.

7 See J. Hall (1980) 'Comparative Law as Basic Research' 4 *Hastings International and Comparative Law Review* 189-200.

II METHODS OF COMPARATIVE LAW

Comparative methods constitute the tools of comparative law. They are the instruments used in the practice of comparative legal studies. The debates of comparative methods are probably as old as the discipline of comparative law itself.[8] They are intricately linked to discussions of the history and functions of comparative law[9] and it is, in fact, not uncommon to equate comparative law with comparative methods.[10]

In the following I propose to distinguish four methods of comparison. These are: country studies, the benchmark approach, the functional approach and the theoretical approach.

1. Country Studies

Country studies are the traditional and still most common approach in comparative law. National legal experts are asked to produce a report on a particular area of law. The area is described in general terms and it is left to the *rapporteur* to portray the national law in a way, and to an extent, which is shared by other members of the national legal culture. The national legal expert might be an eminent legal scholar who partakes of a quality in his or her legal field which is also recognised outside the national boundaries of a particular legal culture. Or the *rapporteur* might be a comparative legal practitioner who specialises in presenting certain fields of law to a foreign audience. These specialists often serve as representatives in formal or informal international networks. They gain reputational advantages in their networks which are beneficial in the selection of participants for new multinational legal surveys.

The country-by-country approach utilises the various scientific methods in existence in the countries under comparison. The aim is 'a scientific

---

[8] See R. David, J.E.C. Brierley (1985) *Major Legal Systems in the World Today* Third ed. London: Stevens, pp. 1-6 (3).

[9] For a discussion of the development of comparative law in Germany after World War II (and after Rabel!) see M. Martinek (1994) 'Wissenschaftsgeschichte der Rechtsvergleichung und des Internationalen Privatrechts in der Bundesrepublik Deutschland', in D. Simon (ed.) *Rechtswissenschaft in der Bonner Republik*. Studien zur Wissenschaftsgeschichte der Jurisprudenz. Frankfurt/Main: Suhrkamp, pp. 529-580.

[10] See M.A. Glendon, M.W. Gordon, and C. Osakwe (1994) *Comaparative Legal Traditions*. Text, Materials and Cases on the Civil and Common Law Traditions, with Special Reference to French, German, English and European Law. Second ed. St. Pauls: West, pp. 1-8. Glendon et al. refer to A. Watson (1993) *Legal Transplants*. Second edition. Athens Georgia: University of Georgia Press.

analysis of law and practice in order to set them side by side'.[11] Country studies often are commissioned by legislators, research institutes or international organisations. They are carried out in rather diverse ways and do not follow a unified method. Their aim is often to emphasise specific national features of a legal system and to support law reforms.[12]

The strength of country studies is that the original, national view on the legal system is presented to the external world. The description of the national law is undistorted by comparative considerations. However, the lack of comparative guidance is also the weakness of this approach. The task of the comparativist is to compile and analyse the reports. His or her role is reduced to ex-post analysis which synthesises and extracts general principles from national reports. The comparative analysis is separated from the description of law, and it used to be guided by a faith in discovering universal natural law principles.[13] However, this belief in 'rules and principles which reason dictates' is no longer shared by modern sceptics to whom it appears in turn rather outmoded and anachronistic.[14]

2. The Benchmark Approach

An approach which assigns the comparativist a more active role is the benchmark approach. The descriptions of different legal orders are conducted by using the same benchmark, e.g., a questionnaire, which has been designed by a professional comparativist. Such a professional might work for a comparative law institute, a ministry or an international or supranational organisation which require systematic information on the legal situation of a particular problem in various countries.

Examples of comparative legal studies using the benchmark approach can be found in the practice of official national and international organisations. The European Commission increasingly prepares new legislative proposals by commissioning surveys of national legal regulations. In certain areas it has become standard practice for the Commission to prepare a questionaire which is sent to national governments or to comparative research institutes.

---

[11] R. Blanpain (1993) 'Comparativism in Labour Law and Industrial Relations', in R. Blanpain, C. Engels (eds.) *Comparative Labour Law and Industrial Relations in Industrialized Market Economies*. Fifth ed. Deventer: Kluwer, p. 4.

[12] See, for example, R.S. Frase (1990) 'Comparative Criminal Justice as a Guide to American Law Reform: How Do the French Do It, How Can We Find Out, and Why Should We Care'? 78 *California Law Review* 539-683.

[13] K. Zweigert (1949-50) 'Rechtsvergleichung als universale Interpretationsmethode' 15 *Rabels Zeitschrift für ausländisches und internationales Privatrecht* 5.

[14] H. Collins (1991) 'Methods and Aims of Comparative Contract Law' 11 *Oxford Journal of Legal Studies* 396-406 (396).

If the responses reveal significant gaps in national legislations and a legal competence for Community-wide legislation exists, the results of the questionnaire can form the basis for the Commission to formulate proposals for new European legislation which are submitted to the Council and the European Parliament.[15]

The reports on national legal developments are essential in areas in which the European Union only has competences to harmonise existing national law and thus cannot impose uniform regulations. Furthermore, the principle of subsidiarity, i.e. the preference for national legal solutions, limits the scope for non-exclusive European measures to cases which can, 'by reason of the scale or effects of the proposed action, be better achieved by the Community' (Art. 3b (2) EC Treaty). This emphasis on subsidiarity forces the European institutions to acquire adequate knowledge of national legal provisions before Community action can be considered.[16] To adopt the benchmark approach seems natural in this situation because the Commission can retain control over the comparative dimensions and the general direction of information gathering.

The strength of the benchmark approach is that it guides the national reports. Information on legal aspects which would not necessarily be portrayed in purely national reports might come to the surface. The comparativist has a more active role. He or she might be motivated by political concerns or a programme adopted by a comparative research organisation and thus can provide guidance in the gathering of information.

A restriction of the benchmark approach is that the questionnaire is often developed on the basis of one or two legal cultures against which the other legal cultures are then measured. The aim is an accurate description rather than an analysis. Thus the danger of this apporach lies in its rigidity. If specific questions are asked for which specific answers are sought, the unique characters or features of the national legal orders might not appear in the report. The importance of certain legal institutions and doctrinal figures might be overestimated while others are understated.

---

[15] A benchmark approach was adopted, for example, by DG V of the European Commission in their assessment of dismissal protection law in the Member States at the end of 1993. The Commission sent a questionnaire of more than 100 pages to all governments of the Member States. The information provided by the governments is still in the process of being evaluated by the Commission. It is likely to create the basis for future supranational legislative proposals in this area of employment protection. See also K. Schömann, R. Rogowski, T. Kruppe (1995) Fixed-Term Contracts and Labour Market Efficiency in the European Union. Final Report for DG V. Discussion paper FS I 95-207. Berlin: Wissenschaftszentrum.

[16] T.C. Hartley (1993) 'Constitutional and institutional aspects of the Maastricht Agreement' 42 *International and Comparative Law Quarterly* 213-237.

3. The Functionalist Approach

Comparative law has long been aware of the weaknesses of country studies and the benchmark approach. In particular academic discussions on methods and the proper foundation of comparative dimensions tend to focus on an alleged neglect of relevant comparative dimensions, including the non-legal context of legal solutions.[17] A prominent proposal to overcome the 'weakness' of technical comparisons is the functionalist approach which emphasises the societal context of law.

Two variants of the functionalist approach can be distinguished: a comparative law functionalism and a socio-legal functionalism.

a. The functionalist method in comparative law

The general idea of comparative law functionalism, as developed by Zweigert and Kötz[18], is that legal regulations should be compared which fulfill similar functions. This approach defines functions as related to social problems. It argues for an extra-legal basis from which the *tertium comparationis*, i.e. the benchmark or the comparative dimension, should be derived. The approach operates with the assumption that, if problems are similar, the legal solutions might nevertheless be different, but they are at least functionally equivalent.

The functionalist method is influenced by legal realism and purports a contextual approach in analysing law. It is explicitly academic. In his inaugural lecture as Professor of Comparative Law at Oxford University, Otto Kahn-Freund described what he saw as the *nobile officium* of any academic lawyer, including the comparative lawyer: 'to place himself both inside the mechanisam which the law uses to maintain its continuity, and outside it, outside the network of legal arguments, and at a detached point from which the law appears in perspective, as a product shaped by society whose needs it is destined to serve'.[19]

The strength of the functionalist approach is the problem-based comparison. It disentangles concepts and increases the complexity of analysis. In particular the assumption of functional equivalence improves the search strategy for adequate comparative dimensions. Comparative law

---

[17] See J. Hall (1963) *Comparative Law and Social Theory*. Baton Rouge: Louisiana State University.

[18] See K. Zweigert and H. Kötz (1987) *An Introduction to Comparative Law*. Second ed.. Oxford: Clarendon, pp. 28-46.

[19] O. Kahn-Freund (1966) 'Comparative Law as an Academic Subject' 82 *Law Quarterly Review* 40-61, reprinted in O. Kahn-Freund (1978) *Selected Writings*. London: Stevens, pp. 275-293 (279).

looks at how social objectives are fulfilled and compares functions rather than structures.[20]

However, the approach has some weaknesses. A major restriction of the functional approach relates to the limited capacity of lawyers to analyse and understand societal developments on their own terms. The social problems and thus the functions of law might be the same only at a technical level.[21] Furthermore, it leaves it to the arbitrary decision of the researcher which institutions or doctrinal figures are called functionally equivalent. Comparative legal functionalism is an inductive method which determines the unit of analysis by way of generalisation rather than theoretical analysis.

b. Socio-legal functionalism

Most comparative sociology of law studies operate in fact either explicitly or implicitly with a variant of functionalism. However, the main difference between legal and socio-legal functionalism is the use of empirical data and statistics. A socio-legal comparison of legal cultures replaces the problem-based approach with a search for legal indicators. Legal indicators are designed on the basis of existing statistical and other empirical data. The socio-legal indicators which create the basis for comparison include data on the legal profession, disputes, caseloads and judicial structures.[22]

The socio-legal approach aims at institutional structures. It challenges a comparative approach which views attitudes and values as explanatory factors for differences in legal systems. Instead it argues that institutional differences and traditions embodied in these institutions create the main comparative dimensions. For socio-legal functionalism the legal infrastructure and the legal behaviour instigated by this infrastructure are the main legal indicators which can be used for a comparison of 'legal cultures'.[23]

---

[20] Ibid. See also Glendon et al., *op.cit* (Fn. 10), p. 11: 'That functional approach ... has been comparative law's principal gift to 20th century legal science.'

[21] '... the legal problem of rent restriction is not the same both in a country where rented accommodation is common and in a country where it is less common; the problem of alimony for divorced wives in a jurisdiction where it is usual for women to work differs from that in a country where women do not have jobs.' Watson, *op .cit.*, (Fn. 10), pp. 4-5.

[22] E. Blankenburg (1995) 'Indikatorenvergleich von Rechtskulturen' in E. Blankenburg *Mobilisierung von Recht.* Berlin: Springer, pp. 95-105.

[23] E. Blankenburg (1994) 'The Infrastructure for Avoiding Civil Litigation: Comparing Cultures of Legal Behavior in the Netherlands and West Germany' 28 *Law and Society Review* 789-808; see also E. Blankenburg (1985) 'Indikatorenvergleich der Rechtskulturen in der Bundesrepublik und den Niederlanden' 6 *Zeitschrift für Rechtssoziologie* 206-254.

Furthermore, law is conceptualised as legal culture which is closely linked to developments in popular culture. This approach focuses on public and professional knowledge of and attitudes and behaviour patterns towards the legal system. Results of population surveys and other social science instruments which are used to study cultural developments are applied in comparisons of legal cultures.[24]

The strength of the comparative socio-legal approach is its scientific rigour. It links comparative legal research to wider discussions in comparative sociology, comparative culture studies and comparative political science.[25] Its weakness lies in the limits of legal indicators which can only portray quantitative data and often lack a qualitative dimension. The comparison itself remains inductive.

4. The Theoretical Approach

A theoretical approach takes functionalism a step further. It is concerned with constructing comparative dimensions based on theoretical hypotheses. It takes the contributions of legal and social theory seriously and uses them as a source of insights into the foundations of law. Comparative hypotheses are deducted from a set of theoretical assumptions and not through inductive sorting of comparative and empirical findings. Thus this approach adds a theoretical basis to functionalism from which functions can be deduced.

Theoretically guided comparative research tends to use sociological paradigms for a reconstruction of legal developments. Mirjan Damaška, for example, refers to Weberian categories in his analysis of criminal procedures in common law and civil law countries. He replaces the traditional distinction between accusatorial and inquisitorial procedure by models of authority which capture structure and process of criminal procedures. Damaška's models are constructed around notions of hierarchy and coordination and broaden the focus of analysis beyond the trial to include pre-trial processes.[26]

---

[24] On the link between legal culture and popular culture see L. Friedman (1975) *The Legal System. A Social Science Perspective*. New York: Sage, pp. 193-268; L. Friedman (1990) *The Republic of Choice*. Law, Authority, and Culture. Cambridge, Mass and London: Harvard University Press.

[25] D. Martiny (1980) 'Rechtsvergleichung und vergleichende Rechtssoziologie' 1 *Zeitschrift für Rechtssoziologie* 65-84. See also U. Drobnig, M. Rehbinder (eds.) (1977) *Rechtssoziologie und Rechtsvergleichung*. Berlin: Duncker & Humblot.

[26] M. Damaška (1974-75) 'Structures of Authority and Comparative Criminal Procedure' 84 *Yale Law Journal* 480-545.

Another example is the sociological concept of law proposed by Niklas Luhmann. His general system theory of law and society creates a basis from which hypotheses are deduced for a comparative analysis of concrete historical processes.[27] Legal developments are analysed at the three levels of society: interaction, organisation and social systems. The legal system can be characterised accordingly as including interaction systems (negotiations, for example) and organisations (courts, for example) and as a function system of society.

It has been suggested that the specific task of comparative law is not the analysis of foreign legal systems but the relationship of legal systems.[28] System theory agrees with this view of the task of comparative law. However, it adds that relationships can occur at various systemic levels and that micro- as well as macro-comparisons need to be carried out in analysing relationships between legal systems.

The social theory perspective enlarges the remit of comparative law beyond the study of foreign legal systems. It advocates the analysis of intersystemic relationships and internal uses of information on foreign legal systems. Furthermore, it insists on including non-legal forms of regulation in comparative legal studies. Richard Abel has forcefully demonstrated this approach with respect to dispute institutions in developed and non-developed societies.[29]

The strengths of the theoretical approach is the founding of functions in theory which can be tested empirically. Legal solutions are analysed in conjunction with non-legal, societal solutions. Social theory suggests to compare legal and non-legal solutions in and across different countries. The weakness of the theoretical approach lies in its abstract exposition.

---

[27] See N. Luhmann (1975) 'Legal Profession: Comments on the Situation in the Federal Republic of Germany' 20 *The Juridical Review* 116-132.

[28] The idea to define the task of comparative law as a study of relationships between legal systems was first suggested by Watson, *op.cit* (Fn. 19), pp. 6-9. However, Watson's approach lacks a proper definition of a legal system. He reduces the analysis of relations between legal systems to a study of historical and 'spiritual' relations surrounding legal transplants.

[29] See R. Abel (1974) 'A Comparative Theory of Dispute Institutions in Society' 8 *Law and Society Review* 217-347.

III SOCIAL THEORY AND THE COMPARISON OF JUDICIAL SYSTEMS

So far comparative law has not managed to develop a comprehensive approach which is able to assist empirical projects. The most advanced approach is still the functionalist method. Its lack of theoretical grounding is gradually acknowledged and a renewed interest in theory can be detected in recent common law and civil law studies.[30]

However, empirical and practical comparative research requires that social and legal theories can be translated into testable middle range assumptions. It is thus necessary to demonstrate how abstract social theories can be used to generate comparative legal hypotheses. The following section introduces some aspects of the theory of social systems, developed by Niklas Luhmann[31], and then uses them for a comparison of court systems.

Luhmann's concept of the modern society rests on the idea of autonomous social systems. Modern societies consist of a number of function systems which include law, the economy, politics, religion, education, health etc. These societies differ from pre-modern societies because their internal structure is no longer characterised by stratification but by functional differentiation. The autonomous function systems are located at the same plane within society and their relationship is based on mutual recognition and structural coupling.

The most radical assumption in Luhmann's system theory of society relates to the constitution of social systems. Social systems do not consist of actions or interactions in the Weberian or Habermasian sense but of communications as their ultimate elements. Each function system is characterised by a specific form of communication and these communications are recursively linked. Communicative self-reference creates the basis for self-reproduction of these systems or, in general systems theory terms, their autopoiesis. They are operationally closed.

Niklas Luhmann's sociological theory analyses society at a national as well as an international level. Since function systems are only operationally closed but cognitively open, their communications cannot be controlled and prevented to flow beyond territorial frontiers. With increasing complexity and intensification of global communications Luhmann sees a world society

---

[30] See R. Rogowski (ed.) (1996) *Civil Law*. International Library of Essays in Law and Legal Theory. Aldershot: Dartmouth, pp. XI-XXII.

[31] N. Luhmann (1984) *Soziale Systeme*. Frankfurt/Main: Suhrkamp (English edition, forthcoming *Social Systems*. Cambridge: Cambridge University Press). N. Luhmann (1993) *Das Recht der Gesellschaft*. Frankfurt/Main: Suhrkamp.

emerging which consists of international social systems which cannot be contained by national political systems.[32]

Luhmann's theory can be used for comparative research. It emphasises new comparative dimensions and provides a framework in which existing judicial research can be reconstructed. Within judicial research, studies have been conducted along a number of comparative dimensions.[33] These include, for example, judicial independence,[34] the political role of courts in modern democracies,[35] judicial control of administrative acts,[36] and styles of interpretative statutes.[37]

Luhmann's theory enables comparative judicial research to transcend the rather narrow focus of these studies. It addresses fundamental questions of function, structure and dynamic change of judicial systems. In the following three dimensions which derive from Luhmann's theory are suggested for the comparative study of judicial systems. These dimensions relate to the ordering of subsystems of the judicial system; the recursivity of judicial decision-making; and the intersystemic relations of the judicial and the political system.

a. The Relation of Subsystems within the Judicial System

Luhmann's idea of the modernization of societies as the transformation from stratification to functional differentiation can be applied to the legal and the judicial system. Functional differentiation of social systems occurs

[32] See N. Luhmann (1990) 'The World Society as a Social System', in N. Luhmann *Essays on Self-Reference*. New York: Columbia University Press, pp. 175-190 (178). See also R. Stichweh (1995) 'Zur Theorie der Weltgesellschaft' 1 *Soziale Systeme* 24-45.

[33] On comparative judicial research in general see M. Shapiro (1981) *Courts. A Comparative and Political Analysis*. Chicago, London: University of Chicago Press; J.R. Schmidhauser (ed.) (1987) *Comparative Judicial Systems*. Challenging Frontiers in Conceptual and Empirical Analysis. London et al.: Butterworths. M. Cappelletti (1971) *Judicial Review in the Contemporary World*. Indianapolis: Bobbs-Merrill.

[34] S. Shetreet, J. Dechênes (eds.) (1985) *Judicial Independence: The Contemporary Debate*. Dordrecht: Nijhoff.

[35] J.L. Waltman, K.M. Holland (eds.) (1988) *The Political Role of Law Courts in Modern Democracies*. London: Macmillan.

[36] For the US see M. Shapiro (1988) *Who Guards the Guardians*. Judicial Control of Administration. Athens: The University of Georgia Press, and for France see F.L. Morton (1988) 'Judicial Review in France: A Comparative Analysis' 36 *The American Journal of Comparative Law* 89-110.

[37] D.N. MacCormick, R. Summers (eds.) (1991) *Interpreting Statutes*. Aldershot: Dartmouth.

both at the level of society at large and at the level of function systems.[38] Function systems of modern societies restructure internally from centralised to decentralised systems. The modern legal system is accordingly characterised by processes of functional differentiation and replacement of hierarchical relations by a structure of horizontally arranged legal fields. Although legal fields differ with respect to autonomy, there is no longer one field, for example private law, which dominates the legal system.

Within the judicial system a similar transformation takes place.[39] It can be described as a transformation from vertical integration by a unitary appeal structure to horizontal integration of independent specialised judiciaries. The relationship of courts is characterised by functional differentiation and the basis of their relation becomes mutual recognition.[40]

Comparative research is invited by this theory to investigate if, and to what extent, the transformation from vertical to horizontal integration of judicial systems has occurred in different national legal systems. Such comparison would focus on specialised judiciaries and their relationship with the so-called ordinary court system.[41] The general hypothesis would be that the distinction between ordinary and specialised courts is replaced by a system of functionally equal courts of different jurisdiction.[42] Judicial systems would be compared with respect to degrees of decentralisation of decision-making and the dissolution of overarching appeal structures.

---

[38] See also H. Willke (1989) *Systemtheorie entwickelter Gesellschaften*. Dynamik und Riskanz moderner gesellschaftlicher Selbstorganisation. Weinheim: Juventa.

[39] N. Luhmann (1990) 'Die Stellung der Gerichte im Rechtssystem' 21 *Rechtstheorie* 459-473.

[40] A similar transformation can be found in advanced legal professions. See R. Rogowski (1995) 'German Corporate Lawyers. Social Closure in Autopoietic Perspective', in Y. Dezalay and D. Sugarman (eds.) *Professional Competition and Professional Power*. Lawyers, Accountants and the Social Construction of Markets. London: Routledge, pp. 114-135.

[41] See S.H. Legomsky (1990) *Specialised Justice*. Courts, Administrative Tribunals, and a Cross-National Theory of Specialisation. Oxford: Clarendon.

[42] See the discussion of function and impact of various national labour courts in R. Rogowski 'Industrial Relations, Labour Conflict Resolution and Reflexive Labour Law', in: R. Rogowski, T. Wilthagen (eds.) *Reflexive Labour Law*. Studies in Industrial Relations and Employment Regulation. Deventer: Kluwer, pp. 53-93. See also E. Blankenburg and R. Rogowski (1986) 'German Labour Courts and the British Industrial Tribunal System: A Socio-legal Comparison of Degrees of Judicialisation' 13 *Journal of Law and Society* 67-92.

b. Recursive Decision-making

A further comparative dimension relates to the core of judicial organisations, i.e., self-referential or recursive decision-making. Judicial systems are organisational systems which are characterised as such by a special form of constitutive communications. These special communications are decisions.[43] If new decisions are found with reference to previous decisions, judicial decision-making has become self-referential and the judicial organisation autopoietic.[44]

Recursive decision-making occurs in many forms. Legal decisions are not confined to judicial decisions. They can be enactments of statutes or treaties, administrative acts, wills, or land registries. However, judicial decisions develop specific mechanisms which guide their autopoiesis. A prominent device is legal argumentation which is used to interpret law in civil law or to decide about the *ratio decidendi* of precedents in common law. Legal argumentation is an invaluble means of recursive closure.[45]

The autopoietic nature of modern court systems offers comparative judicial research a particular challenging comparative dimension. Judicial decision-making can be compared with respect to the extent it is based on self-referential processes. The creation of doctrinal figures and other forms of self-binding devices become objects of comparison. The common law precedent appears in a new light. Furthermore, the interpretatory efforts of courts in implementing statutes are linked to autopoietic concerns.

c. The Relation of the Judicial System and the Political System

A third set of questions relates to the intersystemic relationship of the judicial system and the political system. The theory of autopoietic judiciaries predicts that a radically autonomous judicial system, constituted by recursive decision-making, tends to undermine the traditional hierarchical relationship between the judicial and the legislative system.[46] In advanced societies the view of courts as merely interpreting law which is created by the political system becomes increasingly unrealistic.

---

[43] N. Luhmann (1993) 'Die Paradoxie des Entscheidens' 84 *Verwaltungsarchiv* 287-310.

[44] See N. Luhmann, *op. cit.,* (Fn. 31), pp. 307-310.

[45] N. Luhmann (1995) 'Legal Argumentation: An Analysis of its Form' 58 *Modern Law Review* 285-298. See also Luhmann, *op.cit* (Fn. 43), pp. 365-6, 404.

[46] See the discussion of the impact which the German Federal Constitutional Court had on the West German legislature in T. Gawron, R. Rogowski (1991) 'Drei Seiten des Bundesverfassungsgerichts' in B. Blanke, H. Wollmann (eds.) *Die alte Bundesrepublik.* Kontinuität und Wandel. LEVIATHAN Sonderheft 12/1991. Opladen: Westdeutscher Verlag, pp. 336-353.

In complex, functionally differentiated societies the political system and the democratically elected parliaments lose their role as the initiator of legal change.[47] The courts become the main actors in proposing legal reforms which suit the needs of the legal system. The legislator reacts to judicial demands and imposes political imperatives on the legal system only in exceptional cases.

In fact both the legal and the political system realise that they are structurally coupled. Structural coupling of two systems excludes environmental influences while privileging exchanges between the systems which are structurally linked. However, both systems remain independent and their reciprocal inputs are only irritations which the system might respond to or not. Systemic reactions to irritations are internally controlled and are unlikely to occur simultaneously.[48]

A systems theory of law can provide a new dimension for comparative research which is related to intersystemic relations. The change of roles between the legislator and the judicial system is characteristic of most modern political and legal systems, although it seems more significant in civil law countries in which law is often equated with legislation. However, the study of intersystemic relations requires research techniques in analysing legal realities which transcend the exisiting positivist empirical methodology.

IV OBSERVATION, MIRRORING AND REFLEXION

Within debates on comparative law a new interest in using it as a critical study of law seems to emerge. It coincides with a stronger commitment to theory in comparative legal studies. The aim is thereby to establish comparative legal studies as 'a new perspective, allowing one critically to illuminate a legal system – another's or one's own – much in the same way as, say, critical legal studies, legal semiotics or economic analysis of law'.[49]

A system theory perspective can help to analyse different functions of comparing social phenomena, including foreign legal systems. A comparative assessment of a foreign legal system, be it critical or not, is in the first place a form of *observation*. A theoretical analysis of comparative methods emphasises the dependance of observation on the position of the observer within a particular system. A comparative observation can always

---

[47] See Luhmann, *op. cit.*, (Fn. 31), ch. 7 and ch.. 9.

[48] See Luhmann, *op .cit.*, (Fn. 31), ch. 10.

[49] P. Legrand (1995) 'Comparative Legal Studies and Commitment to Theory' 58 *Modern Law Review* 262-273 (264).

be challenged by asking who the observer is. The observer is bound by the system in which he or she operates. This system reference applies to any form of observation, including academic analysis.[50]

The new commitment to theory in comparative law transcends the boundaries of foreign and self-observation. By restaging a different legal culture within a particular legal setting a paradox arises. If observation of a foreign legal system is used for legal self-description, comparative law encounters the paradox of 'understanding one's own domestic system better'.[51] The comparative method becomes a tool for an assessment of the domestic legal system.

This transformation from pure observation of a foreign legal system to external referencing for domestic purposes shall be called *mirroring*. It is guided by concerns to analyse the observed as well as the observing system.[52] Mirroring means that comparative law becomes aware of its contribution not only to an understanding of a foreign legal system but also of its capacity to analyse the domestic system with the eyes of another system. Comparative law engages in a specific form of contextualisation when mirroring another system.

Mirroring can be described as both a scientific and an aesthetic concept. Human beings use mirrors to find out how they look.[53] A mirror is used by human beings to prepare themselves for participation in the outside world. The mirror objectifies the subject. It contradicts the subject's self-image with the reality of the subject's appearance. In the process of mirroring faults and omissions are detected and can lead, if time and means allow it, to adjustments.

Mirroring is about seeing and being seen. It may lead to learning if the reflected, or the reflector in a two-way reflection, are willing to take advantage of the result of mirroring. Mirroring is a process of reflection. It is said to constitute the basis of love and understanding. It is the reflection of one's own face in the face of the other which founds ethics, according to

---

[50] N. Luhmann (1990) *Die Wissenschaft der Gesellschaft*. Frankfurt Main: Suhrkamp.

[51] Collins, *op. cit.*, (Fn. 14), p. 398.

[52] On the double meaning of observing systems (systems which observe and systems which are observed) see H. von Foerster (1981) *Observing Systems*. Seaside, California: Intersystems Publications.

[53] Indeed, mirroring is, according to J. Lacan's psychoanalytical approach, a crucial formative stage in the early childhood of infants between the age of six and eighteen months. J. Lacan (1949/1977) 'The mirror stage as formative of the function of the I as revealed in psychoanalytic experience' in J. Lacan (1980/1989) *Écrits. A Selection*, London: Tavistock/Routledge, pp. 1-7.

Levinas.[54]   And it is seeing oneself through the eyes of the other which constitutes love, according to von Foerster.[55]

However, the metaphor of mirroring does not suggest that it is a one-way process. It can be constructed as a two-way process in which both parties mirror each other. Furthermore, mirroring can be enlarged when the two mirrors do not only focus on the two legal systems but also scan the surrounding social context.

Reflection becomes a multi-dimensional process if both sides use mirrors. This two-way reflection can lead to a spiral process in which the image of the reflected and the reflector's image in the opposite mirror continuously trigger new insights and adjustments. Mirroring then becomes an infinite source of irritation.

Mirroring is characteristic of an advanced practice of comparative law. Legal comparison is a process in which a legal culture is seen through the eyes of another legal culture. However, there are always different ways to read the mirror. Academic analyses prefer to use theory, including social theory and anthropology.[56]

Mirroring another legal system can produce surprising results and might contribute to a critical assessment of one's own legal system. Developments which were suppressed or simply forgotten might appear in a new light because they developed in another system. Thus comparative law might touch on the 'positive unconscious'[57] of a legal system.   The contribution of comparative law to legal studies in general can be enhanced by theory. By offering within law an external view on law it not only enriches the legal analysis but helps to strengthen legal scholarship as such within the academic context.[58]

Mirroring can be contrasted with *reflexion*. Whereas mirroring maintains a separate activity of analysing a foreign system, albeit for domestic purposes, reflexion forms part of the self-reference of legal systems. From

---

[54] On 'Ethics and the Face' see E. Levinas (1969) *Totality and Infinity*. An Essay on Exteriority. Pittsburgh: Duquesne University Press, pp. 194-219.

[55] H. von Foerster (1993) 'Mit den Augen des anderen' in H. von Foerster (1993) *Wissen und Gewissen*. Versuch einer Brücke. Frankfurt/Main: Suhrkamp, pp. 350-363.

[56] R. Abel (1978) 'Comparative Law and Social Theory' 26 *American Journal of Comparative Law* 219. See also W. Brugger (1994) 'Legal Interpretation, Schools of Jurisprudence, and Anthropology: Some Remarks from a German Point of View' 42 *The American Journal of Comparative Law* 395-421.

[57] See P. Goodrich (1995) *Oedipus Lex*. Psychoanalysis, History, Law. Berkeley: University of California Press, ch. 7. See also P. Goodrich (1990) *Languages of Law*. From Logics of Memory to Nomadic Masks. London: Weidenfeld & Nicolson, p. 16.

[58] G. Frankenberg (1985) 'Critical Comparisons: Re-thinking Comparative Law' 26 *Harvard International Law Journal* 411-455.

a system's perspective mirroring contributes to drawing a distinction between the system and its environment. Reflexion uses the distinction for self-reproduction purposes.

Systems engage in reflexion by orientating themselves at their unity and distancing themselves from their environment. Reflexion is a by-product of normal operations of the system, i.e. in case of the legal system judicial and other legal decision-making. Self-reference of the system occurs if decision-making refers to previous decisions. In order to do so the system must be able to identify previous decisions as relevant for future decision-making. This requires mechanisms of self-observation and self-description. However, reflexion goes beyond basic self-reference and includes external referencing for its autopoiesis. It is a characteristic of advanced autopoietic legal systems that they require knowledge of other legal systems as well as of their non-legal environments in order to match internal structural complexities and enable self-reproduction.

V CONCLUSIONS

Modern social theory, in particular social system theory, argues that differentiation of legal systems is characteristic of internal as well as external relations of legal systems. System theory uses abstract concepts to analyse concrete historical developments. Legal systems develop by becoming self-critical and self-referential. In realising their epistemological shortcomings and their limited capacities to regulate other systems, they become reflexive.[59]

It can be predicted that national legal systems are increasingly forced to mirror their achievements by comparing themselves with other legal systems. Comparative law gains in importance through supranational and international pressures to harmonise laws. In a world of legal pluralism knowledge of other legal systems is vital, in particular socio-legal knowledge which presents a foreign law in its social context.[60] Comparative law can further gain in strength by shifting the focus from

---

[59] G. Teubner (1992) *Law as an Autopoietic System.* Oxford: Blackwell; Luhmann, *op.cit* (Fn. 31); R. Rogowski, T. Wilthagen, *op.cit* (Fn. 42).

[60] There are, of course, practical limits to the conduct of large-scale studies in comparative sociology of law. It requires not only sociological training in data collection and interpretation but equally requires legal expertise in analysing statutes and understanding doctrinal figures. Thus proper comparative sociology of law needs researchers with a double qualification. And these researchers are rare given the structure and orientations which dominate in our higher education systems.

distant observation of foreign legal systems to an analysis of relationships between legal systems.

Comparative law and its methods are still characterised by a tension between the practical requirements in comparing different laws and the scholarly views on proper theoretical underpinnings of these efforts. However, if comparative practice advances from using the country study and the benchmark approach to adopting the functional and theoretical approach, it is able to transcend mere observation and engage in mirroring. It might also be in a position to understand its contribution to reflexion and self-critical assessment of its domestic legal system.